Imaging Education

THE MEDIA AND SCHOOLS
IN AMERICA

*Published in collaboration with the Hechinger Institute
on Education and the Media*

Imaging Education

THE MEDIA AND SCHOOLS
IN AMERICA

Edited by Gene I. Maeroff

Teachers College, Columbia University
New York and London

Published by Teachers College Press, 1234 Amsterdam Avenue, New York, NY 10027

Copyright © 1998 by Teachers College Press

All rights reserved. No part of this publication may be reproduced or transmitted in any form or by any means, electronic or mechanical, including photocopy, or any information storage and retrieval system, without permission from the publisher

Library of Congress Cataloging-in-Publication Data

Imaging education : the media and schools in America / edited by Gene
  I. Maeroff.
       p.   cm.
    "This book is a direct outgrowth of the work of the Hechinger
Institute on Education and the Media, based at Teachers College,
Columbia University"—Pref.
    Includes bibliographical references and index.
    ISBN 0-8077-3735-6 (cloth : alk. paper). — ISBN 0-8077-3734-8
(paper : alk. paper)
    1. Education in mass media—United States.   I. Maeroff, Gene I.
II. Hechinger Institute on Education and the Media.
P96.E292U65   1998
370'.973—dc21   97-51286

ISBN 0-8077-3734-8 (paper)
ISBN 0-8077-3735-6 (cloth)

Printed on acid-free paper
Manufactured in the United States of America

05   04   03   02   01   00   99   98   8   7   6   5   4   3   2   1

Contents

Preface

THIS BOOK is a direct outgrowth of the work of the Hechinger Institute on Education and the Media, based at Teachers College, Columbia University. The Institute's mission is to address issues involving the coverage of education by the press and broadcast media across the country. Primarily, this means sponsoring seminars at which journalists examine topics in education. Other aspects of the program of the Hechinger Institute—which was founded in 1996—are seminars for educators to study their relations with the media, events for the public, and publications.

This collaboration with Teachers College Press marks an additional effort to study the impact that the coverage of education has on the schools and colleges that are the subject of that reporting. A book provides a way to reach the broad audience that ought to be thinking about these matters. The distinguished contributors of the chapters commissioned expressly for this book offer fresh and provocative insights. Their words, we hope, will stir a discussion that will help make education coverage as good as it can possibly be. The media, on the one hand, and education, on the other, have their own needs, goals, and ways of operating. Tension is, perhaps, inevitable.

The Institute honors the memory of Fred M. Hechinger, who during a long and distinguished career was most widely known as the education editor of the *New York Times*.

It's All in the Eye of the Beholder

IN THE EARLY 1980s, a journalist who had written a book about America's schools titled *Don't Blame the Kids* (Maeroff, 1982) was interviewed on NBC's *Today* show. But before Jane Pauley asked him a word, the television monitor filled with wild images of a classroom in Los Angeles in which students had run amok. Then, the scene shifted to the set in the studio and Pauley turned to the journalist, asking the question, "What do you mean, 'Don't blame the kids'?" The remote camera had captured education at its worst, and it seemed readily apparent—whether or not the broadcast had occurred—that this was a particularly egregious example of how bad situations could get inside some schools. These students were clearly blameworthy. Yet, such grotesque conduct in schools is the exception, not the rule, and in airing that footage NBC reinforced the kind of picture that the media have helped perpetuate about education in the United States.

On the other hand, disruption and violence *do* occur in schools, and the educational fortunes of youngsters are sometimes held captive by peers who exact a disproportionate amount of the time of teachers, transforming what should be a joy of childhood into a nightmare for the students they annoy and even terrorize. Can anyone reasonably expect the media to ignore this problem altogether? Or, getting to the heart of the learning enterprise, what about the media's handling of reports on scholastic achievement? Should low test scores, for instance, be overlooked because they paint a negative portrait of schooling?

This is not to say that perceptions about schools will be formed entirely on the basis of what the media choose to portray. Almost everyone who grew up in the United States attended school, and tens of millions of Americans are the parents of schoolchildren. All of these people—not to mention some 50 million currently enrolled in elementary and secondary schools and 14 million attending colleges and universities—have had first-hand experience with formal education. Once out of school, they continue to come in contact with students and recent students on the job, on the streets, and everywhere else that people gather. They do not necessarily need the media to tell them what to think about education. Observers form opinions about the schools when a high school student working part-time counts out change at the supermarket checkout line, when groups of teenagers assemble at the mall, and when recent college graduates show up at the office for their first full-time jobs.

Yet, the media, too, play an undeniable role in fixing impressions about education in the public consciousness. This happens when an actor plays a bumbling principal, such as the one in the old *Our Miss Brooks* television series, or when James Edward Olmos enacts the film role of a heroic math teacher who makes calculus scholars of inner-city students. It happens when CBS airs a back-to-school documentary in September or when the local TV station covers an event in a middle school. It happens, too, as it did on May 21, 1997, when in a single issue of the *New York Times*, readers learned that four teenagers were arrested and charged with gang-raping a 14-year-old girl in a vacant classroom in a Queens high school; charges of aggravated sexual assault were upheld against three former high school football stars who used a broom handle to sexually violate a retarded girl while they were all still students in a New Jersey suburb; and the freshman class at the City University of New York was the best prepared in 27 years because, in part, only 45% were enrolled in remedial courses.

Images of schooling are formed as readers and viewers mingle the impressions they glean from the media with their own personal experiences, producing a melange of opinions about education. This process makes it difficult to tell where perceptions influenced strictly by the media begin and end. Many critics, however, remain persuaded that the media—above all other forces—affect beliefs about schooling. Can this be true? What would happen if the media totally ignored education? Would the negative side of schools suddenly turn rosy? Would students achieve higher test scores? Would disruptions in schools disappear? Would teachers teach better? Would more students learn to their full capacity? Would more citizens approve bond issues? Would dissatisfaction with the schools disappear, causing interest in vouchers and charter schools to dissipate? Would applicants make more informed decisions about which colleges to attend? Would tuition rates hold steady?

It is difficult to believe that anything would be very different—except that Americans would be less informed about education. This is not to say, though, that the media have done an expert job of keeping people knowledgeable about developments in schools and colleges. Or that portrayals of education and learning are always accurate and enlightening. The coverage has many holes and weaknesses. Furthermore, at the nonnews end of the spectrum of coverage, education as depicted in the entertainment media does not always bristle with verisimilitude.

Perhaps the biggest reason why some people believe that the media shape and misshape perceptions about schooling has to do with the aggressive style of journalism that has arisen during the last quarter-century, in the wake of the Watergate scandal. Coverage of incidents surrounding Watergate and the chronicling of the attendant fall of the executive branch of government produced a hard-edged journalistic approach that has now extended to many topics, including education. Institutions generally are reported on with a scrutiny that was unusual before Watergate. This has meant new prominence for stories involving sex abuse by priests, excesses by health maintenance organizations, the peccadilloes of politicians, and even the behavior of sports heroes. A "gotcha" kind of journalism, relatively dormant since Upton Sinclair, Ida Tarbell, and other muckrakers plied their craft in the early 20th century, reasserted itself as every Tom, Dick, and Jane with a pencil or a microphone has tried to make a name for him- or herself. Comity and decorum have fallen victim to a take-no-victims sort of journalism that illuminates the recesses that had remained unobserved when the media was less zealous about its mission.

It may be, though, that the public does not want or appreciate news reports that cast the schools in an unfavorable light, however brilliant the reporting. The main audience of those who appreciate investigative journalism, for instance, may be other journalists. "Readers and viewers typically do not care whether journalists believe that their actions are justified by a sacred constitutional trust or by their notions of the 'public interest,'" said Frederick R. Blevens (1997, p. B7), a professor of mass communications at Southwest Texas State University.

For education, the new style of journalism has meant the piercing of institutional armor. The words of superintendents and school board members, once virtually unchallenged by the press, have become fair game for skepticism, if not outright cynicism. The sanctity of public education, unquestionably accepted for generations, has been stripped away by journalists who report on alternatives to traditional approaches and raise questions about how well consumers are served by the status quo. Are the media leading an assault or merely taking note of events to which the media are no more than passive observers? Probably a little of each, though the evidence one way or the other is rather scanty.

Much of what contributes to the difficulties in the educational enterprise—Watergate or no Watergate—has as much to do with society at large as with changes in the schools. What ails the schools, to a large degree, has its origins in the shifting fortunes and mores of Americans, independent of anything the media do or do not do. In this regard, the blight of drugs that has descended upon a hedonistic America, the dysfunctions of millions of families, and unbridled permissiveness present challenges beyond the scope of what the schools are equipped to handle. The media may be remiss in not doing more to place the problems of education in a social context.

The challenge of covering education is heightened by the complexities of teaching and learning. An understanding of pedagogy and child development adds immeasurably to reports on education. But the tendency among education writers is to simplify—as is the case in all of journalism. As a result, journalists, and even scriptwriters for sitcoms and films dealing with the life of the classroom, sometimes end up producing parodies, squeezing the intellectual juice out of situations that become drained of genuine significance. Brain research, for instance, reveals much that is pertinent to formal education, yet seldom do reports on education in the popular media acknowledge these new understandings. And within the subjects and disciplines themselves, reports on education tend to reduce the issues to caricatures. Television, with its need for sound bites, bears far more of the blame in this regard than does print journalism.

At its worst, this abrogation of responsibility by television news leads to the ignoring of education altogether. An academic study of television news in eight markets found in 1997 that local news time devoted to coverage of education ranged from 0.2% of the broadcasts in Los Angeles to 4.9% in Austin. Miami, Eugene, Syracuse, New York, Indianapolis, and Chicago were at percentages in between. Meanwhile, not surprisingly, the proportion of local broadcasts devoted to crime ranged from 5.7% in Austin to 36.7% in Indianapolis (Local TV News, 1997).

By contrast, when people were asked in another survey to choose "the one thing happening in your community you are most interested in knowing about," 40% opted for education as against 36% for crime (*Good News*, 1997, p. 41). In the same poll, the percentage of the general public saying that that there was not enough attention given to education was 66% in regard to the national broadcast media, 57% in regard to local broadcast media, 54% in regard to national print media, and 35% in regard to local print media (p. 34). An overwhelming finding in this poll was that people say that they want more coverage of education, more substantial coverage of education, and less of what they consider negativity.

Would increased and deeper coverage alter opinions about schools and education? One can hardly tell. Would people bother availing themselves of improved coverage even if it were available? It is difficult to believe that television documentaries about, say, children with learning disabilities or new ways of teaching geography will ever draw large audiences—despite the statements of people who say that they want more substance in education reporting. Possibly attesting to this lack of interest were the findings of a study that had among its sponsors the American Society of Newspaper Editors. It revealed that Americans were more impressed with the advertising in their newspapers than with the reporting, which they said fell short of their expectations in regard to relevance and utility. Readers liked the ads better because they helped them "find products and services, save money and save time" (Ads More Relevant, 1997).

On the other hand, the media surely must exert an influence of some sort when it comes to perceptions of education, if only to bolster negative dispositions. Reinforcement of existing opinions, though, is not the same as molding views in the first place. It is unclear exactly how much the media could sway public opinion in a direction toward which it is not already inclined. People who are leery of the public schools may find credence for their perceptions in the media. The original source of their wariness may have little to do with the media.

Editors and producers at newspapers and television stations usually want to act responsibly in deciding what to cover and how to cover it. But they have time pressures and have to compete for space on a page or minutes in a broadcast, so they know they must encourage reporters to keep their work interesting and compelling. Of course, some critics of the media take a more cynical view of all this. Miles Myers (1997), former executive director of the National Council of Teachers of English, wrote in an article largely chastising the media of "reporters who need educational disasters in order to get promoted" (p. 20).

THE MEDIA'S INFLUENCE FROM A VARIETY OF ANGLES

The authors of the chapters in Part I of this book examine the intriguing phenomenon that results when perfectly rational, well-informed people look at the same event and come to diverse opinions about it. This is certainly the case in regard to the coverage of education by the media. Journalists, for their part, believe that they do a sincere, unbiased job of reporting news about schools and colleges. They would be among the first to concede that the coverage has room for improvement, but, nonetheless, those who work in the media reject the idea that they are interested only in so-called bad news.

Another point of view holds that the media deliberately set out to portray education in an unfavorable light. Those who reach this conclusion cite a variety of explanations for the negative behavior of journalists: They are elitist; they want to make their stories sensational to attract readers and viewers; they simply do not believe that schools and colleges—

especially those under public auspices—are capable of doing a good job; and they are engaged in a conspiracy to undermine public education. The outside world does not realize how little of a conspiratorial nature occurs in journalism, a craft filled with individualists who march to the cadences of their separate drummers. Yet, there is something curious about the ubiquity of the negative slant in the media when it comes to education, and it is no wonder that observers strain for explanations.

Another opinion about the media has it that schools and colleges hardly face the tough scrutiny from the media that they should and that, if anything, the media are too kind to education. This view rankles journalists, but it must be noted that some of those who report on education may not ask the right questions because they do not always know the questions to ask. At too many papers, they pass through the beat like shoppers going through the revolving doors at Macy's. And, worse yet, in television there is hardly ever a full-time education beat, so chances grow that questions about education will not transcend the superficial.

An obvious way to try to gauge the media's impact on what the public thinks about education and the extent to which the media affect those beliefs is to ask people for their opinions and then try to discover where they got their information. The writers of the chapters in Part II do just this. Americans love polls and surveys. Most people cannot resist a request for their opinion, because they think their opinions are so valuable. Look at the explosion in talk radio. Everyone is an instant expert, no matter how poorly informed he or she is. And many people apparently decide what they think about education without taking their cues from the media. One would like to believe that these opinions owe their provenance to facts. Even with their flaws, the media offer information that should be useful to people trying to reach conclusions about the schools. If the public bypasses the media, this may be a sign of cynicism that newspapers, magazines, and television should take seriously.

Another aspect of the surveys is the finding that public opinion, examined over time, may show more constancy on the part of the public, and less fickleness, than the media imagines. A reading of the surveys indicates that Americans are leery of so-called reforms in teaching and learning, probably suspecting that these changes are nothing more than faddism. The media, on the other hand, tend to equate change with improvement. There is an indication here of a limitation on the media's impact on what people think about the schools.

Following up on this matter of opinions, the authors in Part III use three specific areas to focus on the media's influence on perceptions about education—testing, reading, and school desegregation. What comes through again and again is a sense that much of the portrayal of education takes on a negative tinge in the media. The writers of these chapters find that this may be due to such factors as sensationalism, lack of understanding on the part of reporters, and ill-advised headlines. Are the media seeking out the negative, or is this the dominant theme that emerges after careful and objective examination?

Reading instruction, for example, is a field filled with disputes among experts. It may be unreasonable to expect exemplary coverage by the media when the academic community itself is not of one mind about what counts most. And in the coverage of school desegregation, previously held attitudes about race are at stake. Some readers and viewers may approach media coverage mainly with a view to finding reinforcement for deeply felt convictions. The best the media can do under the circumstances is strive for straightforward, impartial reporting, tempered by recognition of a responsibility to help keep extremism at bay.

A recommendation in Part III suggests that improved reporting is apt to follow if educational institutions and agencies do more to help journalists understand the research findings and data that are provided to them. This is a reasonable proposal. Authorities in such organizations as the College Board and the National Assessment of Educational Progress have learned over the years how to present statistics and test scores with contextual information that render them more accessible for interpretation and analysis by reporters. Education writers are not psychometricians; but many of those with experience on the beat are intelligent, savvy people who—with a bit of assistance—generally know how to dig into data on the schools to make them interesting and comprehensible to readers.

Higher education normally gets less attention from the media than does schooling at the precollegiate level. Part IV is devoted to three of the main topics of this limited coverage—tuitions, admissions, and rankings. This tendency of the media to ignore much of what transpires at colleges and universities means the collegiate level does not receive the scrutiny that characterizes the coverage of elementary and secondary schools. Teaching and learning in higher education are virtually invisible as subjects of news and features. The upshot of the media's preoccupation with just a narrow slice of higher education is a kind of coverage that leans toward the hyperbolic, exaggerating what happens at a small number of institutions and leaving the public with the impression that the stories reflect what occurs in all of higher education.

The cost of going to college is perhaps the topic that most fascinates the media when it comes to higher education. This is not an altogether improper obsession given the importance of tuition to the average family budget. Yet, the story, as told by the media, can be distorted. The headline on a *Newsweek* cover in 1996 proclaimed "$1,000 a Week: The Scary Cost of College." This despite the fact that only 60 colleges in the entire United States had an annual tuition exceeding $20,000 in 1996–97, according to the College Board. It is one more way in which the media, in their coverage of education, sometimes seize on subject matter for its shock value. "The editors who want these stories obsess on about 25 schools," said David Breneman (1997), dean of the School of Education at the University of Virginia.

Another way in which the media have affected perceptions of higher education—to the consternation of the institutions themselves—is in their publishing of guides that rate colleges and universities. Stanford University found the guides so objectionable that it posted data on a World Wide Web site to offer an alternative source of information. Gerhard Casper, Stanford's president, encouraged other institutions to follow suit, saying it would enable students and their families to review and compare schools "without the distortion of information that occurs in *U.S. News*'s ranking system" (Geraghty & Guernsey, 1997).

Much of this book is concerned with the print coverage of education, because the overwhelming portion of the reportage appears on the pages of newspapers and magazines. The visual media, however, warrant special attention in Part V. This coverage is examined here through two separate lenses. On the one hand, television—to the extent that it deals with news about education—can be compared with the print media, a comparison in which television fares poorly. The sad fact is that television consigns education to a decidedly marginal position in its list of news priorities. Newton Minow's wasteland has not gotten any less arid; it simply has expanded, as is the wont of deserts. It is worth noting, however, that even though the small amount of coverage it provides is seldom first-rate, television has shown the ability to cover education strikingly well when it so desires.

The other way in which the visual media portray education—and in this case film and television share an approach—veers off entirely from newspapers and magazines; this form is pure entertainment, based on fiction. The only print analogy is found in an occasional novel with an educational setting—and there have been a few good ones lately.

These fictional images of education on the big or the little screen tend to be more powerful and enduring than what appears in print. But what appears tends to be stereotypical and in short supply. Education as subject matter for prime-time series has all the appeal of mumps to producers. They seldom give shows that are built around student or school themes the time to build an audience, yanking them off the air so fast that hardly anyone can remember having seen an episode. The visual media shy away from education, whether the issue is news or entertainment.

And so it is that this examination of the media's handling of education unfolds. This is neither the first nor the last such study of the media and its influence on perceptions. Whether one approves or disapproves of that impact, it is important to recognize its degree and to reflect on how the public interest is or is not served.

BIBLIOGRAPHY

Ads More Relevant Than News? *Editor & Publisher*, May 17, 1997. p. 19.

Blevens, Frederick R. When Journalistic Judgment Outrages Readers. *Chronicle of Higher Education*, May 16, 1997. p. B7.

Breneman, David. Interviewed in a five-part series on the cost of college. National Public Radio, April 21–25, 1997.

Geraghty, Mary, & Guernsey, Lisa. Stanford U. Creates an Alternative to the 'U.S. News' College Guide. *Chronicle of Higher Education*, May 2, 1997. p. A44.

Good News, Bad News: What People Really Think About the Education Press. Public Agenda, 1997.

Local TV News Lacks Substance. *Editor & Publisher*, May 24, 1997. pp. 8–9.

Maeroff, Gene I. (1982). *Don't Blame the Kids*. New York: McGraw-Hill.

Myers, Miles. The Public Press and the Profession. *Council Chronicle*, February 1997. p. 20.

An Overview of the Media's Coverage of Education

ALETA WATSON BRINGS the perspective of a working journalist to Chapter 1 as she details the kind of agonizing that takes place at the city desk as editors and reporters weigh the merits of stories about the schools. What comes through is a sense of the constant pressure facing earnest journalists. She talks about "the Call"—the inevitable voice on the telephone asking why the newspaper does not report the good news. And, like almost all journalists, she dismisses the notion that the media conspire, in the case of education or in any other area of coverage, to paint negative pictures. She wishes that readers had a fuller appreciation of the role of the media. Journalists, unlike novelists, must labor against deadlines that may cause them to compromise and take shortcuts. This is not to say, however, that they knowingly surrender to the forces of dishonesty or humbug.

All of this said, Watson urges her colleagues to produce more work that contributes to the public's understanding about what is happening in schools. She acknowledges that reporters tend to feel uneasy with statistics and she would welcome more time for them to think about and write their articles. "Yet, newspapers arguably remain the most complete and objective general source of information on education . . . , producing as true a picture of schools as possible in limited space and time," she asserts.

David C. Berliner and Bruce J. Biddle, though professors and education insiders, nevertheless are emblematic of many of the average citizens who just plain do not understand why the media give education such a rough ride. In Chapter 2, they go further than some critics, however, in hinting at a conspiracy on the part of the media to place schools in an adverse light. "Too frequently," they say, "a story is found interesting to reporters only if it is critical of the schools." Berliner and Biddle use such words and phrases as *incomplete*, *biased*, and *lack of understanding* to characterize the media's coverage of education. They are particularly dismissive of what they believe to be the media's failure to consider the role of poverty in explaining achievement differences among students.

Denis P. Doyle takes a different tack in Chapter 3, arguing that education gets off with hardly a bruise in its confrontation with the media, because not enough of the bad news is reported. Furthermore, he asserts, what *does* get covered tends to be handled in a shallow fashion. Doyle's view clashes with that of journalists who like to think of themselves as hard-boiled seekers of the truth. Doyle maintains that the education establishment obstructs news coverage of the schools, having created a sprawling enterprise that defies penetration by those seeking to get to the bottom of things. He charges: "Education is not covered in the depth it invites or calls for; neither is it broadly covered." Doyle maintains that the resulting ignorance of education fits comfortably within an anti-intellectual spirit in a public that does not want to think much about education or any other subject of substance.

The Newspaper's Responsibility

ALETA WATSON

EVERY REPORTER or editor who has ever been responsible for the education beat has received "the Call." On the other end of the phone line is a principal, teacher, or even a parent. She is responsible for public relations at a local school and wants your paper to cover this year's sponsored walk, canned-food drive, or reading marathon. "You write so many bad stories about schools," she begins. "Don't you think it's time you printed something good?"

The Call comes in many forms. Sometimes it is from the local superintendent trying to get positive press on a pet project. Sometimes it is from the governor's spokesperson looking for coverage for the latest state education initiative. Teachers, union leaders, college professors, and, of course, professional public relations people make the Call, too. They all deliver the same argument when they phone a newspaper office looking for a story promoting their cause or product: Isn't it time someone wrote something positive about schools?

Exasperated education writers share war stories about the Call whenever they get together at seminars and press events. "Why," they ask one another, "don't people understand that our job is to cover schools, not to make them look good?" They recite all the positive stories they have written about outstanding teachers, curriculum programs that work, and successful students at the same time as they have probed the more difficult issues of dismal test scores, curriculum battles, school violence, and crowded classrooms. "Is it our fault," they ask, "that people only remember the negative stories?"

Just what is the responsibility of newspapers for shaping public perceptions of education? As a line editor supervising education coverage for

Imaging Education: The Media and Schools in America. Copyright © 1998 by Teachers College, Columbia University. All rights reserved. ISBN 0-8077-3734-8 (pbk), ISBN 0-8077-3735-6 (cloth). Prior to photocopying items for classroom use, please contact the Copyright Clearance Center, Customer Service, 222 Rosewood Dr., Danvers, MA 01923, USA, tel. (508) 750-8400.

a large, regional newspaper, I ask myself that question frequently. I have become aware that the public views schools in a harsher light than do either my reporters or I. Parents constantly fret about school violence even though crime statistics show relatively few serious incidents in most schools. Readers worry that children across the board are no longer learning to read or do arithmetic, even though schools in our region generally score well above state and national averages on achievement tests. Families are considering private school even in wealthy districts that send most of their public school graduates on to 4-year colleges. What is going on here?

Research on the subject *is* sparse, and what there is mostly dates back to the past decade, before newspapers caught up with the national preoccupation with education. Furthermore, who can separate the influence of newspapers, magazines, television, radio, and even news groups on the World Wide Web? To what degree are perceptions also shaped by personal experiences and what people hear from their children, friends, and neighbors? We working journalists are left with little more than our own hypotheses, most of which—naturally—reflect favorably on our efforts and intentions.

In any case, there is no question that schools face significant challenges. In well-documented cases such as the school governance reforms in Chicago, inner-city districts appear to be fighting a losing battle against poverty, neglect, and neighborhood violence despite the heroic efforts of some dedicated educators. Students in poor neighborhoods rarely get as good an education as those in affluent communities. Is that the fault of the media? Only the top students take enough math and science to prepare them for the technological age. And universities report a steady increase in entering students who need remedial classes in basic subjects before they can tackle college work.

As journalists, my team of reporters and I try to raise public awareness of such problems as a first step toward solving them. Education has become one of the most visible beats at the *Mercury News,* and the work of those who cover education is often on page 1. Still, in examining the critical issues facing schools, are the media somehow creating the impression that there is nothing worth saving anywhere?

Jim Ritchie, the outspoken superintendent of the respected Moreland elementary school district in suburban San Jose, argued that the *Mercury News,* and newspapers in general, play a strong role in forming public perceptions of school, for both good and bad. In his community, he said, "I haven't seen any other entity that has the ability to change public perceptions for the short term. If it appears there and it appears in a strident and dramatic fashion, it will have an immediate effect on public opinion." The power of specific stories fades over time as parents and readers move on to other issues, in Ritchie's experience, but the impression of critical stories remains strong in the common memory. "I definitely think the image of the public schools reflected in the media is much more negative than it is positive," he said. He pointed to the steady stream of stories about critical reports on education as well as articles about business leaders and politicians who lambaste the schools' inadequacies. In his view, those stories, lumping all schools together in broad, general terms, do little to illuminate the vast differences between schools and even classes within a school. "That constant drumbeat, I really think it's created the impression that public schools do not reflect quality," he said.

Newspapers, indeed, are in the business of news. And ever since 1983, when a blue-ribbon panel warned in *A Nation at Risk* of a "rising tide of mediocrity" in America's schools, there has been a flood of impressive reports cataloging education's ills. The country has learned from the National Assessment of Educational Progress how little its children know about history, geography, reading and math—although their degree of knowledge probably is not significantly different from that of previous generations. Numerous studies, including the Third International Mathematics and Science Study, have found that students in the United States do not rank as well as Americans would like against their counterparts around the world on academic achievement tests. (U.S. eighth graders scored below average in math, where their lessons are not as advanced as in the top-scoring countries, and above average in science, where the curriculum is more focused.) The National Commission on Teaching and America's Future said that many of the nation's teachers are inadequately prepared. There have been so many reports and studies from this or that commission and think tank that the stories rarely get on the front page anymore. Still, they add fuel to the public debate over the future of schools and cannot be ignored by any responsible newspaper or broadcaster.

In their book *The Manufactured Crisis*, David C. Berliner and Bruce J. Biddle (1995) argue that the media have reported the international comparisons, in particular, unfairly, creating the impression that America's schools are failing. The two authors contend that journalists have neglected to ask critical questions about the groups tested and the subject matter covered while ignoring comparative studies in which American students have done well. They insist that schools in the United States, on average, are doing as well or better than ever, although they concede that there is still much room for improvement. "While the media seem quite willing to report bad news about our schools, they are much less willing to report news about the strengths of American education," they write. "One wonders, Why? Is it possible that bad news about education is thought to be more newsworthy? Or have reporters by now been so brainwashed by the critics that they cannot believe good news? Are too many of the reporters' employers friends of powerful people who wish the public schools no good?" (Berliner and Biddle, 1995, p. 62)

I find it hard to swallow such hints of a media conspiracy, and I object to inclinations to paint both print and broadcast reporters in the same light. I suspect, as well, that such criticisms arise from dissatisfaction with the work of the national press rather than of the nation's 1,500 daily newspapers, from which most readers get their news.

There may be some truth, though, in the contention that journalists have not done a good job of analyzing the comparative studies. Few reporters are comfortable with statistics—we joke among ourselves that if we had been good at math, we could have ended up in lucrative jobs instead of in journalism. Also, speed is essential in daily reporting and we do far too much of our analysis on the fly. We do not come back to a topic for deeper consideration nearly often enough. Compounding the problem, newspapers rarely provide enough space in which to analyze the nuances of a huge study. So, at even the best papers, complex stories on all topics become overly simplified more frequently than reporters would like.

All of this said, education itself has shortcomings that it would be irresponsible for the media to ignore. The national anxiety about education appears justified from many perspectives. As we approach the millennium, parents, business leaders, and politicians alike question whether schools on the whole are producing citizens adequately prepared for the information age. Even educators who are proud of what teachers and students are doing in their classrooms would most likely agree that schools need to reach higher to prepare more students for jobs that require academic skills such as advanced math. Economists maintain that students no longer can expect to graduate from high school with minimal skills and move right into well-paying factory jobs that allow them to join the middle class. It is not enough, others suggest, to prepare only our top students for college. At least 2 years of college is becoming the new standard in some eyes.

THE PUBLIC CARES

Education nears the top of the public agenda in most polls, right behind crime and the economy. Even in notoriously tax-stingy California, education is one of the few items on which voters often say they are willing to spend more money. When Policy Analysis for California Education conducted its 1996 poll on public views of education, 38% of the respondents named "improving the quality of public schools" as the most important issue facing the state. In the same poll, 66% said that it was important to increase funding for schools. Education took on even more significance in a 1996 *Mercury News* poll, which found that 88% of the people were concerned with the quality of public schools in their community—a notable departure from national polls, in which people have consistently defended their own schools. With that level of public interest, newspapers should not only report the debate but help inform it with stories that explore the issue from all perspectives.

Those who still believe in public education as a social good propose shifting more resources into the schools, setting high academic standards, and helping all students reach them. President Bill Clinton, in his 1997 State of the Nation speech, set forth a 10-point plan "to ensure that all Americans have the best education in the world." Clinton called for, in addition to setting national standards and drafting examinations tied to those standards, expanding Head Start, creating 3,000 charter schools, spending $5 billion on school construction, and establishing college scholarships. On the other hand, some advocates of choice propose subjecting public schools to market forces by giving students vouchers to attend private schools if they wish. They argue that public schools would have to shape up and compete for students or find themselves out of business for want of customers.

In the midst of the debate, David Mathews (1996), president of the Kettering Foundation, warns that the public's connection to its schools is waning. He says that his research has found what other studies have reported: Whereas Americans believe that the country needs public schools, they are torn between a sense of duty to support these schools and a responsibility to do what is best for children. "They are ambivalent and agonize over the dilemma. And, however reluctantly, many are deciding that public schools aren't best for their children or anyone else's" (p. 3), Mathews writes of the public.

Critics and many educators blame the media for public perceptions that schools are failing because of a combination of growing social problems, declining discipline, and falling standards. Yet, Mathews writes, "the people we talked to based their conclusions on personal experience or the experience of family members and close friends." So discouraged were most of the parents in focus groups conducted for the Kettering Foundation that even those who spoke relatively positively about their public schools said they would send their children to private school if they could receive a "check" to pay for the tuition. It must be noted, though, that voters have consistently rejected voucher proposals that would give parents those checks.

There is no denying that the public has mixed feelings about schools. One of the best indicators is the annual "Phi Delta Kappa/Gallup Poll of the Public's Attitudes Toward the Public Schools." In 1996, 66% of public school parents gave their own school an A or a B—a statistic that gives educators great comfort. But at the same time, only 21% of respondents gave the nation's schools an A or a B grade. Compare that to the 48% who gave top grades to public schools in 1974. Although 54% of the people who responded to the poll in 1996 opposed vouchers that would give families public money to send their children to private schools, most clearly felt that private schools were better: 63% gave private schools an A or a B.

It is hard to tell where the poll respondents obtained the information for that assessment. Most newspapers print very little about private schools, whose business is not conducted in a public forum with taxpayers' dollars. In most cases, private school students do not take the same tests as public school students, so it is tough to compare them on objective criteria. Perhaps it is their word-of-mouth reputation as bastions of discipline, decorum, and traditional curricula—and not portrayals in the media—that makes private schools so popular with a public committed to discipline and basic skills.

This is not the first era of hand-wringing over American education. Stanford University education professors David Tyack and Larry Cuban (1995) point out that the country has been fretting about its schools for more than a century. In *Tinkering Toward Utopia,* they note that the United States has worried most about the effectiveness of schooling at times of crisis, when national leaders obsess about the country's struggle for survival in a competitive world. In the 1890s, the Germans were the source of that anxiety; in the 1950s, the Soviets; and in the 1980s, the Japanese. They write:

> Commentators in the media, muckrakers, leaders in business and unions, government officials, legislators, social reformers, activists in women's associations, foundation officials, leaders of protest movements, and policy makers in education all starkly expose problems and confidently propose educational solutions. Then they pressure legislatures, school boards and public school administrators to adopt their reforms. (p. 44)

What has been different in the latest wave of education debates is the public's current disenchantment with *all* institutions—from their city councils to the Congress. At the same time, college graduation rates are up, and many parents, educated as well or better than are their children's teachers, now appear to be quite comfortable criticizing what goes on in the classroom. For the most part, parents do not buy the education establishment's arguments. They call for a greater emphasis on the basics and turn their noses up at most of the reform proposals from researchers and educators.

The conflicts that arise out of such disagreements are the grist of journalism. It is our job to write about the issues without taking a side. When the media do it right, they help readers and viewers understand what is at stake and explain the arguments. The media must take care, however, not to get caught up in the enthusiasm that educators have for the latest fad or in the ideology of the critics. That role belongs to the editorial writers and commentators. Although it seems difficult for most readers to distinguish the difference between the editorial pages and news sections, good newspapers keep them separated by the journalistic equivalent of a fire wall. Editorial writers tell readers what they should think. Reporters give them the information to make up their own minds.

NEGATIVITY IS IN THE EYE OF THE READER

So, what *should* newspapers be writing about in this time of ferment? Robert Frahm, a prize-winning education reporter with the *Hartford Courant* in Connecticut, says that newspapers have an obligation to help their readers understand what's really going on in schools. That means going into classrooms to show readers how teachers and students try to cope with difficult issues of learning, often against overwhelming odds. It also means holding the people in charge of the schools responsible for education in the community. "We get some complaints from school officials that we are too negative," says Frahm, former president of the Education Writers Association. "I don't believe that's true. I believe that if you were to count our stories and rate them as positive or negative, there would be more positives."

One of the most serious variables, reporters understand, is who is passing judgment on their work. If a story raises critical issues about schools that may lead to the improvement of education for children, most reporters would consider it a positive piece. In 1996, Frahm and fellow *Courant* reporter Rick Green did just that when they wrote a revealing study of the Hartford schools' management after its partnership collapsed with the for-profit corporation Education Alternatives Inc. Their stories, running over 4 days, chronicled the district's deep problems, ranging from serious financial mismanagement to chronic disputes between the union and administration that reverberated in the city's classrooms.

As a result of that series, the Connecticut State Department of Education announced that it would conduct a comprehensive review of the system. Six months later, the state education commissioner called for sweeping changes in management, curriculum, enrollment policies, and union contracts. At last, it appeared, someone was going to make a concerted effort to fix problems that had crippled the inner-city school system for years. Many Hartford readers might well view those events as a positive outcome.

Rarely do reporters get to see such a direct link between their work and a shift in public policy. Frahm took great pride in articles in the series that went beyond the facts and figures of the investigation to look at teachers' struggles to make the system work for their students. For instance, the articles cited a kindergarten teacher whose 22 students—all the children of unmarried mothers—live in some of the city's poorest neighborhoods and arrive at school often not even knowing their colors or the alphabet. This was a reality that few *Courant* readers would recognize. The newspaper's subscribers more often live in the affluent suburbs surrounding Hartford than in the inner city. That is why the story must be told. Educators, however, frequently appear to misunderstand the reporter's role as the public's eyes and ears. "We are conscious of not ignoring things that are going on in school that are good, but we also believe we can't ignore what is bad," Frahm says. "We feel if we were just to create a rosy picture of the schools, it would be a lie."

Although the Hartford stories were exemplary, such journalism is no longer an anomaly in America's newspapers. In Philadelphia, the *Inquirer* cataloged the city schools' failings in such indisputable detail in 1994 that a new superintendent used the series to launch substantial reform. In Denver, the *Rocky Mountain News* in 1995 so graphically outlined conflicts between research and teaching in Colorado universities that the schools ended up giving more attention to undergraduate instruction. Newspapers from Alaska to Kentucky have explored issues ranging from the inequities of special education to the intricacies of school reform. More and more, ambitious reporters go beyond school board meetings to try to explain why schools are working or not.

Steve Barkin is familiar with this trend. Barkin, a journalism professor at the University of Maryland, has judged the National Awards for Education Reporting since 1985. He has read countless education stories over the years. The newspaper stories Barkin read for the contest—admittedly some of the best work in the field—increasingly delved into the reality of what goes on in classrooms. There were still the traditional stories about test scores, budget battles, school board politics, and superintendent searches. But there were also many stories that tried to explain how schools went about their true work—teaching children. "When I was reading about education 20 years ago, I was reading about test scores," Barkin says, "and I'm still reading about test scores but the mix is a little more rich than it used to be. . . . I think you learn a lot more of what's going on in newspapers."

Even George Kaplan, who has censured newspapers for putting too many inexperienced young reporters on the schools beat and then covering education only superficially via school board meetings, modified his tone in a 1997 interview. Although still fairly critical of the national newspapers for inadequately treating trends in education reform, he cited improvement among all papers. "In general, I think the smaller communities are getting a fairly objective picture. They don't care about national trends," Kaplan said. "For the name papers, the reporting is mixed. But overall I think the reporting is good."

Jay Rosen, a New York University professor and an advocate of public journalism, questions the quality of education reporting. He contends that newspapers are still not giving their readers what they need to make informed decisions about education policy and that reporters spend too much time writing about the school board and not enough about schools. "I think the major failing of newspaper coverage of education is the failing of most public institution coverage," Rosen says. "It's institution driven, it's conflict driven and tends to be rarely concerned with the resolution of issues or problem solving." Rosen wants reporters to get away from their dependence on school trustee meetings for day-to-day education coverage.

As an example of a better approach to education coverage, Rosen points to the 40,000-circulation *Bremerton Sun* in Washington State. Editor Mike Phillips became frustrated when the *Sun* education reporter wrote numerous stories about the local school superintendent's salary. Instead, he suggested, the reporter should ask parents what was on their minds and then write about that. The answer that came back was "homework," and the *Sun* responded by looking into why so many Bremerton students didn't bring home homework. A new approach to schools coverage was born. Phillips says: "What happens in a school board has little to do with the rearing of children, the education of children, most of the time. A lot of people recognize the problem with that pattern, but they're not very successful in changing it, simply because it's easier." I would argue that many larger papers have all but abandoned school board-related coverage except in the most dramatic cases—for example, the very public conflict between New York mayor Rudolph Giuliani and former chancellor Ramon Cortines. In an illustration of the new style of education coverage, the *Miami Herald* in 1996 devoted 3 months to producing a 4-day series that answered Dade County parents' most pressing questions about their public schools.

Mercury News reporters rarely attend board meetings. But in countless other newspapers—particularly smaller publications for which reporters are required to churn out several stories a day—such institutional coverage remains the staple of education reporting. What some critics say about newspapers is true: Not all education stories are extensively researched pieces about both the positive and negative aspects of an issue. By necessity, such thorough articles are only a small portion of what we print over time. Even if education reporters fill their articles with context to help readers understand what is really going on, countless stories from other reporters and wire services do not. When Bob Dole attacked teacher unions in the course of his presidential campaign, it made headlines, but there was very little critical analysis of his charges from the political reporters covering the speech. When SAT scores go up or down by a single point, it is news, even though the change is relatively insignificant statistically. And papers still run the Associated Press–produced charts ranking the states by SAT scores even though the College Board notes that only a small proportion of high school students—usually those aiming for elite colleges—take the test in the most high-scoring states. (Average scores tend to decline when more students take the test.) As a nation, we love benchmarks even if they are flawed. Readers demand them and newspapers deliver them, usually with caveats that are routinely ignored.

Yet, newspapers arguably remain the most complete and objective general source of information on education for the public, producing as true a picture of schools as is possible in limited space and time. Look at the case of the move by the school board in Oakland, California, to recognize as a separate language the street dialect of African American students. Within hours of the December 18, 1996, school board vote, Ebonics—a term taken from *ebony* and *phonics*—was Topic number 1 on radio talk shows across the country. Newspapers from Phoenix to London ran stories about the board's action. Within days, Jesse Jackson and Maya Angelou were denouncing the school board's action and Secretary of Education Richard Riley was announcing that there would be no federal funding for bilingual classes in Ebonics.

Throughout it all, newspapers did a far better job than did broadcast media at reporting just what the board did and what this meant. The school board's resolution referred to "genetically based" African language systems and argued that "recognizing the English language acquisition and improvement skills of African American students are as fundamental as is application of bilingual education principles for others whose primary languages are other than English." It also ordered the superintendent to "immediately devise and implement the best possible academic program for imparting instruction to African American students in their primary language" and talked of "maintaining the legitimacy and richness" of Black English. The language of the school board was incendiary and the intent was obvious: At least some people in the district were hoping to get bilingual funding to help raise the dismal achievement levels among African American students. Newspapers reported those facts, and followed up as the school board subtly revised its position to focus solely on improving achievement by acknowledging and working with the dialect that Black children brought into the classroom. Trustees insisted that they never intended for Ebonics to be taught as a separate language in Oakland schools.

Print reporters covered every twist and turn as trustees won Jackson over to their side and then finally backed off some of the most controversial wording of their resolution. But reporters also took a hard look at the problems that Black children face in classrooms across the country when they are expected to speak a language markedly different from their street slang. The *Mercury News* and other California newspapers went into Oakland classrooms to describe just how the district was already using Ebonics to help students master standard English. The *Washington Post* ran a front page story on the search for a solution to the national problem of low academic performance by many poor Black students. It quoted linguists as saying that the use of Black English as a bridge to standard English might be effective in the classrooms, then explored the views of skeptics.

"I think newspapers handled it a lot more responsibly than the school board acknowledged," says Michael Bazeley, then the education reporter of the *Oakland Tribune*. "Television did a horrible job, in my opinion—on Day 6 or 7 they were saying kids were going to be taught black English in the classroom." Rush Limbaugh had a field day. So did editorial writers and columnists from Los Angeles to New York and beyond. As late as February, a *Newsweek* columnist expounded on the topic, and Garry Trudeau lampooned Ebonics in a Sunday *Doonesbury* strip. Yet, readers of the news columns got a fairly clear understanding of one of the most controversial education stories of the year.

EXPLAINING THE NEWS

That is how it should be. Newspaper articles should help readers understand their world better. The huge, controversial stories are exhilarating. Reporters love it when the world hangs onto their words. But they also write smaller, yet important stories that they hope will illuminate pressing issues. Often those articles are good news by almost anyone's interpretation. Early in 1997, the *Mercury News* ran a front page story about a district that consistently performed well against all odds. The report showed how San Jose's Evergreen elementary district, with a large proportion of impoverished students who speak little or no English, had managed to raise test scores and win national recognition for its schools. Evergreen's secret, reporter Maya Suryaraman revealed, was its teachers. The district emphasized teacher training and curriculum planning and gave teachers a strong role in making decisions that affect their classroom. As a result, many teachers took a more professional role in diagnosing and solving their students' learning problems. But the story, focused as it was on solutions, received only slight notice from readers. The public seems to have a better memory for the negative story.

As a case in point, Jodi Berls, education reporter for the *Austin American-Statesman* in Texas, likes to tell the tale of two big projects that her paper produced in 1996. One was on the local district's efforts to get parent volunteers into the schools. The other was on lunchtime violence in schools. "Both packages got front page play, with extensive space inside; both had lots of photos and some graphics; both involved numerous campus visits and myriad phone calls; both took about a month to put together," she says. "The cafeteria violence story got a lot of response—parents, teachers and students called afterward to tell us they liked it, offer us tips and ideas related to it, etc. The volunteering story, response-wise, went down a black hole except for one guy who referred to it in a board meeting in a snide comment suggesting that I'm in the school district's pocket."

Even as they are berated for their work, most reporters realize that public opinion often seems to have a life of its own with little relation to journalistic enterprise. Conventional wisdom quite frequently rules, in spite of evidence to the contrary. To see how newspapers may not sway public opinion, consider the series that the *Mercury News* produced in 1996 looking at the otherwise unquestioned push for more computers in the schools. The newspaper performed its own computer analysis in concert with a University of California researcher, working with data from a national technology data collection firm. When they were finished, the reporters concluded that there was no hard evidence that California schools with large investments in technology performed any better academically than comparable schools without similar equipment—except in low-income neighborhoods.

Few readers, evidently, bought the idea. Letters ran heavily in favor of a bigger investment in school technology in all schools. Local superintendents called for a meeting with the publisher and executive editor to complain that the *Mercury News* was antieducation. And the paper, located in the heart of Silicon Valley, continued to run story after story about high-tech executives trashing the schools for not doing enough with computers, as well as articles on politicians urging greater expenditures on technology. Even though the newspaper included a paragraph in most of those stories about our reporters' findings, it was clear that most people still believed that computers are the answer to schools' academic shortcomings.

Such experiences are frustrating, but journalists are accustomed to them. So most journalists decide that they just have to do their best to keep their minds open, their eyes peeled for good stories, and their judgment unclouded by ideology. Journalists try to keep up with research and the broad range of emerging thought in the field. They look for issues and

trends that may make a difference in their readers' lives as well as interesting features that illuminate what's going on in schools. In the end, journalists cannot allow themselves to be swayed by consideration of whether
a story will be good for the public image of schools. Their job is to tell the
truth and help readers understand the challenges that society is facing. The
truth is often unpleasant.

BIBLIOGRAPHY

Berliner, David C. and Bruce J. Biddle. *The Manufactured Crisis.* Addison-Wesley.
    1995.
Gallup Poll. "The 28th Annual Phi Delta Kappa/Gallup Poll of the Public's Atti-
    tudes Toward the Public Schools." *Phi Delta Kappan.* September, 1996.
Kaplan, George R. *Images of Education: The Mass Media's Version of America's Schools.*
    Institute for Educational Leadership. 1992.
Mathews, David. *Is There a Public for Public Schools?* Kettering Foundation Press.
    1996.
Policy Analysis for California Education. "PACE Poll: Californians' Views on
    Education, Questions and Poll Results." March, 1996.
Tyack, David and Larry Cuban. *Tinkering Toward Utopia.* Harvard University Press.
    1995.
U.S. Department of Education, National Center for Education Statistics. *Pursuing
    Excellence: A Study of U.S. Eighth-Grade Mathematics and Science Teaching, Learn-
    ing, Curriculum and Achievement in International Context.* 1996.

The Lamentable Alliance
Between the Media and School Critics

DAVID C. BERLINER AND BRUCE J. BIDDLE

SPRING, 1997, WAS NOT kind to the press. At the April 1997 meetings of the American Educational Research Association, we asked approximately 200 attendees at a presentation on education and the media four questions about educational reporting and editorial policy in the newspapers they read (Berliner, 1997a). Roughly 95% of this convenience sample believed that news reporting about public education was not neutral, but biased negatively, critical of the schools; reporting about education was simple and incomplete, rather than complex or thoughtful; editorial policy was biased negatively, overly critical of the schools; and editorial policy was simple, not particularly thoughtful.

Shortly thereafter, in May 1997 at the Educational Writers Seminar, the school reform organization Public Agenda released its report *Good News, Bad News: What People Really Think About the Educational Press* (1997). This was a much more rigorous survey, but yielded similar results. Here, educators vilified the press, with 75 to 91% of the respondents agreeing strongly that reporters cover education news according to what sells; report low achievement without contexts for evaluating those findings; unfairly dwell on conflict and failure; use quotes or statistics out of context; and have caused much of the decline in public confidence in public schools. Parents were less negative, but even so, 50% judged news coverage of the schools to be fair or poor.

A little earlier that spring, in February, the Pew Research Center for the People and the Press (1997) conducted a survey of attitudes about the press in general, not just about education reporting. They found broad

Imaging Education: The Media and Schools in America. Copyright © 1998 by Teachers College, Columbia University. All rights reserved. ISBN 0-8077-3734-8 (pbk), ISBN 0-8077-3735-6 (cloth). Prior to photocopying items for classroom use, please contact the Copyright Clearance Center, Customer Service, 222 Rosewood Dr., Danvers, MA 01923, USA, tel. (508) 750-8400.

cynicism about the press. The public characterized the press as more unfair, more inaccurate, and pushier than in previous years. A majority of the public believes that the press is biased and gets in the way of our nation's finding solutions to its problems. The commentary and examples that follow are designed to give substance to these negative perceptions and to point out their unfortunate implications. Before proceeding further, however, we need to acknowledge that educational reporting shows variation from newspaper to newspaper. And reporting varies within the same newspaper, from story to story, and from one reporter to another. It is also true and noteworthy that within the fourth estate are people of great integrity, trying hard to get their stories correct and make their commentary useful. Group and individual data are different, of course, and so we ask your indulgence as we comment on the profession in general, not individual reporters and papers in particular.

We think that too frequently a story is found interesting to reporters only if it is critical of the schools, if it has some scent of blood about it. Using news lingo, "If it bleeds, it leads." And we believe that most of the editorial opinions from the so-called liberal press are in fact, quite conservative. Thus, to us, the newspapers have become a natural ally of those who believe that public education has failed. The school critics believe that public schooling should be abandoned, or should reform itself to find some way of returning to those halcyon days of yesterday (a time better described as the halcyon *haze* of yesterday, we think, much better recalled from memory than actually lived).

We will not explore in depth the problem of who speaks for education to the press. We note only that, for example, some of those who write op-ed articles and are widely quoted are not necessarily objective and have something to gain from, say, the approval of vouchers that could be used at nonpublic schools. It serves their interests to promote the belief that public education is a failure and that privatization is the only sensible solution. Why, when they write or talk, aren't they identified as individuals who may be compromised in regard to their objectivity? Others who criticize the public schools hold strong fundamentalist religious beliefs that lead them to want their children segregated from those in secular schools (Berliner, 1997b). They seek vouchers to fund such schools, and by attacking the public schools, they come a little closer to achieving their goals. Critics with such strong views or with pecuniary interests should be identified by the press when their comments are reported, just as are representatives from the National Education Association and the American Federation of Teachers.

It appears to be great sport to draw blood when reporting the unseemly, the negative, and the absurdities that necessarily occur in a system with nearly 3 million public school teachers, working in about 100,000 public schools. For example, last year the nation's press ridiculed a school that suspended a girl for giving a friend with a headache an aspirin. Very few press reports contained any sympathy for a school dealing with a citizenry that overuses and abuses both legal and illegal drugs. Very few reporters acknowledged that this school was attempting to follow the leads of former first lady Nancy Reagan and President Clinton, hoping to teach children to "Just say no!" and to impose a "zero tolerance" drug policy on their campus. Public school critics have asserted that the schools promote drug use among teenagers. Yet, here was a public school trying its best to guarantee that there would be no drug use or abuse on their campus, and for their efforts, they were made to appear ridiculous.

Last year, the press also ridiculed school officials for suspending a primary school boy who kissed a girl on the cheek. Jokes and cartoons made the rounds, painting the school officials as politically correct fanatics. Few press reports included sympathy for a school trying to deal with the high and ignominious rates of sexual harassment and domestic violence that exist in our society. This is a society where too many males believe that they have a right to make advances to and touch females, though such attention is unwanted. And too many females appear reticent to say no in an unequivocal way and demand that their decisions be respected. When should schools start teaching the serious consequences of these behaviors, after puberty or before? The critics of public schools often assert that our schools do not teach character or develop morals. Yet here was a public school trying to do precisely that, and the media made that school appear ludicrous.

Last year also saw the press ridicule the Oakland, California, school board's Ebonics policy, treating its actions as the demented ravings of foolish African people. In newspapers, newsweeklies, and on the electronic media, cartoons and jokes swept across the country. These not only were designed to ridicule the Oakland School Board, but also incorporated verbal stereotypes and visual images that we thought had died out in polite company 50 years ago. We had to turn to the academic journals to learn something about the rationale for the proposed policy, the reasonable pedagogical principles that were being promoted through the boards' policy, and the linguistically solid grounds for declaring Black English vernacular a language. These arguments were not usually found in the popular press. In general, an unsympathetic press was more interested in a good bloodletting than they were in uncovering any trace of reasonableness in the decision of the Oakland board. The ridicule, of course, provided more ammunition for those who assert that public education has failed.

Please note that we are not defending here the school boards' or administrators' actions in *any* of these three instances. In our estimation, they were each examples of bungled and embarrassing attempts at implementing or developing public policy. These were all public relations nightmares and we cringe when we think about the silliness of some of the school people involved. But schools are about something bigger than the public relations nightmares that inevitably occur. Public schooling is really about ordinary people trying to make reasonable decisions in the best interests of their communities—decisions that will help their young people grow to be knowledgeable, economically productive, and decent citizens. In all three cases, that was the intention of the school policy, and those noble intentions were commonly ignored in the derision and the bloodletting in which the media indulged. Missing from the reporting of all three cases was a modicum of caring, of sympathy, of understanding about what the schools were trying to accomplish, even though in each case they appeared to have bungled it.

Because no quarter was given by the press, those who criticize the schools were given more ammunition; particularly helped were those who claim that the public schools are run by inept bureaucrats. For some, the proposed solution to the allegations of ineptitude is the privatization of our public education system. But, in our view, the most pernicious immediate effect of this kind of reporting was that schoolchildren learned that their school leaders are chumps—people of low prestige, the butt of Jay Leno and David Letterman jokes, people whose words and actions can be easily dismissed. Public perceptions, particularly student perceptions, are shaped by the media through the respect or derision that they display for different groups. Can the routine and undiscriminating ridicule of schoolteachers and administrators be good for the nation? Instead, could the press not find the absurdities of individual educators newsworthy—subject to criticism, laughter, or outrage—and also find ways to preserve the dignity of a few million other professional educators who work so hard for the good of the nation?

DEFICIENCIES GALORE: OUR REBUKE OF THE PRESS

In our opinion, on educational issues, the press—

- Is biased and covers the negative side of news stories much more diligently than the positive side
- Presents too simplistic and incomplete a view of the educational problems and issues that they are reporting
- Is more critical of the schools in its editorial policies than it is complimentary

- Has editorial policies that are biased against public schools, against school change, and in particular, against the schools that serve the poor
- Displays a lack of understanding of the complexity of school life in contemporary America
- Shows an appalling lack of understanding of statistics and social science research, without which reporters cannot properly interpret the huge amount of data that the educational system produces
- Shows an ignorance of the role of poverty as a root cause of many of the difficulties in our schools

The press seems either too scared, too controlled, or too uninformed to raise what we consider the most basic issue confronting education in the United States—achieving a fair distribution of opportunities to succeed. This issue, however, is a close relative of issues associated with redistribution of wealth in our society, a topic that the mainstream press too often avoids.

Over the past few years, we have kept some files about the news reports that have shaped our perceptions. We will use one major recent news event to illustrate why we feel as we do. Then we note some further problems with the coverage of educational stories. Let us start out with the recent reporting of the TIMSS—the Third International Mathematics and Science Study—which first released data to the public in November, 1996 (Beaton, Martin, et al., 1996; Beaton, Mullis, et al., 1996). We read over 100 news stories to get a feel for how the press handles a contemporary and important educational story. The objective facts are clear and not in dispute. In a well-run, 41-nation study of seventh and eighth graders, the United States ranked about average, with Singapore a runaway winner and other Asian nations, in particular, outscoring us. The data on achievement in math and science was presented so that there were three statistically homogeneous groups of nations—those ahead of us, those tied with us, and those behind us. More interesting to the education profession was the data about curriculum and instruction for each nation. But, as expected, more press coverage went to the multination horse race in science and mathematics, a search for winners and losers.

The *New York Times,* along with many other papers, provided perfectly sensible stories based on the release of the data. The *Times* story was thorough, and in our estimation, its headline was accurate and descriptive: "Americans Straddle the Average Mark in Math and Science" (November 21, 1996). But others had different approaches to reporting the same data, provided at the same press conference called to announce the results of the study. For example, the *San Diego Union-Tribune* (November 21, 1996) actually found cause to celebrate, announcing: "Global Test of Pupils Shows

U. S. Improving." This interpretation was an accurate one, but apparently not worth featuring in any other report we could find. The *St. Petersburg Times* article was less positive, but thought provoking, nevertheless (November 21, 1996). It proclaimed: "Science, Math Study Renews Calls for Reform." And that is true, too. There is much of interest in the study that can guide our school improvement efforts. The *Chicago Sun-Times*, however, created a much harsher and unsubstantiated headline to report the same story (November 22, 1996): "U. S. Schools in Crisis; So What Else Is New?" Most of the reporting was closer to the negativism expressed by the *Chicago Sun-Times*, rather than to the single positive and the few thoughtful responses to the study generated by the press.

As we read these stories, we noticed quickly that nobody liked to be average, including Education Secretary Riley, who was quoted as saying that "for U. S. students, average is just not good enough" (*Orange County Register*, November 21, 1996). No reporter or any government official seemed to note the inevitability of *some* nations having to be about average. Moreover, that position in an international comparison of educational achievement will almost always go to one of the more heterogeneous nations, say a country like the United States, which provides for the study a sample from 15,700 designed-to-be-different school systems. These school systems operate independently; receive support through vastly different funding formulas that yield great disparities in per-pupil support; have created different curricula; use different texts; and serve families heavily segregated by social class and ethnicity. Under conditions such as these, if a fair sample is drawn, it should be obvious that it will combine both the excellent performance of children in superb school districts and the abysmal performance of children in awful school districts. A nation such as the United States will inevitably be described by its central characteristics— losing its ability to showcase its pockets of excellence, although hiding, as well, its genuine disasters.

The *Tampa Tribune* (December 1, 1996), however, was not dealing with this subtlety, apparently not even understanding the basic meaning of average, since it proclaimed in a headline: "U. S. Eighth-Graders Far Back in Math." The *San Francisco Chronicle* (December 28, 1996) said that "American Eighth-Graders Are Average, at Best." It added the little zinger at the end to be sure that a negative tone was attached to the headline. The *San Diego Union-Tribune* (December 22, 1996) carried an article by a state legislator noting that such terribly low scores on tests like these are old news. All this negativism was associated with being average in mathematics—a position that statistically tied us with such equally inadequate and equally average countries as Thailand, Israel, Germany, New Zealand, England, Norway, Denmark, Scotland, Spain, and Iceland.

In science, being about average statistically tied us with the inadequate likes of England, Flemish Belgium, Australia, Sweden, Germany, Canada, Norway, New Zealand, Thailand, Israel, Hong Kong, Switzerland, and Scotland. It also tied us with the Russian Federation. That was the awesome economic and military competitor that, 40 years ago, Admiral Rickover predicted would bury us because Russian schools taught rigorous science courses whereas our schools were too lenient. No reports we saw noted the remarkably good company that we were in with "merely" an average score. Apparently, it is the dream of the American press and the American people to have children like those in the Lake Wobegon schools—all above average.

The most obvious distortion of the TIMSS data, however, was offered to the public by the *Orange County Register* (January 8, 1997). Since the nations were placed into three statistically homogeneous groups—above us, tied with us, and below us—this newspaper could honestly say to its readers that "the United States scored in the second lowest group," not even calling it the middle group. The *Register* took a cheap shot in calling this the second lowest group. It is like the description of an Olympic footrace in which all but two runners drop out. The winner could then be described as coming in next to last, and the second fastest runner in the world could be described as coming in dead last!

Ranks were used by most reporters to describe the TIMSS data. But none of the reporters seemed to see any analogy to an Olympic running competition. That is, no one thought that you can be a very competitive racer at the Olympics, come in a few seconds behind the winner of the 10-kilometer race, and rank 24th, though perhaps only a few seconds off a world record. So another way the data from TIMSS might have been looked at was to ask how the United States actually scored, not how the country ranked in the race to mathematics and science gold medals. When that is done in mathematics for the 28th-ranked United States eighth graders, they are seen to have succeeded in getting 53% of the math items right, within 10% of 30 other nations! Only six nations achieved scores higher than those in the United States by 10% or more. *Newsweek* reported this as finishing "way out of the money" in an article describing the mediocrity of the American educational system (December 2, 1996). Actually, *mediocrity* was a word used a lot during the week the TIMSS eighth-grade data report was released, and it was technically used correctly, since mediocre has the same root as *median*. But we think this adjective was chosen less for its technical appropriateness and more for its connotation of failure, which is easier to attach to the rankings but much less convincing if anyone chose to look at the actual scores achieved by the various nations.

The science test showed a similar pattern. Students in the United States got an average of 58% of the items correct. Thirty-three other nations had scores within 10% of what American students attained, and only one scored more than 10% above the United States. In rank, the United States was 17th, a long way out of the money. Nevertheless, only one country exceeded the American average science score by more than 10%, suggesting that the United States ran a pretty good race after all. These kinds of interpretations were lacking in the reports we read.

All that mediocrity on the TIMSS tests led citizens and news reporters to propose solutions. The editorial in the Minneapolis *Star Tribune* (December 9, 1996) suggested that students should use rulers to make every mathematical problem neat, and to use rulers also so that all the equal signs were lined up perfectly. The logic was that if students used the rulers in this way, they would slow down and think more about the mathematics problems they were doing. On the other hand, the *Los Angeles Times* (December 15, 1996) reported that American students needed to be speeded up, developing the facility to do simple multiplication problems in their heads in $8/10$ of a second or less. Then there is the *Orange County Register* (January 8, 1997) reporting that the TIMSS study provided empirical evidence that the new math standards and teaching methods were a total failure. But the *St. Petersberg Times* (November 21, 1996), correctly, we think, reported that the TIMSS data supported the use of the new mathematics standards and teaching methods. Slowing them down or speeding them up, throwing out the standards or putting them in, seems to be a sad kind of search for magic bullets and Holy Grails, a search to assure parents that their children's test scores will be high and competitive with those of other nations. But a little study of the previous international mathematics survey, reported less than a decade ago, reveals most of what we need to know about the causes of high and low mathematics performance in the United States.

We learned in the international mathematics study of 1991–1992 (Berliner & Biddle, 1995) that public school children in such states as Iowa, South Dakota, and Minnesota proved that they were the equal of their Asian counterparts who scored so well, on average, when taking a comparable mathematics test. American public school children of middle- and high-income families also were competitive with students in the highest achieving nations in the world. The average mathematics performance of White children in the United States was quite high, as well. Added to this, and a bit amusing, was that Asian American public school students scored above the average of Asian students in the Asian nations that participated in that study. That is, our Asians outperformed Asian Asians! So we know that the American public system of education, as diverse and incoherent as it is, can turn out world-class young mathematicians if they are raised in certain states, are of a certain income level, and are of a certain ethnicity. But the *average* performance was low in that study because some students in the United States were not achieving well at all. Who were these low performers? Poor children in general, Hispanic and African American children in particular, and the children living in some of the poorest states in the country, particularly Alabama, Louisiana, and Mississippi. In our estimation, there is only one major difference between the schools and students that score well and those that score poorly in the United States. It is the wealth and social conditions that characterize the families, neighborhoods, and districts involved. We saw little evidence that reporters knew any of the history of testing achievement across nations and no TIMSS report we saw even hinted at the fact that poverty might be the single greatest barrier to high achievement in the American public schools.

THE LACK OF DISCUSSION ABOUT WEALTH AND POVERTY

Last year in Phoenix, two schools, one rich and White, the other poor and non-White, had students involved in fights during the same week. The incident at the poor school received days of press coverage by the *Arizona Republic* (February 27, 1997; February 28, 1997), totaling hundreds of lines of prose, including front page stories in the second section of the paper, and pictures of police at the school in riot gear. The story of the fight at the rich school, in which the only injury took place, involved known gang members and adults from the community, but was reported 5 days after the event and received a total of 14 lines on an inside page (March 1, 1997). We believe that more press coverage is given to the negative stories about school problems that plague the poor than about those that plague the rich, even when the problems are the same. This contributes to the perception that "they aren't like us," and fosters segregation of peoples by race and class.

There is dramatic evidence to support the importance of poverty and wealth in explaining the differences within and between countries, some of it coming from a substudy of the TIMSS. A group of 20 public school districts, made up of 32 elementary schools, 17 middle schools, and 6 high schools, primarily on Chicago's North Shore, formed the *First in the World Consortium* (Kroeze & Johnson, 1997). They were responding, in part, to comparative psychologist Harold Stevenson of the University of Michigan. Some time ago, Stevenson made the claim, which we consider ridiculous, that none of the classrooms he studied in the Chicago area was anywhere near as good as the Japanese classrooms that he studied (see Stevenson &

Stigler, 1992; Stevenson, Yee, & Stigler, 1986). The First in the World Consortium bravely set out to prove that American public schools with the resources to do their job can, indeed, do it quite well. These schools serve a wealthy and predominantly White community and that, unfortunately, has meaning for understanding schooling in contemporary America. These were communities where middle- and upper-income families had jobs that paid well, and therefore they provided health care for their children; where parents insured that their children had the physical space and learning tools that were needed to achieve in school; where parents communicated strong educational values and helped create a home environment that was compatible with the school achievement; and where parental values and income combined to provide their local schools with adequate funding, all of which resulted in competent teachers working for decent rates of pay in well-maintained physical plants. These conditions are typical of the public schools in communities all over this nation where it is possible for people to pursue and realize the American dream. They are prevalent in the multitude of communities where families have some stability and dignity in their lives, and where parents therefore raise children who have some vision of themselves as competent, useful, and well-remunerated adults. In communities such as these, teachers talk about standards, set high expectations, receive good training, and are given the chance to implement a rigorous and successful curriculum.

So what happened to these exemplary American public schools when they said to the TIMSS directorate, "Test us if you dare, we'll pay the bill"? They got their way and entered the study. Students of theirs were randomly selected to be tested in the same way that a national sample would have been tested in any of the other participating countries. When their mathematics test results were announced, they ranked fifth overall, but their score was exceeded statistically by only one other nation! And in science, the First in the World Consortium ranked second in the world, but statistically no nation scored any higher than they did. Not bad, we think, for a set of public schools that is said by its critics to be unable to deliver.

Did the press rejoice about this? No. Was there much attention given to this fabulous public school performance? No. Did this study generate anywhere near as much press as the overall TIMSS where our nation's eighth graders were described as behind the pack, mediocre, or just giving one more poor performance? No. The press provided limited coverage of this event even though the president of the United States, the secretary of education and the head of the House committee overseeing education all traveled to Illinois to proudly announce the significant and completely unambiguous good news about the performance of some of the nation's public school students. Teachers we meet all over the nation have never heard of these heartening results. Moreover, in the stories we read, the spin that was put on these results was that it was okay for these schools to do well; after all, they were predominantly "rich and White." But implicit in this view is a terrible form of racism and classism, implying by the very same logic that it is also okay for schools not to do well because they are populated by the Black and the poor. Color and income are not indicators of ability, but of resources available.

The modest performance of American students on the TIMSS led to hypotheses about the causes for the failure of the United States to achieve scores as high as those in some other countries. The secretary of education and the various professional education groups in the United States suggested that the problems were caused by poor preparation of teachers, that is, teaching these teachers procedures for doing mathematics, rather than the conceptual knowledge needed to understand mathematics; a national lack of standards; a lack of a focused curriculum; a lack of high expectations for performance; a lack of time for teachers to prepare lessons; a lack of an apprenticeship in teaching that helps novice teachers learn their craft; and some others. All of these factors probably contribute to our modest level of performance in the international competition. But history and the data from the First in the World Consortium tell us that one whopping big factor is also affecting the performance of American kids, namely, the economics of family, neighborhood, and school district. Poverty in school district budgets and in the neighborhoods and among the families of our urban ethnic minorities and our rural poor is strongly related to test performance. And the United States has the highest rate of childhood poverty among all the industrialized democracies—21.5%. No other industrialized nation is even close, and many nations (e.g., Sweden, Finland, Switzerland) have a rate of childen in poverty of around 3% (Rainwater & Smeedling, 1995). These statistics—not the nation's rank in math or science—are more likely the cause of America's educational problems, but these statistics do not receive much attention.

So one perfectly sensible suggestion for improving the mathematics and science performance of America's youth is to provide decent-paying jobs for the members of a community whose children are not doing well. This suggestion is perfectly compatible with existing data but was never mentioned by analysts of the TIMSS reports. Families and neighborhoods that have wealth buy the talent to teach their children well (e.g., Ferguson, 1991). They buy the resources to enable their students to do well, and provide a family life that is supportive of educational advancement. Among the best predictors of achievement in the Second International Math Study (SIMS) was the level of a district's funding, its poverty rate, and the rigor of the curriculum (Payne & Biddle, 1997) These are the kinds of advantage that accrue to being rich and White, the kinds of advantage that were capitalized on by the First in the World Consortium.

What can we conclude from the recent TIMSS reporting? Certainly some of it was fair and reasoned. But we think there were some problems, too. There was bias against suggesting that relative wealth and poverty is a causal factor in achievement; there was a lack of historical understanding of the international tests; there was a widespread misunderstanding about the difference between ranks and scores and the difference in interpretations that accompany each of these ways of presenting the same data; there was ignorance about the concept of standard error of measurement and the nature of social science data in general; there was confusion, or bias, in interpreting the meaning of the average performance of the United States; there was bias in the lack of space given to the extremely high performance of the students in the well-supported public schools of the First in the World Consortium.

This lack of reporting on the good news, we might add, is not new. In July 1992, the parent organization of the TIMSS study, the International Association for the Assessment of Educational Achievement (IEA) released the news about a 31-nation study of reading. In that study, our 9-year-olds ranked second, whereas our 14-year-olds ranked ninth but were tied, statistically, with the second-place finisher. Essentially the United States placed second—behind tiny, homogeneous, family-friendly, medically well-covered Finland. The press conference to announce the excellent achievement of the remarkably heterogeneous United States drew zero reporters. No one showed. Nobody. If Europeans hadn't carried the story and made so much out of it, the American press would never have heard of it. But the European stories soon drifted over, and *USA Today* finally broke this story of high academic achievement to the public, though months after the original press conference had been called and failed to attract reporters (Bracey, 1994). Most newspapers had nothing to say about this noteworthy and positive accomplishment by our public school students.

THE NATIONAL ADULT LITERACY STUDY (NALS)

Now, let us look briefly at literacy in the United States through the reporting of the well-regarded National Adult Literacy Study (NALS) (Kirsch, Jungeblut, Jenkins, & Kolstad, 1993). This study was conducted by the Educational Testing Service for the National Center for Education Statistics. The press conference accompanying the release of this report resulted in a front page story in the *New York Times* (September 9, 1993) with a headline that read: "Half of adults in US lack reading and mathematics ability." The *Wash-*

ington Post also reported the story. Its headline was "Literacy of 90 million is deficient." (September 9, 1993). The nation's weekly newsmagazines joined the pileup, along with hundreds of newspapers, to decry the awful state of literacy in America and the obvious failure of public education. The reporting suggested that the nation was imperiled. We will always remain puzzled, however, about why these periodicals all chose to publish written versions of this terrible news, when it was apparent from the research that so few in the nation could read their reports.

Let us look closer at the study than did the press. First, the tests of prose, document, and quantitative literacy were just that, formal tests, and therefore not part of the daily lives of the people involved. The literacy skills of this sample were not evaluated in the contexts of their everyday lives. Except for academics, who have come to value literacy for itself, literacy is best thought of as instrumental and cannot be understood when it is removed and abstracted from the environments in which it operates. Second, the test was 15 minutes in length. Short tests can be used to profile the performance of groups of people, but a 15-minute test cannot provide an accurate assessment of the literacy skills of an individual who is unaccustomed to formal testing. And most of this sample were not accustomed to testing. We hypothesize that the combination of a 15-minute formal test and the lack of a measure of literacy in context leads to a large *under*estimation of the true level of literacy of the individuals who comprised the sample. But no reporter brought up this likelihood.

In each area of literacy assessed, five levels of ability were created. Level 1 and level 2, scoring low, were deemed inadequate by the test developers and were labeled illiterates by the press. By extrapolation from the sample to the general population, almost 50% of the American adult population were then declared to be illiterate. This was the basis for the broad assertions made by the media. Obviously, any nation with 50% of its people so terribly handicapped in reading is a nation in peril. According to the study, the United States is a nation comprised of around half dunces and half functional literates, with hardly anybody highly proficient at understanding complex prose. The report claimed that around 97% of the adults in America are unable to "interpret a brief phrase from a lengthy news article" (Kirsch et al., 1993, p. 11). So, the press wrote unhesitatingly and uncritically about a study that concluded that their reading audience was severely handicapped. Didn't reporters wonder who was reading their newspapers and magazines? Couldn't they smell that something was fishy?

We believe that the media misled the public in interpreting this study due to laziness, or a lack of a critical sensitivity, or, dare we say it, their illiteracy in reading social science documents. Reporters seemed content to read only the brief executive summary of the report, and accepted the interpretations of the department of education, especially its esteemed secretary of education, Richard Riley. He commented that the schools had to do better, because illiteracy was causing poverty. This potentially serious distortion of the data, to be commented on below, passed unnoticed at the time.

What did we learn that reporters did not from reading the full report about the NALS sample performing at levels 1 and 2—those dubbed illiterates? The persons at levels 1 and 2 are much more frequently poor minorities, though almost half the White population were found to be illiterate too (Kirsch et al., 1993, p. 113). It looks like prose literacy scores are related to family incomes, ethnicity, level of parental education, and so forth. Hardly a surprise. Scores on the test also revealed that around half the 16- to 54-year-olds are fully literate, scoring at level 3 or above. But the 55- to 64-year-olds in the nation, the age of most of the leaders in government and industry, scored on average much lower. Fifty-seven percent of them scored at level 1 or 2. This means, according to the researchers, that only a little over 40% of the 55- to 64-year-olds in the nation have the ability to make sense of the documents they read. According to the researchers, however, they are not America's worst problem: Fully 76% of those over 65 years of age were classified as illiterate, as well (Kirsch et al., 1993, p. 116). We might infer that because of their severe inability to function as readers, most in this age group should not bother with books and magazines, but be counseled instead into TV viewing. Since this age group contains a high proportion of American voters, perhaps they should also be barred from voting until poll testing is reinstituted.

Is this starting to sound ludicrous? We hope so. We think a little common sense would have gone a long way toward dismissing the charges of widespread illiteracy in the United States. If anyone had looked closely at the report, they would have discovered in the appendix that among those classified as illiterate—the levels 1 and 2 respondents—were

- 76% of all those in the entire sample who were physically or mentally impaired
- 80% of those in the entire sample who were visually impaired
- 66% of those in the entire sample who had hearing difficulties
- 80% of those in the entire sample who had learning disabilities
- 72% of those in the entire sample who had a mental or emotional condition
- 90% of those in the entire sample who were mentally retarded
- 79% of those in the entire sample who had speech disabilities
- 74% of those in the entire sample who had physical disabilities
- 70% of all those in the sample who had long-term illnesses of 6 months or more (Kirsch et al., 1993, p. 135)

And finally, we learn that 25% of those who scored at the lowest level of prose literacy were not born in this country and presumably not native speakers of English (Kirsch et al., 1993, p. 119). The upshot of all this is that the two lowest levels of tested prose literacy, particularly those in level 1, comprised people who have overwhelming health problems and contained a disproportionate number of recent immigrants. The health of these people should be a concern for the nation; their prose literacy performance, however, should not be used to judge how well public schools are doing, or how our economy will fare in the future.

An inference about how American public schools are really doing could have been obtained by comparing recent immigrants in the sample with those of similar background who were born in the United States. We found that American citizens born in Central or South America scored very low. But we also found that those with Central or South American parentage who were born in the United States scored at level 3, demonstrating adequate levels of literacy in English, at least according to the researchers. This difference in scores between generations provides a markedly different picture of literacy and schooling in America than that suggested by the news media and some government officials. Obviously, the larger the number of recent immigrants, the larger the number of people who are likely not to do well in a formal test of English literacy. In recent years, this country has had a large surge of immigration, and therefore now has a larger than usual non-English-speaking population. Pooled data containing such individuals are likely, therefore, to *under*estimate the literacy levels of others in the pool, particularly those who were born and educated in the United States. The possibility that underestimations of American literacy might have taken place was not usually reported.

The illiterates had many interesting characteristics—some of them shared by the reporters themselves. The tables included with the report disclose, for example, that 54% of those at level 1—the real dunces—read a newspaper every day or a few times a week. Eighty-three percent of those at level 2—the other group of illiterates—read a newspaper every day or a few times a week. Apparently, the great Italian writer Alberto Moravia was right when he once muttered, "Nowadays, even the illiterates read and write." We now have empirical proof that this is so.

The first meaning of literacy in virtually any dictionary is "the ability to read and write." Thus, one should suspect a problem when illiterates are reading newspapers on a regular basis. Is it possible that the levels 1 and 2 individuals had read about how illiterate they were? Probably, since 93% of those who did read regularly attended to the editorials. Moreover, whereas the researchers declared these people to be greatly impaired, over two thirds of those at level 1 and over 95% of those at level 2 reported that they believe that they read and write well or very well. In our business, we call this a validity problem. The researchers declared this subgroup of the sample to be incompetent, but the individuals in the sample feel quite competent. One of them—the researchers or participants in the study— must be wrong. But not one news reporter thought to ask why these poor illiterates felt so comfortable with their literacy skills or would read the newspapers on a daily basis. It seems clear to us that if the reporters had possessed a higher level of prose, document, and quantitative literacy, or at least had been curious enough to read the report itself, they might have inferred that something was amiss.

Although Secretary Riley commented that illiteracy causes poverty, over two thirds of those at levels 1 and 2 were not poor by the government's own standards. In fact, over two thirds of the illiterates received interest from their own savings accounts, and around 85% received no food stamps. Secretary Riley actually would do better to think of the causal flow in this correlation as going in the other direction. That is, it is quite likely that poverty causes illiteracy more frequently than illiteracy causes poverty. And, if this is true, vastly different social policies are needed. For example, *if* illiteracy causes poverty, as claimed by the secretary and accepted by those reporting this story, *then* more aid to schools is needed and greater efforts by school people are required to reduce or eliminate the scourge of illiteracy from the nation. But if poverty is more often the cause of illiteracy, as we believe, then the agenda to reduce illiteracy is necessarily outside and not inside the schoolhouse door.

This analysis of the nation's biggest contemporary study of literacy and illiteracy leads us to several conclusions. We think Secretary Riley's interpretation of the NALS data is wrong and misdirects the media's attention away from the real problems of America. The news stories that carried the secretary's interpretation were negligent in not pointing out the obvious alternative, namely, that poverty probably causes illiteracy at least as often as illiteracy causes poverty—although the high correlation between the two is not in doubt.

We also think the NALS data demonstrates that the individuals that score at level 2 are really quite competent to perform any employment task if they were familiar with or trained in the task, and motivated to learn. In fact, if the researchers and Secretary Riley had thought more about it, they might have concluded that the many craftspeople and tradespeople who were in level 2 were not earning a great deal, nor working all year long, because of something other than the level of literacy that they displayed. These men and women are also overwhelmingly nonunionized. We would hypothesize that this accounts more for their lower incomes and reduced time in the workforce each year than does their literacy skill, but the press never seems to interpret the data that way. The skills of the level 2 people are vastly underestimated, we think, and they should be reclassified as literate enough for the needs that they and their employers have.

The danger in studies such as this one is the implicit suggestion that measures of literacy represent a fixed trait. Of course, this is not the case. A measure of literacy tells us where a person is on a continuum between decoding with minimum comprehension and the critical literacy expected of those who successfully live in a world dominated by prose literacy— college professors, lawyers, scientists, and so forth. A measure of literacy is a measure of a developing skill, not of a relatively fixed characteristic. We think many people at levels 1 and 2 seem quite capable of demonstrating higher level skills should their life circumstances require it. We must remember that this is a nation where the economy has become service oriented. About two thirds of the workforce is in service, and this sector of the economy is growing while the manufacturing sector is declining. So this is not a nation that requires the highest levels of critical literacy from all its citizens as they perform their daily work. Rather, we seem to require increasing amounts of domain- and job-specific prose, document, quantitative, and technological literacy, the kind of literacy that is taught on the job and not in schools.

This analysis of NALS also suggests that America might improve its overall level of literacy if it could do better in providing for the mental and physical health of its citizens. The United States is a nation with around 40 million people who have no health insurance, and millions of others are too poor to seek medical or psychological help for which some copayments are needed. As we have seen, the level 1 sample is disproportionately made up of the physically disabled and the mentally confused. Level 1 contains recent immigrants, too. And it also contains disproportionate numbers of those who have been subject to discrimination and poverty, with too many of these individuals living in neighborhoods filled with despair and desperation. The neighborhoods that most often have the sick, the poor, and the recent immigrants are also those with the most inadequate schools, least qualified teachers, and lower-than-average levels of school funding. These are *not* the schools that made up the First in the World Consortium. In our interpretive framework, America has not got much of a literacy problem at all—it has health, equity, employment, and unionization problems and a problem in the distribution of quality education to those who have the greatest need of good public schools. Finally, our interpretation of the NALS reporting suggests that many in the American media are in desperate need of literacy training programs. They failed the prose, document, and quantitative test that NALS provided them.

ADDITIONAL CONCERNS WITH THE PRESS

We are concerned about the problems that occur when an uncritical press promotes myths that serve to demonize youth (Males, 1996). Examples of this include the distortions about the sexual activity of teenagers and their high pregnancy rate. Almost all of the early sexual activity and ensuing pregnancies of young females is the result of predatory, fully adult males, often family members. It is not necessarily female teenage sexual morals that are our national problem, it is adult male morality to which we need to attend. But one would never know it from the newspapers. Moreover, the well-publicized violence of youth is almost fully explained by the poverty of youth in the United States. America is the undisputed leader in the industrialized world in percentage of youth in poverty (Rainwater & Smeeding, 1995). It is the pernicious effects of this poverty and the easy availability of weapons, not the uncontrollable hormones of puberty, that result in youth violence. But one would never know it from the newspapers, because not many reporters know how correlations and other statistics really work. The great youth drug culture is still another myth that is promulgated. But 99% of the illegal-drug deaths recorded in the United States in 1993 were of adults; only 1% of the deaths were of teens. All of these deaths are tragic, to be sure, but it is hardly a teen drug problem that the nation faces.

What harm is there in demonizing youth? It is done, after all, to sell papers. We think it does more than that. Either by implication, or sometimes quite directly, the schools are held to blame for our youths' alleged licentiousness, violence, and drug use. Those schools are thus deemed unworthy of support. Demonizing teens through lurid headlines and vivid prose, therefore, results in a loss of confidence in the public schools and aids those who promote privatization.

We think it is inappropriate to expect a democratic free press to be anything but highly critical of the society in which it exists. That is one of its functions. But it is not inappropriate to ask for balance. And we do not think we have that. It seems to us that democracy depends just as much on a free and efficient public school system as it does on a free press. It would be ironic, as well as tragic, if the imbalance in the reporting that exists were to lead to the abandonment of public schools and a dramatic rise in private school rates of attendance. We are sure that this would result in greater privilege for a few and less of a chance for success in life for the many. And when those circumstances occur, the press is always captured by the power of the few, and no longer can claim to be totally free. We may be well on the way to that sad state now, as recent critics contend.

By continuing the unfair, unremitting negative characterization of the nation's schools and youth, by searching for the blood and too often avoiding the more reasonable interpretations that are possible, and by failing to describe the magnificent achievements that also characterize public education, the nation's free press may ultimately become less free. The natural alliance between the media and public school critics could destroy both the free press and the free public educational system that we now enjoy in this nation. It may be in the interest of the press to ponder this line of reasoning, and think about providing more balance in educational reporting— not just because it is justified, but because it is in their own self-interest.

BIBLIOGRAPHY

Astronaut praises science teachers. He disputes notion that U. S. lags behind. (1996, December 28). *San Francisco Chronicle*, p. A18.

Americans straddle the average mark in math and science. (1996, November 21). *The New York Times*, p. B14.

Beaton, A. E., Martin, M. O., Mullis, I. V. S., Gonzalez, E. J., Smith, T. A., & Kelly, D. L. (1996). *Science achievement in the middle school years.* Chestnut Hill: Boston College.

Beaton, A. E., Mullis, I. V. S., Martin, M. O., Gonzalez, E. J., Kelly, D. L., & Smith, T. A. (1996). *Mathematics achievement in the middle school years.* Chestnut Hill: Boston College.

Berliner, D. C. (1997a, March). *If it bleeds, it leads: The natural alliance between school critics and the media.* Paper presented at the meetings of the American Educational Research Association, Chicago, Illinois.

Berliner, D. C. (1997b). Educational psychology meets the Christian right: Differing views of children, schooling, teaching and learning. *Teachers College Record, 98,* 381–416.

Berliner, D. C., & Biddle, B. J. (1995). *The manufactured crisis.* Reading, MA: Addison-Wesley.

Bracey, G. W. (1994, September). The media's myth of school failure. *Educational Leadership,* 80–83.

California education: math movement robs generation of basic skills. (1996, December 22). *San Diego Union-Tribune,* pp. 1–2, G1.

Collective responsibility part of lesson plan in Japanese schools (1996, December 9). *Minneapolis Star Tribune,* p. 13A.

Ferguson, R. F. (1991). Paying for public education: new evidence on how and why money matters. *Harvard Journal on Legislation, 28,* 465–498.

Friedman, J. (1992, February 17). The Whittle-Alexander nexus: big business goes to school. *The Nation,* pp. 188–192.

Global test of pupils shows U. S. improving. (1996, November 21). *The San Diego Union-Tribune,* pp. 1–8, A1.

Half of adults in U.S. lack reading and mathematics ability. (1993, September 9). *The New York Times*, pp. A1, A22.

Kirsch, I. S., Jungeblut, A., Jenkins, L., & Kolstad, A. (1993). *Adult literacy in America*. Princeton, NJ: Educational Testing Service; and Washington, DC: U. S. Department of Education, Office of Educational Research and Improvement, National Center for Education Statistics.

Kroeze, D. J., & Johnson, D. P. (1997). *Achieving excellence. A report on the First in the World Consortium*. Oak Brook, IL: North Central Regional Educational Laboratory.

Literacy of 90 million is deficient. (1993, September 9). *The Washington Post*, pp. A1, A15.

Low student test scores, push for vouchers reflect inadequacy of Americas public schools. (1996, December 1). *Tampa Tribune*, p. 3.

Males, M. (1996). *The scapegoat generation: America's war on adolescents*. Monroe, ME: Common Courage Press.

Molnar, A. (1996). *Giving kids the business*. Boulder, CO: Westview Press.

New math counts for little in the real world. (1997, January 8). *The Orange County Register*, p. B6.

Payne, K., & Biddle, B. J. (1997, under review). *Poor school funding, child poverty, and mathematics ability*. Columbia, MO: Psychology Department, University of Missouri.

Pew Research Center for the People and the Press (1997, February). *National Social Trust Survey*. Philadelphia, PA: Author.

Public Agenda (1997, May). *Good news, bad news: What people really think about the educational press*. Paper presented at the meetings of the Educational Writers Association, Washington, DC.

Rainwater, L., & Smeeding, T. M. (1995). *Doing poorly: The real income of American children in a comparative perspective*. Luxembourg Income Study Working paper No. 127. Syracuse, NY: Maxwell School of Citizenship and Public Affairs, Syracuse University.

Rifkin, J (1995). *The end of work*. New York: Putnam.

7 youths, 2 adults arrested in fight at Scottsdale park. (1997, March 1). *The Arizona Republic*, p. B2.

School study hints at U. S. flaw. (1996, November 21). *Orange County Register*, p. A1.

School suspends 8 more. (1997, February 28). *The Arizona Republic*, p. B1.

Science, math study renews call for reform. (1996, November 21). *St. Petersburg Times*, p. 1A.

Stevenson, H. W., & Stigler, J. W. (1992). *The learning gap*. New York: Touchstone.

Stevenson, H. W., Yee, S. Y., & Stigler, J. W. (1986). Mathematics achievement of Chinese, Japanese, and American children.

The sum of mediocrity. (1996, December 2). *Newsweek*, p. 96.

Turf war erupts at high school. (1997, February 27). *The Arizona Republic*, pp. B1–2.

U. S. schools in crisis; so what else is new? (1996, November 22). *Chicago Sun-Times*, p. 39.

Education and the Press: Ignorance Is Bliss

DENIS P. DOYLE

RUMINATING ON the role of the press and education nearly 15 years ago, I did a piece for the American Federation of Teachers (AFT) magazine, *American Educator,* which I irreverently titled "Education and the Press: Malign Neglect?" (Doyle, 1985). I concluded that the press was indifferent, not malicious, and although the consequences might be the same, the motive, at least, was benign. Because prognostications have such a short shelf life, I continue to ponder the question, Why does the press treat education so casually? In all fairness, I am convinced that today's coverage is better than it was a decade and a half ago; there is more space devoted to education, the reporters are given more latitude, and many of the stories offer greater depth. But the coverage is still not extensive enough or good enough. In reaching this conclusion, I put four factors on the scale to weigh education coverage: the education enterprise, the media, the reporters, and the audience.

As big as the education enterprise is, and it is very big indeed, it is a moving, even elusive, target. (An important parenthetical note is in order: Serious school reformers, of whom there are never enough, are, by definition, out of the mainstream. They are hard to find and harder still to report on in a systematic way, and I do not include them in my general comments about schools. They are to be encouraged and applauded, however.) The main subject of this essay, then, is the great bureaucratic engine comprising most of the nation's schools and represented by their myriad professional associations, what former secretary of education William Bennett unceremoniously called the "blob." While they do not make up a formal system—school districts are independent, states differ greatly, and there is only limited federal control over schooling—their common culture al-

Imaging Education: The Media and Schools in America. Copyright © 1998 by Teachers College, Columbia University. All rights reserved. ISBN 0-8077-3734-8 (pbk), ISBN 0-8077-3735-6 (cloth). Prior to photocopying items for classroom use, please contact the Copyright Clearance Center, Customer Service, 222 Rosewood Dr., Danvers, MA 01923, USA, tel. (508) 750-8400.

lows them to be discussed as though they were a system. And it is this "system" that controls much if not most of what we know about schools. Accordingly, it is critically important to know how schools want to be covered, if, indeed, they want to be covered at all. Few educators understand the old political adage that the only thing worse than bad publicity is no publicity. I, for one, am convinced that no one in our society is more interested in spin control than the typical school official. He or she would make a political consultant blush.

Second, there is the media itself, print and electronic, in all its glory and vainglory. I am concerned here largely with the daily print media (and to some extent, commercial radio and TV, though they are simply sound bite heaven and not much can be expected of them) and a few education publications that reporters and educators might be expected to read, for example, *Education Week* or the AFT's *American Educator*.

Third are the laborers in the media vineyard, the reporters who fret about stories and wonder who will attend to them. Like the teachers they cover, few are in it for the money. To the contrary, most begin their professional lives with a sense of public service, determined to "comfort the afflicted and afflict the comfortable," as H. L. Mencken would have it.

Fourth is the audience—the public and the educators—the readers, listeners, and viewers for whom the stories are ostensibly reported in the first instance. Unlike sports fans or financial page readers, they are a relatively passive group with little capacity to influence the way education is covered.

THE ENORMITY OF THE EDUCATION ENTERPRISE

Let me turn first to the education enterprise. There is nothing about this vast conglomerate that would lead one, a priori, to expect casual treatment by the press. The sheer size of the enterprise would lead one to expect probing coverage. When it comes to coverage of the schools, the numbers alone are staggering: nearly 52 million youngsters attend public and private elementary and secondary schools across the country. Three million adults teach in them and an equal number work in them in other capacities. More than 80,000 public school buildings are situated in more than 15,000 school districts. They are complemented by more than 26,000 private schools. In turn, the public schools are overseen by more than 90,000 school board members. Ninety percent of these board members are elected in local elections, the most amazing example of citizen democracy in the world. Together the whole enterprise spends about $335 billion per year, a lot of money even by Washington standards. To complete the sense of scale, education is typically the biggest single expenditure that the 7,500 state legislators must concern themselves with.

Add in 14 million postsecondary students in 3,500 colleges, universities, and trade and technical schools—one third of the world's supply—and the expenditures continue to spiral upward. In addition, at any point in time, 500,000 foreign students are studying here full-time, while we send about 80,000 a year abroad. The investment banking house Lehman Brothers estimates that the United States spends $670 billion a year for prekindergarten through postgraduate education, more than 9% of the GNP (Lehman Brothers, 1997). Add in workplace-based training and education, and the nation approaches $1 trillion a year in education spending. Indeed, Rand economists estimated that by the mid-1980s, America was already investing more in human capital formation than our total investment in physical capital.

More important than the raw numbers, big as they are, is the role education plays in the modern world. Without fear of exaggeration, it is fair to say that education is the principal if not final arbiter of wealth and status today. What you become is largely determined by what you know (and where you learned it). The work of Finis Welch, Marvin Kosters, John Bishop, and other economists paints a compelling picture of rewards for education and penalties for its lack. Their findings can be neatly summarized: Education pays and pays handsomely. And lack of education exacts a high price: As former Harvard president Derek Bok wryly notes, "If you think education is expensive, try ignorance." To be sure, there is the occasional millionaire who dropped out of formal education. Microsoft's Bill Gates got tired of Harvard, and Steve Jobs returned to Berkeley (where he got Bs in engineering) after creating Apple, but they are autodidacts par excellence. That their education was informal as well as formal does not detract from the overall point. To the contrary, no greater example of the importance of human capital can be imagined than the computer revolution of which Gates and Jobs are among the most conspicuous participants.

Who, 20 years ago, besides Peter Drucker, would have predicted that the most robust part of the economy would be "mind work," for which school is supposed to prepare students? The power of the telecommunications revolution is not the glass, wire, and plastic in the PC, but the upstream intelligence that designs and produces it and the downstream intelligence that uses it. The personal computer is the perfect metaphor for human capital. The PC provides intellectual leverage just as Archimedes' lever produced mechanical leverage. What has human capital to do with the issue? It is the story of the 1990s and beyond. In economic terms, the value-added of schooling is applied human intelligence. "Why is Harvard such a vast repository of knowledge?" President Elliot was asked. "Because the freshmen bring so much when they arrive and take so little when they graduate," he is said to have answered.

Finally, with among the highest literacy rates in the world, most Americans have gone to school. At least some school. And the nation's great non-school-goers, such as Eric Hoffer (who went not at all, not a day) and Erik Erickson (who earned no degree), are celebrated as thinkers and writers. Those of us who went to school may read them to our heart's content.

But if what "comes out of school" is the important story, it is hard to tell, because the numbers that schools reveal about themselves are typically restricted to "inputs." The education enterprise reports what goes into schooling—the number of dollars spent, the number of youngsters enrolled, the number of buildings, the number of districts. To use a dreadful term from computer art, we even know something about school "throughput": what goes on in school. Thanks to the U.S. Department of Education's National Center for Education Statistics, we know a good deal about what classes students take, how many students drop out, and the like. But we know precious little about the "output" of schooling. Yet, it is this issue that most concerns parents, taxpayers, and school critics, and it is this issue that the press has the hardest time with. Why is this the case? There are several pieces to the answer, which has to include the media and what it chooses to write about or not write about.

At this point, however, some evidence for this assertion might be offered. It is, after all, a rather sweeping point to make that little is known about the results of the collective investment in this huge enterprise. And it is compounded by a phenomenon that I am convinced is widespread: the deeply held conviction that your own field (whatever it may be) is poorly covered by the press. The more you know, whether it is architecture or zoology, the weaker that subject's coverage appears to you. We are all familiar with the phenomenon; it is particularly acute when the subject is complex or controversial; it is most acute when we know more than the reporter. Even with this caveat, however, I still think that the assertion that education coverage is weak withstands scrutiny. In defense, I not only offer personal observation but invite the reader to consider his or her own experience.

THE INADEQUACY OF COVERAGE

How much coverage is there and what is its quality? There is, to be sure, coverage of disasters and fiascoes, teachers who are set upon by students, students who are set upon by one another, teachers who set upon students, teachers who set upon other teachers, principals who set upon teachers, board members who set upon superintendents and so on ad nauseum.

The permutations are nearly endless. There is also coverage of athletic triumphs and losses, honors, awards and feel-good celebrations—and feel-bad stories. When half of St. Anselm's Abbey's graduating class earns merit scholarships, the information makes its way into the Metro section of the *Washington Post*. Athletic scores are faithfully reported on the sports pages (after the professional and college scores). Local broadsheets will cover prospective fundraisers. And so on. Although it is easy to make light of this, it is news, and it is proper to report it. So, too, there is coverage of the nuts and bolts. Small-town papers may even print the menus from the school cafeteria, and the most important school story of all is faithfully reported by local radio and TV: snow days.

What is missing, though, is what is important. It is the education counterpart of the dog that didn't bark. First, there are no national education columnists. Interestingly, the late Albert Shanker filled that role in his weekly, paid advertisement in the *New York Times* (and the *New Republic*), which offers a fascinating commentary on my theme. Shanker had to pay to get his ideas published. Imitation being the sincerest form of flattery, the National Education Association now sponsors a column by its president, Bob Chase, which runs in many more papers, as befits the wealthier of the two unions. It is not too much, though, to assert that were a paper willing, someone, somewhere, could be found to write about education, not as a paid advertisement, with almost as much sophistication and interest as Shanker did. To my knowledge, no editor or syndicate seeks such a columnist. Bridge, chess, astrology, and gardening get their own columnists, not to mention national defense, politics, and advice for the lovelorn. The second point is a reverse spin on the first; everyone whom I know in education read Shanker's column faithfully, not just because it was the AFT party line, which it frequently was, but because it was so good. Perhaps this reveals a reverse spin on Gresham's law, that bad money forces out good. Does good money for ads force out paid columnists?

To come at this question of the adequacy of education coverage another way, consider the case of *Education Week*. As the education newspaper of record, it is very good indeed, but it has very few subscribers, at least relatively—55,000 to be exact. Remember the dread numbers I opened with? The point is that education in the United States is big business, but it is not self-reflective. By and large, teachers and administrators don't read about their own enterprise. And if the *Education Week* numbers are not sobering, consider this: The AFT has a subscription service for its members, enabling them to subscribe at a deep discount to almost any magazine you can imagine. So banal was the taste of AFT members that Al Shanker refused to reveal the names of the magazines for which they signed up. In this respect, it should be noted that they perfectly mirror their fellow citizens. They are not alone.

I could go on, but consider the point made. Education is not covered in the depth it invites or calls for; neither is it broadly covered. Indeed, the editorial judgment appears to reflect the audience's tastes and interests because there appears to be little interest in serious education coverage even from educators. What accounts for the sounds of silence? One theory is that there is simply no demand for education reporting; that is what editors and reporters say. But this view is not supported by public opinion polling. Year after year, the public puts education high on the list of problems that cry out for solution, precisely the kind of attitude that should lead editors to increase coverage. It was once widely believed that no one, or too few people, to be precise, wanted to read about anything as dull as education. In light of the public's concern with education, however, this may say as much about the way the story is presented (or not presented, as the case may be) as the audience.

Or it may be that editors, who are typically older than their reporters and less in touch, think that the stories on education are intrinsically dull and do not wish to foist them on their readers, even if they might be good for them. In regard to dealings with editors, the reporter's lament is a familiar one: The editor's idea of an education story is to fill the 8 inches of space left on page 10. (It is the "all the news that fits, we print" approach to journalism.) And then there is the nature of the beat itself. Almost without exception, the education beat is one step up from obituaries. A reporter must work through it on the way to something interesting. It is like the dread third world posting a diplomat must accept on the way to Paris or London. Or it is all of the above.

That, of course, is the more realistic answer. The phenomenon of shallow coverage is itself deep. In a democracy with a market-driven economy and a free press, it is difficult to advance a compelling argument that we do not get what we want and deserve. Who is denying us? What do we want and deserve that is being withheld? One is left with the dismal conclusion that two-time Pulitzer prizewinner Richard Hofstadter is right; America is profoundly anti-intellectual (1964). Americans do not ask for much in the way of education coverage and do not expect much and, consequently, do not get much. More to the point, a recent book reached an absolute fever pitch of anti-intellectualism. In *The Manufactured Crisis* (Berliner and Biddle, 1995), the authors stated in their preface:

> This book was written in outrage. . . . Slowly . . . we began to suspect that something was not quite right, that organized malevolence might actually be underway . . . federal politicians and their allies were throttling research and misusing evidence about education. . . . Some who accepted hostile myths about education have been genuinely worried about our schools,

some have misunderstood evidence, some have been duped. . . . Powerful
people were . . . pursuing a political agenda designed to weaken the nation's
public schools. . . . To this end they have been prepared to tell lies, suppress
evidence, scapegoat educators, and sow endless confusion. We consider this
conduct particularly despicable. (p. xi)

If these charges were true, it would be despicable. But the claim is
errant nonsense. The book advanced, among other absurdities, the assertion that Chester Finn, Bill Bennett, Diane Ravitch, and others (me included)
were engaged in a conspiracy against the public schools and that, in effect, the media have provided us with a platform. The book's subtitle is
Myths, Fraud and the Attack on America's Public Schools. Doubters might think
that I single out *The Manufactured Crisis* because it treats my friends, colleagues, and me shabbily. I would not have it any other way. Indeed, I am
reminded of Art Buchwald's column the day after Nixon's "enemies list"
was published. To Buchwald's horror, his name was not on it. He was convinced that Nixon was trying to destroy his reputation.

The more important issue is the book's reception among educators,
some of whom actually believed it and hailed it. In endorsements on the
book's dust jacket, Jonathan Kozol, an author in his own right, called it "a
very important book," and Keith Geiger, a former president of the National
Education Association, "a powerful piece of truth-telling." One of the
authors, David Berliner, received the NEA's 1994 Friends of Education
Award.

On the other hand, let me quote a dispassionate observer, Ron Wolk
(1995), founding publisher of the *Chronicle of Higher Education* and former
publisher of *Education Week* and *Teacher*: "In what is either paranoia or an
effort to sell copies, the authors premise their book on the absurd charge
that government officials, business leaders, and the media have conspired
to destroy America's public schools by deliberately spreading lies and
pressing a harmful agenda for reform" (p. 3). The simple fact is that there
is no media conspiracy against the education enterprise. This explanation
does not hold water. Anti-intellectualism, however, offers a compelling,
culturally based explanation. Permit me to offer three more observations
to further illuminate this point.

THE AMERICAN CONDITION

First, there is an American penchant to not take schools seriously
as academic institutions. In some respects, this is an echo of anti-
intellectualism, but it is also a point of view in its own right. In a practi-

cal society, schools are meant to be practical institutions. Henry Steele Commager said that Americans expect of education what they expect of religion—"that it be practical and pay dividends" (1950, p. 10). More to the point, the schools reflect the culture and economy of which they are a part. For example, when 80% of the nation lived on the land, school days were few and absences many. Kids were valuable parts of the economy. They were able to do chores and farm work, and their strong backs, deft hands, and a willing attitude were more important than formal education.

Indeed, in the second half of the 19th century, when the U.S. Office of Education did little more than collect numbers, the length of the school year was reported in two ways: the number of days school was open and the number of days most students actually showed up. In 1869–70, for example, the average school was open 132 days per year but the average student attended 78 days (Digest, 1996). Today's push to lengthen the school day and school year simply reflects the economic, social, and cultural realities of the end of the century. But it is important to note that if schooling is meant to be exclusively practical, emphasizing training rather than education, the country is getting the coverage it needs and wants; as a people we are more concerned about snow days than intellectual excellence, more interested in football scores than academic test scores, more involved in cafeteria menus than curriculum. For example, lack of interest in matters academic reflects the larger culture in which a pernicious notion has gained general credence: Bright children will do well no matter what. Ironically, the logical extension of this proposition is that schooling doesn't matter; what matters is luck of the socioeconomic and genetic draw. This in turn reflects the view that academic success is not a matter of discipline, diligence, or hard work, but native talent. You've got it or you don't. Effort doesn't make a difference.

Once upon a time, Americans believed in hard work. But this no longer seems to be the case. Merry White, author of *The Japanese Education Challenge*, says that when a Japanese mother is asked what accounts for academic success, she answers immediately that it is effort, hard work (White, 1987). Ask a Japanese child how much he or she knows. Not much, is the short answer. Yet, they earn among the highest math and science scores in the world. They understate their knowledge and have, in American parlance, low self-esteem. In Japan, knowledge and self-esteem correlate inversely. Try the same routine with Americans. The American mother will tell you the secret is talent, native intelligence, aptitude. That's what makes the difference. Ask an American student what he or she knows, and the tendency is to overestimate the degree of knowledge. Then administer a self-esteem test. The American student feels good about him- or herself. Self-esteem and knowledge correlate inversely in America as well.

A second example of anti-intellectualism is the increasing credulity that characterizes the modern era. From new-age spiritualism and crystal gazing to fantastical conspiracy theories, Americans appear to be entering a postrational age. And if anything is possible, anything goes. (Flying saucer cults flourish and Do's Rancho Sante Fe cult members commit mass suicide in anticipation of being beamed up to a rendezvous behind the Hale-Bopp comet; Oliver Stone rewrites history with impunity and, mirabile dictu, produces a sympathetic Nixon. Will wonders never cease.) And in what is most emblematic of all, there are new-age uses for science and technology. On April 21, 1997, Timothy Leary's remains were put into orbit around the earth. As one of his disciples noted, how high can you get? What an irony that the great triumphs of the scientific revolution would be followed by a period that renounces the intellect in favor of sensation and feeling.

Third, and most important, is the resolute position taken by most schools across the country that they will not report anything about themselves that can be quantified or measured. They stalwartly resist providing the kind of information that permits thoughtful analysis and complain mightily when analysis is attempted with weak data. Nor do they use achievement data to inform themselves about how they might improve their own performance. The classic example is the use by the press of Scholastic Assessment Test (SAT) scores to draw inferences about school performance. Educational Testing Service (ETS), which administers the SAT, leads the school chorus of complaint that the SAT does not measure school effects and should not be used to draw conclusions about what schools are up to. Yet, SAT cram courses are big business, and ironically, the biggest provider of such services, Stanley Kaplan, is owned by the Washington Post Company. Needless to say, the reporter and the public are put at a significant disadvantage by institutions that refuse to submit to measurement.

Perhaps most telling is that Americans know less about their own schools than they know about schools in Bonn and Tokyo. As Stedman (1996) points out:

> Andrew Coulson makes an intriguing . . . argument—namely, that citizens are better informed about the national condition of education than they are about the local one. Every few years, for example, the National Assessment of Educational Progress reports on students' knowledge and skills in major academic areas—history, civics, geography, reading, mathematics, writing, etc.—and the findings are widely distributed in the media. It could well be that, if parents had the same kind of detailed achievement information about local students' knowledge and performance, they would be just as critical of their local schools. (p. 83)

Knowing less, parents and other observers are less critical than they might otherwise be. Restricted to rumor, guesses, and intimations, they make judgments on what little information they do possess. Thus, a resident of Montgomery County, Maryland, feels good about local schools because they are demonstrably better than Washington, DC, schools. Sophisticated parents and educators should find no consolation in such a finding. To the contrary, they should be comparing Montgomery County schools to the best public and private schools in the nation and the world. Indeed, the Montgomery County schools and other systems in its league should be the first to assert that they need improvement.

The problem is clear. We know less because our schools tell us less. Not only are there no national standards, there is no national evaluation of school quality. Indeed, the one national barometer we have, the National Assessment of Educational Progress (NAEP), reveals precisely what the problem is. NAEP uses the word *assessment* in its name because the word is neutral, nonthreatening. That this group exists at all is a minor miracle. Indeed, the major problem with American schools is not low test scores—to be sure, that is problem enough—it is the fact that our schools do not want to be measured and evaluated. They do not measure and evaluate themselves, and they do not want anyone else to do so either.

This kind of self-protection can exist only when the subject is a protected monopoly. In the case of its own institutions, the school "system" prefers ignorance to knowledge. When reporters attempt to use school "box scores" (test score comparisons, for example) they are accused of trivializing an important enterprise. This charge might be credible if the schools offered more sensitive and useful measures. But by and large, the schools themselves are obdurate; they neither report on themselves nor provide opportunities for third parties—in this case the press and its readers—to dip beneath the surface. And that, in the final analysis, is why education coverage in the press is so weak. There is not much of substance to report. Why? Because for too many educators, concerned with spin, not with results, ignorance is bliss.

Let me close with a famous poem about education that makes the point—Thomas Gray's *Ode on a Distant Prospect of Eton College*. It is a prelapsarian, Edenic paean to innocence. School is innocence personified; it precedes the cruelty and treachery that life after school necessarily brings. And Eton, the Platonic ideal of schooling, should be left in its sublime innocence, which is to say, ignorance:

Yet ah! Why should they know their fate?
Since sorrow never comes too late,

And happiness too swiftly flies.
Thought would destroy their paradise.
No more; where ignorance is bliss,
'Tis folly to be wise. (Wain, 1969, p. 559)

Too many American educators have taken Gray's ode to heart.

BIBLIOGRAPHY

David C. Berliner & Bruce J. Biddle, *The Manufactured Crisis* (Reading, MA: Addison-Wesley, 1995).

Henry Steele Commager, *The American Mind* (New Haven: Yale University Press, 1950).

Denis P. Doyle, "Education and the Press: Malign Neglect?" *American Educator*, Vol. 9, No. 1, Spring, 1985, pp. 28–33.

Digest of Education Statistics 1996, Table 38, Historical Summary of Public Elementary and Secondary Schools 1869–70 to 1993–94, National Center for Education Statistics, Washington, DC, 1996.

Lehman Brothers, Emerging Trends in the $670 Billion Education Market, Lehman Brothers, New York, March 17, 1997.

Richard Hofstadter, *Anti-intellectualism in American Life* (New York: Knopf, 1964).

Lawrence Stedman, Respecting the Evidence: The Achievement Crisis Remains Real, *Education Policy Analysis Archives*, Vol. 4, No. 7, April 4, 1996.

John Wain, ed., *Oxford Anthology of English Poetry: Spenser to Crabbe* (New York: Oxford University Press, 1990).

Merry White, *The Japanese Education Challenge: A Commitment to Children* (New York: Free Press, 1987).

Ron Wolk, *Teacher*, November/December 1995, p. 3.

What the Surveys Say

PUBLIC AGENDA, a New York-based organization headed by Deborah Wadsworth, has looked at opinions about education over an extended period. In Chapter 4, Wadsworth writes that feelings about the schools are very much linked to the public's overarching mood, which is shaped by economic anxiety, moral ambiguity, and institutional mistrust. Any diagnosis of what ails education, she feels, must encompass these larger realities. The metal detectors in school vestibules symbolize a national mood that has been depressed by corporate downsizing, family dysfunction, and a loss of confidence in institutions.

Wadsworth contends that attitudes about education are not necessarily driven by media coverage. The public has its own sources of information about the schools, and media portrayals may be irrelevant to some of these people. Taking this argument a step further, Wadsworth says that research does not support the view that the media's bad-news bias—and Public Agenda confirms the existence of such a slant—is primarily responsible for the public's negative attitudes toward the schools. Opinions about the schools have a basis in experience for many people. On the other hand, Americans tend to be cynical about the media's treatment of education, saying that reporters cover bad news because "it's their job."

In Chapter 5, Larry Cuban finds, after examining responses to surveys conducted over many years, that public concerns about the schools have remained remarkably stable. What Americans have persistently wanted in the schools are profoundly conservative institutions that are safe and teach respect for authority, proper moral behavior, and basic literacy. The news media, however, would have readers and viewers believe that the public is fickle, flitting from issue to issue.

Actually, according to Cuban, it is the media that are flighty, seeking "excitement in what they present to the public to attract readers and viewers." This approach by the media accounts for the differing issues that rise to the top of its agenda from one year to the next—career education, performance contracting, instructional television, and alternative schools, for instance. The media gravitate to what they define as the problem of the moment, evidence of their short attention span. Cuban's view seems consistent with Wadsworth's finding that the public cares little about the disputes of adults in education and is uninterested in many of the controversies to which the media are drawn in their coverage of education. Cuban says that the media have written about academic achievement as if they were reporting scores in athletic contests, minimizing and simplifying the issues. This approach, meant to attract readers and viewers, is perhaps the most convenient way for uninformed reporters to handle news when they do not take the time to convey complexities. The average television news program, after all, leaves few minutes in which to deal with nuances.

Do Media Shape Public Perceptions of America's Schools?

DEBORAH WADSWORTH

THE FIRST STEP in determining the role that media coverage plays in shaping public attitudes about any issue is to separate perception from reality. This is especially difficult, however, when it comes to attitudes about America's public schools, where the proverbial chicken-and-egg debate plays itself out with particular intensity. Educators blame the media for planting bleak images of schools in the public's mind, while journalists insist that they are simply doing their job.

The findings of Public Agenda, a nonprofit, nonpartisan research and education organization founded in 1975, shed some light on this debate. Public Agenda has abundant evidence about the sources of the public's information about education and about opinions on how well the media do their work. These findings come from more than 100 focus groups, four national surveys, and a study in 1997 of the opinions of the parents of schoolchildren, the general public, and even journalists themselves. But before we leap into this archive of findings, it may be useful to consider the broader societal context in which these attitudes have been shaped.

In early 1996, Public Agenda's cofounder, author and social scientist Dan Yankelovich, characterized the country's mood as uncertain, anxious, and mistrustful. The public's troubled state of mind, he suggested, stemmed from several sources, including a high degree of economic insecurity occasioned by corporate America's adjustment to fierce global competition and the need to deliver products and services at the lowest possible cost. The pain of downsizing and restructuring, along with that of stagnating wages, guaranteed that Americans would feel off balance, buffeted by forces be-

Imaging Education: The Media and Schools in America. Copyright © 1998 by Teachers College, Columbia University. All rights reserved. ISBN 0-8077-3734-8 (pbk), ISBN 0-8077-3735-6 (cloth). Prior to photocopying items for classroom use, please contact the Copyright Clearance Center, Customer Service, 222 Rosewood Dr., Danvers, MA 01923, USA, tel. (508) 750-8400.

yond their control, and unsure of their future. Interestingly, this uncertainty has continued even though the economy has grown more robust and many more new jobs have been created. People seem to have learned that even good times can be precarious and that, whereas life may be better at the moment, no improvement can be considered as permanent.

This attitude was captured in a Public Agenda study that probed views of retirement and saving. Two thirds of those Americans surveyed voiced fears that the economy in general will sour and undermine their efforts to save for retirement (Farkas, 1997b). Adults worry that even if they are resilient and manage to succeed financially, their children may have a very difficult time in the future, particularly if they are inadequately prepared. As if this economic insecurity were not enough, vast numbers of people also worry about the state of the American family and the moral ambiguity that characterizes modern life. They believe that traditional values no longer apply, and that those who cheat and refuse to play by the rules seem increasingly able to get ahead. People suspect that honesty, integrity, and respect are declining. They see evidence of a lack of civility in the behavior of the young and in the unruly, undisciplined environment that they associate with today's public schools.

Added to this volatile mix is a growing mistrust of the very institutions that have shaped the nation. This mistrust is occasioned, at least in part, by the failure of America's leaders and experts to engage the public in serious and thoughtful dialogue about potential solutions to many of the most severe problems. Some of those who are the strongest advocates for reform in education inspire the most mistrust among the public, for they speak in an impenetrable jargon, and their priorities bear little resemblance to those of ordinary people.

THREE PREVAILING IMAGES

These overarching moods—economic anxiety, moral ambiguity, and institutional mistrust—pervade Americans' diagnosis of what is wrong with public education today. The moods are manifested in three images that Americans evoke in all of Public Agenda's research to convey what troubles them about the schools. Over and over, people complain bitterly about the existence of metal detectors at the entrance to schools; about kids hanging around the high school parking lot when they ought to be in class; and about checkout clerks at the local supermarket who lack the skills even to make change. Again and again, they evoke these images almost as metaphors to transmit their authentic concerns—those driven not primarily by the media but by events they experience in their daily lives.

It is valuable to examine each of these images carefully, to better understand the attitudes that they reflect, attitudes that Public Agenda has documented with parents, grandparents, and those without any direct school experience, as well as teachers, principals, superintendents, school board members, business and community leaders, and, most recently, students themselves. Then, it is appropriate to determine the degree to which these images are or are not shaped by journalistic coverage.

Although most Americans have passed through a metal detector at a local airport, few have actually confronted one face-to-face at the entrance to a local school. Nonetheless, the knowledge that even *a single metal detector* exists at the entrance to *a single school* evokes a powerful response. The image may have appeared originally on a television screen or in a newspaper photograph, but its existence has been burned into public consciousness. It signifies to people that their schools—the one institution that had always been safe and inviolate—have been invaded by the violence and drugs that pervade contemporary society. Even the sanctity of schools has been violated by societal upheaval.

In conveying this image, were the media responsible for disseminating untruths or manipulating incipient fears? Did they implant in the public's mind this idea that the schools are unsafe? On the surface, it seems reasonable to assume that media coverage is the culprit, but research does not support that interpretation. Rather, the research reveals that this image, deeply ingrained in the public mind, has a basis in reality. Seventy-two percent of the general public and 80% of African American parents identified the presence of too many drugs and too much violence as a serious problem in the public schools in *their own community* (Johnson, 1994).

In other words, people are thinking in terms of their neighborhood schools, not some distant, abstract schools, when they express these concerns. Perhaps more importantly, almost half of teachers and students—47% of teachers and 48% of students—say drugs and violence are a serious problem in their schools (Johnson, 1997). Those who conclude that media coverage has affected the perceptions of the general public can hardly dismiss the views of significant numbers of teachers and students, who spend their days in the schools and do not have to rely on the media for those perceptions. They are neither out of touch nor responding to a bad-news bias.

With such opinions rampant, every group surveyed by Public Agenda demands that, before tackling curricular reforms or introducing innovative teaching techniques, schools should be made safe and drug free. Moreover, 76% of the public and 84% of teachers want youngsters who are caught with weapons or drugs removed from the classrooms. Support for this position is very high among teens themselves—66% among White students,

77% among African American students, and 74% among Hispanic students (Johnson, 1997).

The image of students hanging out in the school parking lot is another metaphor conveying what people think ails public education today. Whereas I suspect that most recent generations have spent time in such activity—or inactivity—and have probably irritated neighborhood residents in the process, until recently teenagers were considered harmless. Today, however, the very presence of seemingly idle teenagers makes adults uneasy, for they symbolize the lack of order and discipline that most people believe should characterize the lives of young people. In a Public Agenda study conducted on behalf of the Advertising Council, two in three (67%) of those surveyed, when asked to describe the first thing that comes to mind about teens, responded with negative impressions (Farkas, 1997a). Similarly, the teens interviewed for the recent national study *Getting By: What American Teenagers Really Think About Their Schools* (Johnson, 1997) acknowledged that they often behave badly and know they are threatening to many adults.

Are *these* attitudes driven by media coverage? Hardly. The scenes people describe, which they say they confront on a daily basis, convey in shorthand much that they believe is wrong with our schools. "Why," people ask in focus groups, "aren't these kids in class?" "Doesn't anyone know that they're not in school?" "Who's in charge?" "Why doesn't someone do something about this?"

In *Getting By*, teenagers themselves describe an atmosphere that is unruly, coarse, rough, and not conducive to learning. Seven in 10 say that there are too many disruptive students in *their* classes, and, not unexpectedly, 82% say they would learn more in school if these unruly youngsters were removed from regular classes (Johnson, 1997). This is based upon firsthand experience; they don't have to rely on the media for these impressions. It is no surprise that adults list, following safety, the removal of disruptive students as their next highest priority—73% of the general public and 88% of teachers support this idea (Johnson, 1997). There is a prevailing sense that classrooms are being held hostage by the few who have made it impossible to teach the many who really would like to learn.

And, finally, there are the countless stories from people's personal experiences of the ubiquitous checkout clerk who can't make change or the telephone operator who can't find a number in Des Moines, which she can't spell, either. Anecdotes about such individuals multiply daily, and while they, too, may have become metaphors—dramatically symbolizing the academic inadequacies of our schools—they are based not on stories from the media but on real life experiences. These experiences lead the public to conclude that the schools are failing to deliver on their most important responsibility.

This failure of the public schools to deliver even the most basic education to all youngsters drives people mad with frustration. Adults wonder how youngsters without adequate skills can possibly succeed in a world that they see as increasingly competitive and unforgiving. They worry about the cost to society of functionally illiterate young people on whom they themselves will shortly be dependent. There is no need for media verification on this matter.

When a *Newsweek* poll, released in April 1997, asked people, "Which of the following is a bigger threat to the U.S.?" only 18% responded, "Foreign nations working against us," whereas a resounding 74% said, "Young Americans without education, job prospects, or connections to mainstream American life." The public's demand that all youngsters master basic skills, including the new computer technologies needed for the next century, grows out of this anxiety, which is compounded by people's belief that their local neighborhood's schools are currently failing to deliver.

Thus, mastery of the basics remains at the top of the public's reform agenda—along with safety, order, and discipline. Regrettably, many school reformers continue to resist these public priorities, sometimes dismissing such concerns as simplistic and out of touch. Public Agenda has documented a gap between experts and the public over the years on many issues, welfare and health reform included. But nowhere is the disconnect more profound than on the issue of education reform.

First Things First: What Americans Expect from Their Public Schools documented the public's concerns in 1994. The study clarified why the public is not more positively engaged in the process of reform and detailed their lack of confidence in the reformers' agenda. How, people asked then and continue to ask, can learning take place in such a chaotic environment, and shouldn't the environment be fixed before curricular reform and innovative techniques are introduced? Reformers and educators continue to point accusingly at the media for distorting the problems and instilling attitudes that they believe are destroying the public's confidence in the schools. But the reality is that reformers have been slow to accord the highest priority to the issues that most distress the public.

ARE THE MEDIA BIASED—OR IRRELEVANT?

As already noted, Public Agenda included journalists in a study conducted on behalf of the Education Writers Association (EWA) in the spring of 1997 (Farkas, 1997a). In this study, Public Agenda interviewed members of the general public, parents of public school students, and educators. Everyone was asked about where they get information about their schools; whom they trust to inform them; and whether they think their local media do a good job in covering education and the public schools. Separate questions were asked of journalists who cover education.

This study contains both good news and bad news for journalists. Though educators claim that the media's bad news bias is responsible for the public's negative attitudes toward the schools, the research does not support that point of view. Further, the study indicates that most people are neither furious with the press nor downright disaffected. Rather, for most people, media coverage about the schools is largely irrelevant (Farkas, 1997a). Fewer than one in four parents say they rely on local media for the most useful information about their community's schools. Almost three quarters told us they rely instead on personal observations, experiences, and conversations with real estate agents and others for their information.

At the same time, even among members of the community who are not themselves searching for good schools for their children, there is evidence of considerable skepticism about media coverage. Sixty-nine percent of the general public—in commenting on news about education—believe that reporters cover news according to what sells; 70% believe that journalists use quotes and statistics out of context; and an astonishing 8 in 10 believe that reporters cover "bad news" because "it's their job" (Farkas, 1997a).

In focus group after focus group, people relayed anecdotes that explain the basis for their beliefs. Yet, the public's mistrust of the media does not typically translate into public outrage at the press for bad-mouthing the local schools. Instead, people seem to shrug off the coverage, noting that if media are going to provide news only about the politics or process of education, there is no reason to rely on them for information. Thus, the public is dismissive of the media; if not deeming them entirely irrelevant, certainly considering media coverage far from central in shaping their attitudes toward local schools. To be fair to educators, 86% of whom told Public Agenda that reporters dwell unfairly on conflict and failure (Farkas, 1997a), there are moments when irresponsible coverage of a singular incident can cause real damage in a community and frustrate educators who are struggling to address the public's concerns about its schools.

I recall an early morning meeting of educators and business leaders in 1996, in a community with a diverse population and many of the problems of a large urban environment. The superintendent of schools was late to arrive, and when he did appear he was frantic. The local paper that morning had carried a headline about a scuffle in the local public high school, which had, in fact, been resolved several weeks before. The incident had not been serious; teachers had intervened appropriately, and parents had been responsive. Nonetheless, for whatever reasons, an editor had run this story under a banner headline proclaiming yet another violent episode in the local high school.

The superintendent's anguish was palpable and understandable. He had worked for months to bring the school's diverse community together to talk about how to handle the occasional incidents that do occur, and how to ensure the safety and well-being of all students. He and his staff had faced uncertain, if not hostile, parents and invited them to visit and talk— to join conversations about how best to protect all the community's youngsters. Having handled the incident under scrutiny well, the superintendent was justifiably enraged by coverage that he believed would undo the good work that had been done. In reading the article that morning, I had found it strange that the reporter had not provided context for what had happened, how the incident was handled, and what the school system, with the community's support, was attempting to do. It was, instead, a largely provocative piece of journalism that confirmed many citizens' deepest fears. This particular incident is surely not unique and undoubtedly provides evidence to substantiate some research findings about educators' critical views of the media.

Parents say time and again in various Public Agenda studies that they feel personally responsible for obtaining key information about their children's schools. They believe that critical information about what the schools are teaching their children is not forthcoming, and they yearn for some real substance. In the research conducted for the Education Writers Association, parents and members of the general public were pretty clear about the role they wished local media might play in helping them make sense of their local schools. The father of a public school student in San Jose, California, put it most succinctly. He said, "What the newspapers report has nothing to do with how my daughter is being educated. I would love for them to talk about how the schools are different. But they're not. Let's talk about education."

In this study, people complain that present coverage is shallow, deeply wanting in substance about possible solutions to problems. In large numbers, people are *less* interested in hearing and reading about school politics and *more* interested in learning about their schools' academic standards, programs, and curricula. They want to know more about the qualifications of their children's teachers and about safety and discipline efforts (Farkas, 1997a).

People are also interested in the schools' spending priorities, particularly as they relate to available resources. At the very bottom of the public's list are articles about disputes between members of the educational establishment. A comment heard in one focus group was echoed in one form or another throughout the research:

Both TV and the papers don't deal with education. The press deals with school board members fighting each other. It deals with the superintendents being fired or under suspicion for this or that . . . but I can't recall an article about whether they're doing their job in the education field. (Farkas, 1997a, p. 14)

Thus, while media may not be a major part of the problem, they may be missing an opportunity to be part of the solution.

WILL THEY READ—OR NOT?

Public Agenda has been working in communities around the country to demonstrate a new kind of public conversation about education and the public's schools. In locally sponsored town meetings, members of the public, community leaders, and educators are being helped to engage in a lengthy and productive dialogue about solutions. People who have participated, from Maine to California, express real enthusiasm at having experienced such serious dialogue and a willingness to work hard to see to it that it continues.

People say they have tired of acrimonious debates that are not central to their concerns about the schools. They believe that coverage, like local meetings, has become captive of highly partisan individuals who are always ready to respond to reporters' phone calls and requests for interviews. For its part, the public seems capable of threading its way between scandalous articles and local boosterism, craving instead serious and balanced coverage about how to improve the schools. Seventy percent of the public in this study acknowledged honestly that, given a choice between very good or very bad stories about the schools, they thought most people would be attracted to the bad news first. Further probing reveals, however, a public that is emotionally tired of the bad news and hungering for real substance. "I don't live in a fantasy world," said one participant. "If everything [in the coverage] was just rosy, we'd be looking at the world through rose-colored glasses. But we have to have balance." (Farkas, 1997a, p. 24)

One might assume that journalists would respond defensively to this criticism of their coverage. They might be expected to say: "We're simply telling it like it is." But that is not what Public Agenda found. To the contrary, the majority of education writers interviewed for Public Agenda's study were particularly self-critical when describing their coverage of the substance of education. Almost three quarters (74%) rated their coverage of the quality of teaching in their communities as fair to poor, with 58% saying that this also describes their coverage of curricular issues. Only one in five thinks the public is "very satisfied" with the local media's coverage of the public schools (Farkas, 1997a).

It is fair to ask, I believe, why journalists do nothing about the inadequacies to which they admit. Education writers say they are too dependent on superintendents and school board officials for information, yet they seem incapable of casting a wider net. In interviews for *Good News, Bad News*, as well as in more informal conversations with members of the press, journalists frequently compain about having inadequate time or insufficient resources to thoroughly probe complex issues. Bill Kovach of the Nieman Foundation was recently quoted as saying:

> There's a rising level of concern about the degree to which work in the newsroom is pressured and shaped and interfered with by the pressures of the marketplace. It's mutated into a virus that's begun to destroy journalism. (*Washington Post*, May 12, 1997, p. B1)

Frankly, I suspect that increasingly, journalists won't know how to do anything other than "business as usual" in a culture that consistently reinforces the "gotcha" mentality.

WHAT THE MEDIA DON'T DO—AND COULD

To return to the opening question of the chicken and the egg, it's clear that media do help shape Americans' perceptions about almost any issue imaginable. The degree of influence that the media exert, however, is directly related to the amount of confidence that the public possesses in its own understanding of a particular issue.

Education is an issue that most citizens believe they are qualified to discuss. Public Agenda's research, both quantitative and qualitative, repeatedly indicates that most people—and parents in particular—have a pretty good fix on the strengths and weaknesses of schooling in America. The extraordinary consensus among all groups, including the students, over the need for more rigor, higher standards, greater accountability, and, above all, a safe and civil environment conducive to learning, is neither the result of media coverage nor susceptible to manipulation by it.

But that is not to deny the media a role in the nation's attempt to improve the quality of education. People are hungry for content, and when asked to choose the one thing happening in a community that they would be most interested in knowing about, the public selects coverage of the public schools over the issues of crime and the local economy (Farkas,

1997a). Clearly, people are desperate for help in evaluating what really occurs in their local schools. Everyone agrees that more in-depth reporting is essential—68% of the general public and 81% of parents would be "very interested" in seeing more stories on curriculum, and 74% call for coverage on the quality and training of teachers (Farkas, 1997a). Said one parent: "I'd like to see stories about what they [the schools] are going to teach, what the curriculum is for the upcoming year" (p. 14).

This is not a call for boosterism or cheerleading alone. When asked to choose among four categories of coverage, 54% of the general public called for articles on ideas and programs that offer solutions; 22% requested good news; 15% wanted articles on problems; and only 6% favored more coverage of politics (Farkas, 1997a). But, even when people call for accurate reporting on problems, they simultaneously ask for a discussion of possible solutions, saying it is difficult to absorb a barrage of problems without alternative ideas on how to deal with them.

In summary, I think it's fair to conclude that educators are mistaken and at risk if they continue to ascribe the public's attitudes toward the schools to the bad-news bias of the media. Concurrently, however, I believe that Public Agenda's research provides a wake-up call to all journalists, emphasizing how isolated they are from the public's concerns and how dominated they are by their own interests. The public is telling us loudly and clearly that it is prepared to deal with the problems of education in America—if only journalists would also provide some insight into possible solutions.

BIBLIOGRAPHY

Farkas, Steve (1997a). *Good News, Bad News.* New York: Public Agenda.
Farkas, Steve (1997b). *Miles to Go.* New York: Public Agenda.
Johnson, Jean (1994). *First Things First: What Americans Expect from the Public Schools.* New York: Public Agenda.
Johnson, Jean (1997). *Getting By: What American Teenagers Really Think About Their Schools.* New York: Public Agenda.

The Media and Polls on Education— Over the Years

LARRY CUBAN

Is PUBLIC OPINION fickle? Reading the polls about problems in America in the late-1980s would lead one to answer yes. In September 1989, pollsters for a New York Times/CBS News poll asked Americans to identify the most important problem facing the country. The questions required no forced-choice answers. There was no picking out a problem from a list offered by the poll taker. Each person who was asked the question volunteered an answer. Sixty-four percent said that drugs were the most important problem. Yet, a year later, poll takers asked the same question and only 10% of those who responded said drugs were primary (Oreskes 1990; Kagay 1991). What happened?

Although many federal and state efforts to end the explosion of crack-cocaine traffic had been launched, no noticeable dent in drug-connected street crime had occurred within those 12 months. Nor had drug consumption changed materially. So those surveyed in 1990 who named national problems other than drugs were not responding to any major drop in supply or demand for drugs or in drug-associated crime. Perhaps a more convincing explanation for the sharp drop in the naming of drugs as a national problem can be found in the following events:

- July 1989. In a national poll, 22% of the public said that drugs were the nation's most important problem.
- Mid-August 1989. The White House announced that President George Bush would address the problem of drugs on prime-time television.

Imaging Education: The Media and Schools in America. Copyright © 1998 by Teachers College, Columbia University. All rights reserved. ISBN 0-8077-3734-8 (pbk), ISBN 0-8077-3735-6 (cloth). Prior to photocopying items for classroom use, please contact the Copyright Clearance Center, Customer Service, 222 Rosewood Dr., Danvers, MA 01923, USA, tel. (508) 750-8400.

- August–September 1989. Each of the three network news programs averaged almost three stories per evening about drugs (compared to less than one a night prior to the White House announcement).
- September 6, 1989. President Bush spoke on television and declared a war on drugs.
- September 6–13, 1989. Each of the three network news programs produced four stories per night on drugs.
- Mid-September 1989. A New York Times/CBS News poll registered 64% of Americans putting drugs at the top of their list of national problems.
- August 1990. Almost a year later, a New York Times/CBS News poll found that only 10% said drugs was the top national problem.
- September 9, 1990. President Bush held a news conference to say that reducing drug use is still the nation's top priority even if "other subjects preoccupy all of us these days" (Kagay 1991, p. E3).

Maybe the president was referring to the collapse of communism in Eastern Europe and in the Soviet Union, or the Persian Gulf crisis, or the economy. Whatever he meant, he knew as an experienced politician that holding the public's attention on a subject that initially had concerned his fellow Americans was no easy task. The reporters who wrote these stories for the *New York Times*, many media officials, and national policy makers are aware that public opinion is mercurial. Just look at what happened to opinions registered in the two polls in 1989 and 1990, they might say. To others, including myself, the quicksilver nature of public opinion may be as much due to how and what the media (including polling firms), public officials, and bands of experts communicate to Americans as it is to Americans' presumed short attention span.

In this chapter, I will argue that there is an issue-attention cycle in America to the identifying and framing of most, but not all, problems, including those of an educational nature. The cycle itself is largely driven by professional elites comprised of top public officials and their expert advisers, poll takers, and media leaders who identify and frame particular problems (and not others). It is this cycle driven by elite groups and the unique linking role of media that largely account for the portrayal of public opinion as ever changing. When it comes to educational problems in the last half-century, however, I will argue that it is not skittishness that marks public opinion about schools but a constancy in beliefs about discipline, basic skills, respect for authority, and accountability. These stable beliefs about what constitutes a "good" school, documented over a quarter-century of polling, differ in marked degree from those of policy makers, experts, and media leaders.

HOW PUBLIC PROBLEMS GET FRAMED:
THE ISSUE-ATTENTION CYCLE

There are five stages to the cycle of public perceptions of key national problems (Downs 1972):

1. *The preproblem stage.* An undesirable situation exists that affects millions of people (but a relatively small percentage of the population), such as increasing poverty, a new disease, or an outbreak of racism. The continuing plight of rural and urban schools enrolling large numbers of children from poor families in need of varied social services offers one example in education. The problem has yet to capture sustained public notice.

2. *Sudden arousal and enthusiasm for solving the problem.* Dramatic events, amplified by the media, bring attention to the problem (e.g., the 1992 riots in Los Angeles following the verdict in the Rodney King case; pornography on the Internet accessible to children; industries dumping toxic waste in lakes). Four decades ago, in the midst of the cold war, the shock of the Soviets' launching of Sputnik led critics to identify America's anemic supply of scientists and engineers as the problem and pointed to the public schools' inadequate math and science curricula as the reason why the Soviet Union forged ahead of the United States in the space race. Something had to be done! Public officials respond to such aroused attention and rush to solve the problem. Time and money are invested in figuring out what to do, and confidence grows that the situation can be remedied by a new law, a new program, or a new technology, or, in the case of the fallout from Sputnik, curricula such as "new math" and "new physics."

3. *Growing awareness that the cost of solving the problem is high.* Since most national problems are rooted in society's institutional structures and cultures, it is not too long before Americans realize that much money and substantial sacrifice would be needed to "solve" the problem. Calculations of trade-offs begin to diminish the earlier enthusiasm. Solving immigration from Latin America, for example, involves compromises between powerful economic interests that fear losing migrant labor needed to harvest billion-dollar crops and other groups who worry about the social costs of educating and caring for illegal immigrants. As awareness of the price that has to be paid to solve the problem rises, determination to craft solutions declines.

4. *Diminished public enthusiasm for the problem.* As more Americans realize how many compromises have to be struck or how difficult and complex the problem really is, disappointment and boredom grow. Consider the matter of air pollution. Scientists throughout the 1960s and 1970s raised serious issues about the effects of pollution upon life on earth.

Throughout these decades, media had aroused the public's awareness of polluted air from smokestack industries and from smog caused by car exhausts. They alerted the public to the dangers of acid rain and the hole in the ozone layer. All of these were lumped together under the label *greenhouse effect*—a shorthand term that became popularized in the media in the early 1980s. These media-designated issues caused much consternation and calls for solutions (stage 2). The Clean Air Act (1970), getting rid of aerosol cans, establishing the Environmental Protection Agency became "solutions" (stage 3). But the costs involved in a total reform that meant strong enforcement of vehicle emissions and swift changes in industrial practices of dumping wastes in the air and water ran too high in substantial loss in profits to large corporations and increased unemployment. So only a few changes were made. Enthusiasm for ending the greenhouse effect slipped (stage 4) as new problems replaced environmental concerns (Yankelovich 1991).

For public schooling, the issue of desegregation also went through these stages. After the *Brown* decision in 1954, initial enthusiasm for solving the problem of racial segregation in schools swept the nation (stage 2). That support began to dissolve in the South in 1956 with massive resistance in Virginia. A year later, there was a standoff between the governor of Arkansas and President Dwight D. Eisenhower over the desegregation of Central High School in Little Rock. After violence erupted, Eisenhower sent in federal troops to escort the nine black students into the school to enforce the Supreme Court decision (stage 3). In the late 1950s and early 1960s, it was clear that many southern and northern politicians would seek ways of circumventing *Brown* and subsequent court decisions. Racial violence in and out of schools and families deciding to leave neighborhoods revealed the price that had to be paid for obeying the law; public support for desegregation evaporated over the following two decades (stage 4) (Kluger 1976).

5. *Postproblem stage.* The problem slips off the public radar screen into limbo to be resurrected, perhaps, when dramatic events again seize public attention. Terrorist-directed attacks on U.S. airplanes in the late 1970s and early 1980s, to cite a dramatic example, became a national problem when Americans were involved and led to an increase in monitoring devices at airports and closer surveillance of passengers. After awhile, the "problem" faded only to be resurrected when a hostage-taking incident occurred or when hundreds of passengers died in a plane crash triggered by a bomb.

Similarly, in big-city schools with large percentages of low-income youth, gang involvement in drugs, assaults, and robbery momentarily seize the attention of the media and of school officials. Gang colors and distinctive clothes are banned; weapons are confiscated in schools; order is restored. Then a teacher is beaten up in her classroom by three gang members and renewed attention to gangs surges again. In this case, as in other instances of the postproblem stage, there were new policies, programs, and technologies that had been originally introduced to deal with possible terrorist threats to passenger safety and gangs in schools that left a residue after public attention shifted to another problem.

HOW THE AGENDA GETS SET

What all of these stages have in common is the role of the media in helping shape public opinion by identifying problems to be solved and suggesting solutions. Historically, most Americans have formed their opinions about political, economic, educational, and social problems beyond their immediate experiences from information that they have received from travelers and family and read about in the newspapers, and later, from radio and television.

As commercial ventures, however, print and visual media in America must compete for audiences to deliver to advertisers. Because readers and viewers have other demands and attractions that divert their attention, there is a daily struggle for limited space in newsprint and for prime television-viewing time. Media, then, seek excitement in what they present to the public to attract readers and viewers. Those problems that have dramatic appeal and conflict are identified and presented to the public. As an early-warning system, media sound an alarm for situations that suggest serious consequences for the public: threats from another nation, epidemics, terrorists, corrupt government, and so forth. Because there are so many problems (e.g., drugs, inflation, welfare, crime, malnutrition, loss of forests, homelessness), editors make choices in what to assign to reporters and what is printed and televised. In making those choices, media awake consciousness about problems and thereby help set the agenda for what gets noticed by public officials and what issues many Americans discuss.

Consider media attention in news articles, long magazine pieces, and televised reports given to home schooling, which involves a tiny fraction of less than 1% of all school-age children. By calling attention to the few parents in a community who home school their children, media highlight alternatives to public schools and legitimize the criticism that home schoolers make of public schools to justify their decision to educate their children at home. Thus, the accusation that media shape what Americans think is much less true than the statement that media are "stunningly successful in telling readers [and viewers] what to think *about*" (emphasis in original) (B. C. Cohen, cited in Iyengar and Kinder 1987, p. 2).

The traffic in identifying and framing problems, however, is circular: Public officials and the experts who advise them also help define what

Americans talk about, through news releases and press conferences to journalists about government responses to problems, shaping the stories that
are broadcast and published. Also, pollsters survey public opinion and
report their results to newspapers and television, offering yet another way
of defining what problems and solutions will get discussed. Newspapers
and television stations have since taken the process a step further by con-
ducting their own polls.

Public officials, pollsters, or even interest groups engaged in spontaneous or planned protests, then, need media to raise public consciousness
about particular problems. The audience-seeking media form a crucial link
in the circularity of the agenda-setting process and the elaborate dance of
attracting and sustaining public notice. A critic of this daisy chain relationship among public officials, pollsters, and the media described the symbiosis during the 1996 presidential campaign:

> Today . . . the first flicker of change in the popular mood shows up instantly
> on the pollsters' charts, and becomes the subject of immediate nonstop dis-
> cussion on ABC's *Nightline*, CNN's *Inside Politics*, PBS's *Washington Week in
> Review*, and so forth. Neither the news analysts nor campaign strategists have
> the will or the capacity to do anything as ambitious as engineer public opin-
> ion. . . . But they can and do detect changes that are under way, and they
> rapidly and gigantically inflate them, usually without meaning. (Schell 1996,
> pp. 72–73)

Media critics have also pointed to the convergence of class interests
among editors, reporters, pundits, public officials, and pollsters that reveal
much social distance in both education and tastes between these elites and
most middle- and lower-income Americans. To highly paid journalists who
spend $4,000 a year to send their children to nursery school and $25,000 a
year to college, President Clinton's proposal to offer a $10,000 annual schol-
arship sounds trivial and nonnewsworthy. Social-class affinity among
media and elite interests in the society can distort decisions about what
gets defined as news (Fallows 1996, p. 80).

What is often overlooked in this symbiotic relationship that so deli-
cately measures every twitch in the public mood and often produces the
stages in the issue-attention cycle described earlier are the enduring issues
on which Americans have strong beliefs, not just impressions. Since 1935,
perennial issues have dominated American responses to the poll questions
written by the George Gallup organization, one of the first in the field. For
over a half-century, serious economic and political problems of war and
peace, of unemployment and inflation, have consistently shown up strongly
in polls. Each of these mirror real-life matters and values related to first-
hand experiences that millions of individual Americans have had. They

have beliefs and opinions based on these experiences. Issues may ebb and flow as media attention shifts to the problems of the moment, but in the public's mind, they are connected to what directly affects their private lives: earning a living, having a family, raising children, making and keeping friends, and being a decent person. Other less salient issues also have a constancy to them that surge to the top of polls when a news event triggers public notice, such as troubled race relations revealed by the murder trial of a celebrity, deaths from toxic waste, or cloning a lamb (Kagay 1991).

And so it has been with education. Instances of the issue-attention cycle have tossed up educational problems that have caught the public eye for a moment—career education, performance contracting, instructional television, and alternative schools—and with a blink have disappeared. Often illustrating the symbiosis between pollsters, policy makers, experts, and media, the sudden rise of Americans' temperature about such problems on poll takers' charts masks the trend line of beliefs and value judgments that have a history beyond yesterday's headline or last week's news program. Here, again, what editors choose to print or air seldom persuades the public what to think; the choices provide the public with material to discuss.

Since the mid-1930s, polling organizations have asked different questions on education, and since 1969, the Gallup polls on education have annually tracked issues that Americans have noted about their public schools. It is to these that I now turn.

CONSTANCY IN PUBLIC OPINION ON EDUCATION

One abiding belief held by Americans prior to the invention of polling was that education was important both to individuals and society. The establishment of tax-supported public schools and the steady expansion of public schooling to include ages from toddlers to young adults speak to the historic faith that Americans have had in the social and personal power of formal education. Since surveys of opinion with scientifically drawn samples were introduced in the middle of the Great Depression, questions have been asked about schooling. Although questions have been worded differently over the past 6 decades, Americans' faith in education registered strongly in each survey.

Of the 3,000 Americans in 1939 who answered the question, "Do you want your children to have more education than you did?", 87% said yes. The Gallup/Phi Delta Kappa polls asked Americans in the 1970s and 1980s, "How important are schools to one's future success?" The responses are shown in Table 5.1. To a question in the 1982 poll that asked how impor-

TABLE 5.1. Responses to "How Important Are Schools to One's Future Success?"

Year	Extremely Important	Fairly Important	Not Too Important	No Opinion
	Percent Responding:			
1973	76	19	4	1
1980	82	15	2	1
1982	80	18	1	1

Source: Elam, 1989.

tant it was to develop either the best educational system, the highest industrial productivity, or the strongest military force in the world in regard to America's strength in the next quarter-century, 84% said the educational system was "very important," compared with 66% for high industrial productivity and 47% for a strong military (Cantril 1951, p. 178; Elam 1989, p. 134).

This publicly expressed value about the individual and social importance of schooling has not prevented Americans from being critical of the quality of what is taught, of how classrooms are run, or of life in schools. In their criticism, there has been a notable stability in what Americans have said to poll takers over the past 3 decades about what they value in schooling for their children. In the Gallup/Phi Delta Kappa polls between 1969 and 1996, for example, Americans told pollsters year after year that the "biggest problem in local public schools" was lack of discipline. In 18 of those 28 years, it was ranked first; in the other years, it was second or third. This is a remarkable uniformity in a country with dramatic regional differences in race, ethnicity, and social class and a highly decentralized system of education dispersed in 15,000 school districts across 50 states. In addition to lack of discipline, fears about drugs in schools (drugs first showed up in the top three problems in polls in 1978 and have been ranked there since) suggest that Americans connect the quality of their schools with the degree to which their children learn to respect authority and go to schools that are safe from the street crime and violence that plague many urban neighborhoods (Elam 1989).

According to polls published in the 1970s and 1980s, Americans also believed that the schools should teach the academic basics and that students should acquire sound moral character, become useful citizens, and possess marketable skills for the workplace. Poll after poll registered the high value that Americans placed upon basic and moral literacy. Polls have revealed clear trends in interviewees' strong preferences for mastering reading, math, writing, and, more recently, how to use computers. When asked directly about what schools should be teaching, those polled told

Gallup interviewers that imparting the "basics" was the most important academic task of the school, topping even their call for stricter discipline. For high schools, those interviewed decade after decade supported overwhelmingly (between 75 and 95%) that all students, whether they go to college or not, should be required to take mathematics, English, and history/U.S. government. Just over half to three-fourths of those polled endorsed science as a required subject (Elam 1989)

Those polled also expected improved moral behavior in students. There was near unanimity (range of support from those polled went from 90 to 95%) in 1993 and 1994 for such virtues as respect for others, hard work, persistence, fairness, compassion, and politeness. Buried within the demands for stricter discipline, of course, is the moral imperative of respecting authority. The importance of schools teaching moral literacy was underscored further by the large majorities that still wanted public schools to have prayer even though the practice is unconstitutional (Elam, Rose, and Gallup 1994).

Americans, according to these polls, also want their schools to be accountable. Having national standards for what students should learn enforced by national tests has been as overwhelmingly endorsed in the past 3 decades as, more locally, having students pass tests to move from one grade to another. Moreover, in five separate polls between 1958 and 1988, poll takers asked whether all high school students should be required to pass a national exam in order to get a diploma. In 1958, half of those polled said yes. Since then it has moved from two thirds to about three quarters of those polled favoring such a test. That parents also favor their local schools using nationally standardized tests to compare their students' performance with those of students in other places is one belief that has been constant. Seventy-five percent wanted schools to make the comparison in 1970. In repeated use of the same question in polls for 1971, 1983, and 1986, the response ranged from 70 to 77% in favor of comparing local students with their national peers (Elam, Rose, and Gallup 1992).

Differences in some judgments among Americans, however, have existed. On racial integration, busing, equal educational opportunity, and the seriousness of problems in schools attended by low-income minorities, responses varied, with Blacks being moderately more in favor of integration, busing, and enhanced funding of schools than Whites. In some years, Blacks gave lower grades to schools than did Whites and expressed a strong opinion that their children did not have the same educational chance that White children had. Yet, apart from these differences, both Blacks and Whites largely share a common picture of what constitutes a good school (Elam 1989). According to these polls, what Americans have persistently wanted in public schools are profoundly conservative institutions that are safe and teach respect for authority, proper moral behavior, and basic literacy. Such schools are good ones if they regularly measure student academic achievement and give parents reports on how their children compare to others locally and nationally. There has been a remarkable constancy in these values over the last 30 years.

Such an emerging picture of good schools derived from polls over 3 decades agrees with some educational researchers, policy makers, and practitioners who have called for "effective schools" in the 1980s and 1990s. But other experts disagree. They call effective schools inadequate. They propose that public schools be completely reorganized to encourage students to actively, rather than passively, learn not only the basics but how to solve problems, make independent decisions, learn collaboratively, help the community, and be creative. Other experts see the problem as too much bureaucracy suffocating principals and teachers. Only when schools guided by enlightened teachers and principals are freed from such restraints to work closely with parents and children can they become good. The disagreement among educational authorities extends even to such basic skills as reading (Bliss, Firestone, and Richards 1991).

For example, at the turn of the century and in the 1920s, 1960s, and 1980s, many educators said that children should learn to read for understanding and enjoyment. Reading, of course, includes decoding the sounds of vowels and consonants. But the thrust of instruction in reading, they argued, should be connected to other subjects such as math, science, art, and history. All of these subjects can be integrated when students work together on projects investigating other cultures, the past, or the present, such as inadequate transportation, polluted rivers, and even neighborhood problems. Projects bring students together in real-life situations to learn content from across disciplines that integrates basic skills. Other reading experts, however, then and since, have said that instruction in decoding the language—teaching phonics directly and with much practice—should be emphasized. Of course, reading for understanding is essential, and projects are a fine idea, they pointed out, but without direct instruction for 6- and 7-year-olds to learn the sounds and connect them to letters and words, children will not fully break the code and master other skills of reading (Langer and Allington 1992).

Beyond identifying reading, experts have disagreed among themselves for decades about what the major educational problems are and, of course, the best solutions for schools. Moreover, definitions of a good school vary greatly among educators. Some agree with the beliefs of parents about what constitutes a good school that have emerged from these many polls over the last half-century. Many others, however, diverge in their views from these enduring public beliefs and assert very different versions of what makes a school good.

What these differences reveal is a mismatch of beliefs among lead-ers, experts, and the public about what constitutes good schools. These divergent beliefs produce conflict. In identifying particular problems that will arouse the public (e.g., schools lack new technology, students aren't learning to read and do math, too much bureaucracy) expert-designed "solutions" are advanced (e.g., buying more computers and wiring schools, a whole language curriculum, vouchers, the new math). Fre-quently, these are technical solutions, containing specialized vocabulary, that are either vaguely understood by the public or run counter to the deeply embedded and enduring beliefs cited above. Consequently, to the dismay of policy makers and educational experts, the public loses interest —moving from one stage of the issue-attention cycle to the next. Another problem, identified and then amplified by leaders, media, and pollsters, disappears. The stereotype of a fickle public gains further credibility (Yankelovich 1991).

A QUESTION OF WHOSE VALUES GET NOTICED

What I have argued is that public beliefs about schooling are far from mercurial. The issue-attention cycle is what accounts for the indictment that public opinion is fickle. And that cycle is the unintentional consequence of the convergence and symbiosis of pollsters, media, and public officials in their agendas, ones driven by values of efficiency and of the marketplace. Such values account for frequent shifts in expert opinion about what ought to be done to improve schools. Paradoxically, it is the public's value judg-ments that have been steadfast on the individual and social purposes of tax-supported public schools and what makes a good school. Certainly, some public beliefs have been modified—there is less support for corpo-ral punishment than a quarter-century ago, for example—but the constancy in core values about what should be taught, how schools ought to be run, the importance of teachers, and accountability have been enduring. I would be hard-pressed to make such a statement about the opinions of experts over what makes schooling good (Elam 1989).

I have argued that there has been a constancy, not sudden changes, in public beliefs about good schooling. I have underscored disagreements between the public and experts and policy makers over what makes a school good. And I have pointed out how expedient, interlocking ties be-tween elite groups of media officials, pollsters, and policy makers have sustained the fiction of public fickleness. So what? An implication of this argument is that the institution of schooling is about *whose* values get noticed. The public's belief in core values has been constant. Yet, it has been the ever shifting opinions, anchored in different values, of public officials and their experts, amplified by the media, that have driven the identification of problems and solutions for education. Seldom does this gap in values get examined. Nor is there sufficient study of how access to the media produces expert-designed solutions that ultimately lack credibility with the public.

One example will help make this point. Public faith in the importance of a diploma to an individual's future wages has been remarkably constant. In the early 1980s, however, national experts, blue-ribbon commissions, and presidents of this country began a steady drumbeat of criticism of public schools that linked inadequate education to America's sinking global economic position. "Education," U.S. Secretary of Education Richard Riley said eventually, "is the engine that drives our economy." In the 1980s, Japan and Germany were the shining examples of how a first-rate educational system could create an economy that outperformed that of the United States. National and state leaders (drawn from both political parties) spliced falling economic productivity in America to falling standardized test scores in math and reading (Applebome 1997, p. 5).

The media produced story after story about how poor were American schools compared to those of successful nations in Europe and Asia; how annual scores on national tests barely improved; and how new solutions of restructuring schools, curricular frameworks, national standards, and national tests could solve the problem. As critics have pointed out, media reporters and editors treated the complex issues of educating children in the same way as they treated the World Series or an NFL football game, looking at how the game is played and who wins and loses. The deep story line that the media follow in reporting on schools is the sports contest (Fallows 1996). Rare, indeed, were in-depth analyses of school budgets, resource allocations, and conflicting purposes for public schools. Poll takers registered Americans' dismay with public school performance in their annual report card by giving lower grades.

Yet, almost 2 decades after the issue of competition arose, national productivity has risen and the nation's economy is outperforming those of Germany and Japan. Unemployment and inflation remain lower than in the early 1980s. Have public schools dramatically improved in their test scores or in their performance in relation to other nations? If media reporting and public officials' announcements are any evidence, the answer is no. The underlying narrative remains the win-lose syndrome of football's Super Bowl. Thus, the link between education and the economy is far more complex than what the elite opinion shapers since the early 1980s would have the public believe. The strategy of national and state leaders of linking economic productivity to standardized test scores has left untouched most Americans' confidence in the individual benefits of gaining more education. But people are increasingly confused or even skeptical about claims that their schools are terrible or that higher test scores mean national prosperity.

Public officials and their experts have laid out their beliefs about strengthening the economy through education. Media have amplified and displayed both the criticism of schools and elite-crafted solutions for improvement. The solutions, however, have not easily gained the public's embrace, because many of them diverge from the rock-hard beliefs about good schools that the public has had for decades. The issues are this gap in beliefs between elites and the public and how access to the media is negotiated to continually produce expert-designed solutions.

Fickle public opinion about education is *not* the issue; public beliefs about what makes schools good have been stable. It is public officials, policy experts, and media leaders' value-driven agendas for exerting influence and attracting audiences that have, albeit unintentionally, created rollercoaster cycles and the myth of mercurial public opinion. That is where the light of public debate should shine.

BIBLIOGRAPHY

Applebome, P. (1997). Better schools, uncertain returns. *New York Times*. March 16.

Bliss, J., Firestone, W., and Richards, C. (1991). *Rethinking effective schools: Research and practice*. Englewoods Cliffs, N.J.: Prentice-Hall.

Cantril, H. (1951). *Public opinion, 1935–1946*. Princeton, N.J.: Princeton University Press.

Downs, A. (1972). Up and down with ecology—the issue-attention cycle. *Public Interest*, 28: 38–50.

Elam, S. (ed.) (1989). *The Gallup/Phi Delta Kappa polls of attitudes toward the public schools, 1969–1988*. Bloomington, Indiana. Phi Delta Kappa.

Elam, S. Rose, L., and Gallup, A. (1992). Twenty-fourth annual Phi Delta Kappa poll. *Phi Delta Kappan*. September: 41–52.

Elam, S., Rose, L., and Gallup, A. (1994). Twenty-sixth annual Phi Delta Kappa poll. *Phi Delta Kappan*. September: 41–56.

Fallows, J. (1996). *Breaking the news*. New York: Vintage.

Iyengar, S. and Kinder, D. (1987). *News that matters: Television and American opinion*. Chicago: University of Chicago Press.

Kagay, M. (1991). As candidates hunt the big issue, polls can give them a few clues. *New York Times*. October 20.

Kluger, R. (1976). *Simple Justice*. New York: Knopf.

Langer, J. and Allington, R. (1992). Curriculum research in writing and reading.

   In P. Jackson (ed.) *Handbook of research on curriculum*. New York: Macmillan,
      687–725.
Oreskes, M. (1990). Drug war underlines fickleness of public. *New York Times*.
      September 6.
Schell, J. (1996). The uncertain leviathan. *Atlantic Monthly*. 277(2): 70–78.
Yankelovich, D. (1991). *Making democracy work in a complex world*. Syracuse, N.Y.:
      Syracuse University Press.

The Media's Impact
in Three Areas—Testing,
Learning to Read, Desegregation

A MAJOR PART of the media's reporting on education has to do with the test scores of students. In Chapter 6, Laurence T. Ogle and Patricia Dabbs give the media neither an A nor an F on the way they have carried out this assignment. The grade is mixed, they say. The authors look, in particular, at the media performance in reporting on the results of two tests, the National Assessment of Educational Progress (NAEP) and the Third International Mathematics and Science Study (TIMSS). "By the 1990s," write Ogle and Dabbs, "the negative tilt in the media was overwhelming, to the point that some journalists apparently had difficulty believing any good news about achievement." They maintain that these allegedly unbalanced reports contributed to a general perception of crisis in the schools, sometimes leading educators to act precipitously. They identify the hiring of a private corporation to run the schools in Baltimore as one such action.

In Chapter 7, Dorothy S. Strickland continues in a similar vein as she examines the ways in which the media have depicted reading instruction. She begins from the premise that educators complain of one-sided reporting, slanted toward the negative, in which issues surrounding learning to read are reduced to simplistic formulations. She provides a historical context for her argument. Strickland uses the coverage of the whole language-phonics debate in California during the 1990s as a prism through which to focus on the media's performance. She concludes, along with Ogle and Dabbs, that media pressure pushes educators toward decisions that may not be thoroughly considered. "Public discussion about reading instruction and literacy is commonly conducted within a framework of hotly contested arguments," writes Strickland. "Many reading educators believe that the media are to blame."

Leonard B. Stevens turns in Chapter 8 to one of education's most controversial issues, school desegregation, in one city, Cleveland, to study the media's influence. Stevens, a former journalist, was appointed by the federal court to direct the school monitoring office in Cleveland. Specifically, for this chapter, he conducted an analysis of the articles that appeared in Cleveland's two daily newspapers during a 13-month period as the desegregation order was first implemented. Readers were "exposed to emotion-laden descriptors of school desegregation regularly," he concludes in analyzing the articles and headlines for their use of subjective and objective language. He combines his examination of the reporting with the findings of polls that were conducted at the time to compare the reactions of Black and White parents to school desegregation. Acknowledging that newspaper accounts were not the only sources that shaped impressions, he nonetheless wonders about the media's possibly negative impact on attitudes toward school desegregation.

The Media's Mixed Record in Reporting Test Results

LAURENCE T. OGLE AND PATRICIA A. DABBS

MILLIONS OF STUDENTS take tests every day in America. Many, probably most, are teacher-prepared tests, but a large and growing number are such standardized examinations as the Iowa Test of Basic Skills or the Scholastic Assessment Test, better known by its acronym SAT. Because standardized tests serve as convenient yardsticks for measuring the schools, the media often seize on the results. And since standardized tests *appear* to be an easily interpreted, ready-made indicator for all of American education, they have taken on an unusual importance, sometimes with unfortunate consequences. Investigations of principals are launched for tampering with tests, accusations are lodged against teachers for manipulating scores, and charges of cheating are filed against students for having answers in advance. Indeed, tests have taken on such importance in this country that some commentators see the United States as a nation obsessed with tests. Given this atmosphere, one wonders about the role that the media play in these contretemps.

Some anecdotal accounts are not encouraging. A former testing company executive speaks of "a lot of wasted time" in his efforts to provide meaningful reports to journalists. A reporter recounts his story of a statewide high school exit exam in which he emphasized that the scores of local students had greatly exceeded those of students in more affluent districts. But in the hands of his paper's assistant city editor, the story became an article "about how one out of every 10 young people roaming the streets was stupid" (McQuaid, 1989, p. K2). That is only part of the picture, how-

Imaging Education: The Media and Schools in America. Copyright © 1998 by Teachers College, Columbia University. All rights reserved. ISBN 0-8077-3734-8 (pbk), ISBN 0-8077-3735-6 (cloth). Prior to photocopying items for classroom use, please contact the Copyright Clearance Center, Customer Service, 222 Rosewood Dr., Danvers, MA 01923, USA, tel. (508) 750-8400.

ever. Reporting about education and testing, according to some, has improved remarkably. One media analyst claims that education writers today, "are better informed, better educated, and willing to go the extra mile" (Walsh, 1994). Better journalists may be writing better articles.

Who's right, and more to the point, what changes will be needed to generate better reporting on test results? These become critically important questions as the debate about the quality of education in this country more and more focuses on test scores. This chapter examines the issue in connection with media coverage of the results on two major tests: a national assessment and an international examination. Our analysis indicates that there is much to be concerned about. We found examples of a media preoccupied with the negative, an approach that produces devastating consequences. But we also found some antidotes to this type of reporting. As we hope to demonstrate, reporting about tests is not as easy as might be supposed and requires much more than publishing a few numbers or a set of rankings. When journalists are given additional tools for looking at test scores, the resulting stories can be quite useful to the vigorous ongoing debate about American education.

Prior to and during the 1996 elections, a host of national polls were conducted in which the public was asked about its major concerns. What would top the lists: taxes, American troops in Bosnia, unemployment, crime, or always-troublesome race relations? None of the above. Results consistently showed that the number 1 concern of Americans was their belief that schools were getting worse rather than better. The candidates apparently listened as education issues quickly moved to the fore. But this finding left some unanswered questions. Were the perceptions about the condition of American education correct, and what role did the media play in shaping these perceptions? John F. Jennings offers an emphatic answer to the latter question. After years as a senior staffer for congressional education committees and later as a consultant on Capitol Hill, Jennings was determined to remove himself from the Washington scene and experience firsthand the educational state of mind of the American people. Logging over 80,000 miles in crisscrossing the country, Jennings reported: "Everywhere I went I found the major news media to be extremely negative about public schools. . . . ignoring the good and focusing on the bad" (1996, pp. 12–13). A 1997 poll commissioned by the Education Writers Association found a similar sentiment among educators. "Educators say [that the media] are killing them with bad news. . . . They feel bitterness and anger, coupled with a sense of impotence" (Bowler, 1997, p. 2B).

Are these allegations correct, or are they merely another case of ubiquitous media bashing, of blaming the messenger? Certainly, there is much going on in American schools that is less than desirable. American students have finished last or near last in some international comparisons of educational achievement; increasing numbers of students are concerned about weapons and fights in schools; many minority students continue to lag behind their nonminority counterparts in academic achievement; horror stories continue to emerge especially from some of the nation's poorest schools.

But there is also some surprisingly good news, too. Since the middle 1980s, many more students have been undertaking a significantly more rigorous course of studies; fewer students are taking remedial courses; dropout rates are falling; and the basic reading literacy of some American students compares quite well internationally. Reflecting this mixed picture, the Educational Testing Service released a pamphlet using arrows to describe the movement of student achievement in recent years. Some arrows pointed up, some down, others were flat. In short, it was difficult to decipher a trend in any direction. In addition, a detailed study of mathematics achievement released by the National Council of Teachers of Mathematics concluded that test scores point to real improvement in math education, but cautioned that much work remained. Even some of the most severe critics of public education recently gave the schools an overall average of C (Finn & Ravitch, 1996). Not outstanding, to be sure, but certainly not as dismal as the polls would suggest.

THE NATIONAL ASSESSMENT OF EDUCATIONAL PROGRESS

Unfortunately, although the performance of students on tests would appear to be mixed, the message in the media typically is not. There, Jennings and the educators appear to be correct: The negative slant is quite strong. Test results, in particular, seem to bear the brunt of this negativity. As evidence, we present an example of media coverage of the National Assessment of Educational Progress (NAEP). This test is the only measure of its kind to produce nationally representative and continuing results of student achievement in the country. It is widely respected by educators and researchers alike for its technical rigor and substantive contributions to the understanding of student achievement. Further, the testing profession is in agreement that it is NAEP rather than the better-known Scholastic Assessment Test that should be used to evaluate national and state student achievement. In short, this test has an unusual degree of credibility and importance, which should translate into critical attention to its results and a high level of visibility in the media.

In a 2-week span in the autumn of 1995, NAEP released new U.S. history and geography results. The geography report was issued at the headquarters of the National Geographic Society in a press conference attended by the president of that institution, Gilbert M. Grosvenor, the secretary of education, Richard Riley, and others. Most speakers stressed that this was a "tough test" that went well beyond the memorization of state capitals or the location of national borders. Yet, the results looked promising. Grosvenor (1995), who had been critical of earlier NAEP geography results, emphasized both the high level of performance and the difficulty of the NAEP test when he stated, "American students are becoming *good at good geography*" (p. 1). Riley (1995) said that he was "encouraged by the results of this tough new test" and pointed out that more than 70% of students at the 4th, 8th, and 12th grades had attained at least a basic level of proficiency in geography. The overriding impression from the news conference should have been one of progress.

The reporting in the media, however, was sparse and left the impression that student performance was lackluster at best. Only a handful of the nation's leading newspapers reported the findings—and those that did usually buried the story well beyond the front page. Moreover, in those few stories, the generally positive comments by Grosvenor and Riley were typically overshadowed by the observations of the only speaker to provide a negative take on the results, William Moloney (1995), a superintendent of a Maryland school district and a member of the NAEP governing board. Given the relative prestige of the other speakers, their comments would usually receive more attention from the media, but this time they did not. The reporting in *USA Today* was typical. The first sentence read: "About three quarters of U.S. students have a basic knowledge of geography," but in the same sentence, the reporter cited Moloney's "serious concern," for the 30% "who are barely geographically literate" (Henry, 1995, p. 4). In fact, this statement went further than Moloney's comments. High school students, it said flatly "are not geographically illiterate" (p. 1). Only the last sentence of the article captured some of the positive mood of the press conference: Grosvenor was quoted as saying, "We are seeing progress" (Henry, 1995, p. 4). The article was brief, placed on page 4, and presented only a few of the major issues.

Publications aimed at educators themselves, which do not circulate widely among the general public but have a direct impact on members of the education community, were particularly attuned to negative findings in NAEP. One newsletter, *Education Daily*, headlined "NAEP Shows Most Students Lack Geographic Skills" (NAEP shows, p. 1), a demonstrably false statement. Meanwhile, *Education Week*, in possibly the most penetrating article on the geography assessment, nevertheless left out a crucial positive statement to accentuate the negative (Lawton, 1995). Grosvenor was correctly cited as saying "We are not at the head of the class yet, not by a stretch." The excerpt, however, omitted his next sentence: "But it's a good start" (Grosvenor, 1995, p. 2).

The good news so evident at the press conference was lost on most of the media, replaced with the perception that geography education is not faring well. This inaccurate representation has serious implications. It might erroneously lead readers to conclude that the geography curriculum is in a shambles and should be junked. In fact, the geography results indicate the opposite. There is, of course, need for improvement, as Moloney correctly noted. But ironically, the way to improvement might be to stay the course—and this is a story worth telling. Unfortunately, it was not told.

At the U.S. history press conference two weeks later, the results reported were significantly worse: More than half of the nation's high school seniors scored below the basic level of achievement in history. The news spread like the proverbial wildfire. Within an hour, results were on the radio and the Internet. Requests for additional information flooded into the Department of Education from radio and television stations, newspapers, and a few talk show hosts. Stories about the history performance were on the national news broadcasts and public television that evening, and were a subject of discussion later in the week on Washington weekly review shows. The next day, the history results made the front page of the *Washington Post* and *USA Today,* and the *New York Times,* the *Boston Globe,* and most other large newspapers also prominently featured the story. Later in the week, the editorial pages of the *Washington Post* and the *Christian Science Monitor* carried solemn warnings. As the results moved beyond the "serious media," they became fair game for pundits across the spectrum. Late-night comedy king Jay Leno found time to ridicule the results in his monologue, and at least one radio station led into the morning news report with the pop lyrics "Don't know much about history. . . ."

Clearly, the coverage of the negative news about U.S. history overshadowed the relatively good news about geography. Possibly this is due to the "record-setting" dismal performance of the 12th graders. But evidence suggests that this tilt to the negative was not an isolated phenomenon. The results of an earlier NAEP geography assessment that produced scores significantly worse than the 1994 test scores received greater play in the media. The National Academy of Education (1996) reported that in 1992 the majority of states receiving the most press coverage on that assessment had performed poorly, and that the results in only two states were reported in a positive light.

Perhaps the negative slant of the media was most egregiously exemplified by what happened to the results from a 1992 international assessment in basic literacy. On that test, American 9-year-olds scored second in the world in reading—only Finland performed better. This was a world-class performance by any standard, and one that suggests that maybe our reading methods are showing some promise. It was also a story that should have compelled press attention because it was so surprising—a true man-bites-dog story. But *USA Today* was the only mainstream newspaper to carry the story, belatedly picking it up from *Education Week*. Eventually, the *Los Angeles Times* wrote an article on the test, *4 years later*. Their reason for running the story so late is instructive. "We were initially suspicious about the story because of its age, but when we checked around, we found out that no one knew about the study, so it was still news," said a spokesperson for the *Los Angeles Times* (Bracey, 1997, p. 19). Good news about education appears to be of little interest to many in the nation's newsrooms.

THE MEDIA'S SLANT

This raises two questions. First, why is the reporting about achievement test news so negative, and second, does it matter? To the first question, we suggest that although there are probably many factors at play, one seems to stand out: The concept of successful schools does not fit well with the widely accepted notion (reflected in the national polls) that schools are universally failing. This idea of failing schools has gained renewed and unusual strength in recent years. In 1983, the U.S. Department of Education issued a slender volume entitled *A Nation at Risk*, a blistering attack on the quality of the nation's schools that received wide attention in the media. By the 1990s, the negative tilt in the media was overwhelming, to the point that some journalists apparently had difficulty believing any good news about achievement. In February 1997, for example, the Department of Education released NAEP mathematics results that showed statistically significant improvement at every grade tested. Government officials said this was "good news." It was, and again it indicated that math educators might be moving in the right direction. But some in the media did not see it that way. ABC news anchor Peter Jennings editorialized that the gains were only modest and that the government was "cheerleading" the results (1997). Not likely. While government officials and politicians have their own political agendas, and now might want to accentuate the positive, in this case they simply had no choice; the news was good, and it should have been reported as such.

This brings us back to our second question: Does it matter if the media is negative in reporting test results? After all, most news in the media is negative; aberrations make news. (Although, as we have seen, that argument did not carry the day with the standout international reading test results.) Furthermore, the media have a responsibility to reveal the shortcomings of the system so it can be fixed. The history results, for example, suggest that a great deal of work needs to be done if the United States is to produce a knowledgeable electorate. In addition, some highly regarded educational reformers point out that the bad news can actually have a salutary effect. They argue that the negative news almost guarantees that a critical spotlight will remain on education. Reform will proceed apace of the bad news. Finally, others indicate that positive reports are simply not newsworthy. Even some educational reformers who admit to gains in achievement say that this improvement is of little consequence. According to them, quantum leaps in achievement will be required to maneuver successfully in the 21st century, and the gains students are making today are unimpressive by that standard. Good news about education, then, amounts to nothing more than a rearrangement of the deck chairs on the Titanic, providing a more pleasant view as the ship slips into the gurgling sea.

Nevertheless, there are serious problems with negative reporting. Consistently unbalanced accounts in the media contribute to a general perception of crisis, and crises allow little time for careful reflection and analysis. In such an atmosphere, prudent discussions of the issues give way to the compulsion for immediate solutions. Public officials, pressured to respond, might try something—anything—to improve their education system, and in their haste, focus on the wrong problem, the wrong solution. Baltimore's experiment with school privatization is an example of a solution sought through panic.

The crisis atmosphere was much in evidence (as it is in many large urban districts) when that city decided to hire a private firm to run the day-to-day operations, including instruction, at nine public schools. Privatization, as it is called, had never before been tried on such a large scale in one school system. Still, some research had been done in this area, and its findings could have aided the Baltimore officials in their decision making. Instead of carefully considering these findings, officials in Baltimore, in full crisis mode, rushed through the proposal. Results from that experiment show that achievement in privatized schools was at about the same level as in nonprivatized schools, but at much greater cost. Later, some accounts in the local paper referred to the experiment as a "disaster." UCLA professor Mike Rose describes the situation that prods experiments such as that in Baltimore: "This [negative] kind of talk fosters neither critique nor analysis but rather a grand dismissiveness or despair [which leads to] . . . one dimensional proposals for single-shot magic bullets" (1997).

The broad sweep of unfair negative press can also dispose citizens to believe that public education is failing *in every aspect,* suggesting the need for scattershot remedies. Sensing a problem too large to control, citizens might simply give up on the public schools altogether—putting a gun to their collective head. Newspapers have the power to bring citizens together to work on issues of concern to them, as Tocqueville argued, but if they fail to report accurately, they may generate inaccurate perceptions that lead the public in risky directions. The call for the elimination of public schools is one such example. Unbalanced negative reporting can lead to other, less extreme scenarios. It might, ironically, reinforce the status quo. Sensing that everything is wrong with the schools, concerned readers might simply continue to do what they have been doing: throw money at the public schools. Because everything is wrong, the real problems are not targeted and nothing is changed. In either case, the schools and the students do not improve.

To proceed more rationally, citizens first need to know what works and what does not. For the media, this should mean probing test results more carefully and in more depth to determine both strengths and weaknesses so that changes can be made. Press reports, for example, could indicate how and in what ways students are "getting good at geography." But here's the rub. To do that well, journalists will need reports that are both detailed and comprehensible. The NAEP documents certainly contained a great deal of data, but as we will see later, the reports were not always presented in a accessible format. Consequently, much of it never got reported, and, instead, a shallow negativity filled many columns. What happens when "media-friendly" test data are well presented to journalists? Our next section offers a promising glimpse.

THE THIRD INTERNATIONAL
MATHEMATICS AND SCIENCE STUDY

How can the media do a better job of reporting test results and thereby help schools improve? The coverage of the Third International Mathematics and Science Study (TIMSS), released about one year after the NAEP history and geography scores were announced, shows a way. The largest study of its kind, TIMSS tested more than 500,000 mostly 13-year-olds worldwide, generating math and science scores from 41 countries. Overall, the United States scored slightly above the international average in science and slightly below the average in mathematics. Japanese, French, and Canadian students scored significantly higher than U.S. students in math, but American students scored about the same (3 points higher) on the science test as both German and Canadian students, and significantly higher than French students. In sum, the results indicated that American students scored near the middle of the international pack.

The comparisons just presented are inevitable in any international competition, be it educational or Olympian. A number of the presenters at the press conference, however, were quick to emphasize that there was much more to the story than an educational horse race, and came equipped to explain why. In fact, the TIMSS press conference turned into a veritable data feast complete with easy-to-read tables on a host of issues, compact discs filled with information, and even a video of actual classroom instruction in Germany, Japan, and the United States. Educational myths were exploded, and experts discussed not just the test, but curricular issues that might have influenced performance on the test. The TIMSS press packets contained an accessible and rich set of data that could be easily mined by journalists. And many journalists took advantage. *USA Today*, a paper sometimes criticized for its brevity, used this occasion to carry the TIMSS story on page 1, and then devoted two stories with large graphics and special columns to explaining why American students performed the way they did. An article in the *New York Times* explored complex cultural issues, among other topics, that might have contributed to differences in test scores. The *Los Angeles Times* even sent a journalist to Singapore to try and uncover why that country had scored at the top in both math and science.

The reporting was at its best when it took the data to the schools. The *Washington Post* and the *Detroit Free Press*, for example, sent journalists into classrooms to uncover what was being taught and how it matched up with TIMSS findings. The story in the Detroit paper cited a wide variety of officials and academics associated with the test (Van Moorlehem, 1996). But it also went well beyond these, presenting a scene from teacher Lauren Isotalo's class at the Macomb Mathematics, Science, and Technology Center. Isotalo's class is part of a program attempting to avoid piecemeal approaches to the teaching of math and science, a central piece of the story because that type of teaching was strongly recommended by the TIMSS study. The article demonstrated just how fascinating and difficult learning can be in such an atmosphere, and it reported on teachers' and administrators' successes and frustrations with this type of instruction. By couching the TIMSS findings in an enlightening and helpful discussion of local educational practice, the article gave Detroit citizens a model that might help at their local school. This is no small accomplishment!

In a few cases, media reports went beyond the data to pose really difficult questions. One newspaper that showed both how to and how not to do it was the *Los Angeles Times*. In an early commentary on TIMSS, the paper claimed that a lack of discipline was the culprit in the "poor" scores produced by American students. This is a provocative point, and may have some legitimacy. Unfortunately, the paper cited no evidence to buttress its argument, presenting scare tactics instead: "Tests showing Asian students at the top of the heap and America lodged in the middle should awaken us as did Sputnik" (Plate,1996). But was discipline the deciding factor? To its credit, the *Los Angeles Times* decided to find out by sending a reporter to Singapore (Colvin, 1997). A front page article showed that not only was discipline a key part of the educational mix, but so were competition and central government control, factors rarely discussed in the United States. By going to such lengths, the *Los Angeles Times* provided its readership with a way to begin the discussion, and in so doing, exemplified the still vital role that newspapers have in engaging public debate about education.

One of the more complex and detailed discussions of TIMSS occurred in the British journal the *Economist* (Who's top?, 1997). There, the writer freely used research findings and a variety of test results to produce one of the better articles on TIMSS, even though its major thesis was questionable. The article intoned that the TIMMS data reveal that money spent on education was not a factor in determining how well or poorly countries performed—an important area of discussion. Unfortunately, this was the least convincing part of the article, as TIMSS is not particularly well suited for that analysis. But in arriving at that conclusion, the author passed through some fascinating terrain. A selected review of how TIMSS results played out in Europe was presented (e.g., a German network ran a program titled "Education Emergency in Germany" after the TIMSS results were released. After all, the United States had scored 3 points higher than Germany in science). Findings from previous international studies were presented, as were other countries' use of these. Questions about the utility of TIMSS and other international tests were raised, and teaching methods among the nations were examined. Findings were placed in a context that helped readers understand why students performed the way they did, and research was highlighted and interpreted. It is important that the author did not shy away from some fairly complex research studies; indeed, the article was informative precisely because the author took the data so seriously, looking into a wide range of causes of achievement.

Potentially important also was the coverage of the TIMSS results in the nontraditional media. The World Wide Web pages of the mainstream media were particularly exciting. Many newspapers and electronic media placed the TIMSS findings on their Web sites, which guaranteed worldwide dissemination. But Internet technology is rich. It provides important services an "ordinary" newspaper cannot. The *New York Times,* for example, incorporated audio recordings from the press conference on its site, whereas the *Washington Post* linked readers to related on-line studies. The *Detroit Free Press*, in a move that could substantially aid reform-minded educators, placed a teaching guide on its site. These are examples of truly innovative journalism, and they portend an exciting future for education reporting. Providing useful and accessible data to journalists appeared to improve many articles and stories. Yet, other journalists who had access to the same data were less successful. Why? The failure of these writers was typically due to one of three factors: They ignored the data, they reported them erroneously, or they failed to ask the right questions.

First, the *Chicago Sun-Times*, like many other papers, produced a fairly accurate report on the TIMSS findings, but one day after that story was published, a surprising editorial headlined in the same paper: "U.S. schools in crisis; so what else is new?" ("U.S. Schools in Crisis," 1996). The editorialists declared that TIMSS results showed American schools to be "on the brink of catastrophe" because they learned their science less well than students in Bulgaria. What the writers failed to mention was that Bulgaria was the fifth leading scorer in the world in science (out of 41 countries), and that it had scored better than most developed Western European nations. The *Sun-Times* article also noted that the study had found American education deficient in a number of areas, and concluded sarcastically that "no one needed an international study to know that." Had the *Sun-Times* taken the time to analyze rather than ridicule the study, the resulting story could have added to rather than detracted from the ongoing debate about public education in Chicago.

Second, favored ideas were erroneously presented as findings from TIMSS. The late Albert Shanker, then president of the American Federation of Teachers, stated in his weekly advertisement in the *New York Times* that America did "about average" basically because it has failed to adopt tough national standards as many of the higher-scoring Asian nations had (Shanker, 1996). He was not alone; several prominent newspapers expressed similar sentiments. Shanker was a strong supporter of standards, but his analysis of the TIMSS data was flawed. In a televised interview that was broadcast several months after Shanker's comments were made, Columbia University professor Richard Wolf noted that there was no relationship between a country's score on TIMSS and whether it had national standards (Wolf, 1997). Wolf pointed out that of the countries scoring higher than America, some had standards, whereas others did not. The same was true for those countries that scored about the same or lower than the United States. Although this does not necessarily argue against implementing standards, it does imply that it is inappropriate to use TIMSS results as a premise for supporting the development of standards.

Third, conventional wisdom was rarely questioned. One typical part of test reporting is to gather comments from the business community—an important practice since it is they who will be hiring many of those taking the tests. TIMSS results provided another opportunity. In a number of articles, business leaders were quoted expressing their disappointment. Typical were these comments in the *Sacramento Bee*: "The study met with dismay, but not surprise, from state and national leaders, who said American students were increasingly unprepared for the technological jobs on which the economy depends" (Anderluh, 1996). Did the data lead inexorably to that conclusion? The answer is not straightforward. There was no identifiable technology component on either test, though the science exam contained elements of technology. American students performed above average on that test and as well or better than students in some European technological powerhouses, such as Germany and France. Aside from the important Asian nations, some of the countries that scored highest in science, such as the Czech Republic, Slovakia, Bulgaria, and Slovenia, are not nations typically known for their technological prowess. Business leaders may not be at their best in interpreting test results. While their input contributes to the debate, it should not go unquestioned.

The coverage of the TIMSS data, then, was far from monolithic. Some stories were excellent, others were poor; some explained the findings well, others did a shoddy job with the data, or simply ignored them. But, taken together, media reporting was better than in the coverage of previous test results. A number of stories contained creative insights into the data, and gave their audiences more to think about than simply where the United States placed on the international scale. By moving beyond the horse race and the associated national self-flagellation typical of so many testing articles, journalists brought, not despair, but ideas and models of success to the thinking public. Not all journalists were successful at this. The atmosphere of crisis pervades some of these reports, even some of the better ones. Some reporters seemed too inhibited by this mind-set to create a fresh and careful consideration of the data. But, given the times, that is to be expected. Indeed, it was impressive to see so many journalists move so quickly beyond the rankings to a careful discussion of their causes.

WHAT'S NEXT?

The conclusion to our brief study, then, would seem obvious. For better reporting and to move away from an obsession with the negative, journalists need more and better data. The TIMSS reporting seems to show this. These data were unusual in both their depth and accessibility. Many articles about NAEP, on the other hand, demonstrate that the public, policy makers, and journalists simply do not understand test results. To simply give out more data may not be enough. Journalists need assistance with both context and interpretation. Professor Ronald Hambleton, a researcher at the University of Massachusetts, has experienced much frustration in trying to make test results more understandable, a frustration that was probably not assuaged by the findings of his own recent studies (Hambleton & Slater, 1995). Hambleton's research team took a copy of the most "reader-friendly" part of a NAEP report, the executive summary, and asked the lay public and policy makers to explain what they read. Hambleton found that these individuals made many errors in interpretation.

In earlier studies, Hambleton had discovered that journalists fell prey to many of the same mistakes. This is not surprising. The reports are full of mention of "standard errors," "significance levels," and other test and statistical jargon that few outside the fields of statistics and psychometrics understand easily. Although the "stats" inject an important and necessary element of technical rigor, they also add confusion for the lay reader. And for journalists there is an added complication. Because of the pressure of deadlines, concepts that took years to develop, and years of advanced graduate training to understand, must be grasped in an afternoon—a seemingly impossible task.

Clearly, then, those who release test results must do a better job of explaining them, consistently presenting complex data in clear and easily digested form. Many are now calling for such action. An assessment panel of the National Academy of Education (1997) studied NAEP for more than 6 years, recommending in the end that if NAEP is to have a voice in the educational debate of the future, it must vastly improve its reporting mechanisms. The National Center for Education Statistics, which releases both the TIMSS and NAEP reports, has commissioned numerous studies analyzing the presentation of test results and ways to improve them. While there are some promising avenues being explored, much work, perhaps radical rethinking, needs to be done. Not an easy task. Test professionals, statisticians, and technical experts are usually trained to write for their own constituencies, not for the general public. Branching out to lay readers, including journalists, is quite challenging, and some are not eager to try. In addition, translating highly complex sophisticated and technical language into understandable prose can be a daunting task and, in the end, may not be completely possible. But if tests play a significant role in the education debates of the future (and it looks like they could be central), that task must begin.

Ensuring that test developers create more accessible test results is only part of the solution. The media also have an important role to play. Simply put, reporters need to become better at interpreting the test results. This means putting able journalists on the education beat and letting them remain long after they get a solid grasp of the issues in testing. Laments James W. Guthrie, an education professor at the University of California at Berkeley, "I am always bringing a new cohort [of reporters] up to speed. They don't understand." Too many lack "the background against which to make judgments" (Walsh, 1994). The media need to invest in education reporters' training and place a higher premium on keeping good writers in the fold. This, of course, will cost time and money.

So, both journalists and test developers must work together at improving test reporting. But this could be difficult. A focus group of journalists and test developers meeting in New Jersey in 1992 illustrated one of the potential problems. The gathering took place just after the release of the first NAEP "state reports," and the results had been widely disseminated by the media. But at this meeting, neither test developers nor the media were happy. The test people had spent months creating the most important chart in the book. It showed which states were statistically significant from each other, but in deference to the media, it was compact, a one-pager. The psychometricians considered it to be a breakthrough: technical data presented in an attractive format—surely it would capture the imagination of the media, and be widely used. To their dismay, it was not, and the reasons were obvious. Whereas the chart made eminent sense to the testing contingent who deal with complex data sets daily, the same graphic of more than 40 rows and 40 columns with various levels of shadings (which illustrated the concept of statistical significance) drew blank stares from the media. It was, claimed the reporters, indecipherable. They wanted a table that people could understand in 10 seconds, or they would lose their readers. This chart did not meet that criteria. Each side had a legitimate point, but both left disappointed as neither side budged. Five years later the same type of chart was used in a NAEP report, and again it was ignored by the media.

Yet, even if the media and test designers join forces to match comprehensible test reports with knowledgeable journalists, there is no guarantee that these tests will get the coverage they demand. This is due in large measure to the nature of the instruments themselves. In testing parlance, neither NAEP nor TIMSS is a "high-stakes" measure; that is, neither test produces individual scores, and so students have little at stake in the outcomes . Because this factor limits household interest in the test results, the media and the public have generally displayed varying levels of interest in these test results.

This may change rather quickly and dramatically. In his 1997 State of the Union message, President Clinton set in motion the development of new national tests in fourth-grade reading and eighth-grade mathematics. Although development of the tests is only in the formative stage, the intent is to produce individual scores that inform parents and school officials about the academic performance of their fourth and eighth graders. Further, the test would be linked to both NAEP and TIMSS so that individuals' scores could be compared to both national and international scores. Of course, this type of testing presents both desirable and undesirable elements, and there are many practical and political roadblocks on the way to implementation, if, in fact, it does occur. But one thing is clear. If the policy were to be implemented at some point in the future, these tests would be watched much more closely than examinations in the past. Both test developers and reporters would need to join forces to display the highest level of skill to report the results. Much would be at stake for the public.

BIBLIOGRAPHY

Anderluh, D. (1996, November 21). Special report: U.S. students do so-so in global testing. *The Sacramento Bee* [online]. Available Internet: http://sacbee.com/news/.

Bowler, M. (1997, May 11). Blaming the media messenger. *The Baltimore Sun,* p. 2B.

Bracey, G. W. (1997). On comparing the incomparable: A response to Baker and Stedman. *Educational Researcher, 26* (3), 19–26.

Colvin, R. L. (1997, February 23). Column one: Why tiny Singapore is at top of class. *The Los Angeles Times,* Part A, p. 1.

Finn, C. E., & Ravitch, D. (1996). Report card on American education: U.S. education reform, 1995–96. *Education Excellence Network* [online]. Available Internet: http://www.edexcellence.net/.

Grosvenor, G. M. (1995, October 17). Remarks by Gilbert M. Grosvenor, President, National Geographic Society. National Assessment of Educational Progress, Geography, pp. 1–4.

Hambleton, R. K., & Slater, S. C. (1995, August). *Are NAEP executive summary reports understandable to policy makers and educators?* National Center for Research on Evaluation, Standards, and Student Testing. Technical Review Panel for Assessing the Validity of the National Assessment of Educational Progress. Los Angeles, Center for the Study of Evaluation.

Henry, T. (1995, October 18). Mapping geography knowledge. *USA Today,* p. 4.

Jennings, J. F. (1996). Travels without Charley. *Phi Delta Kappan, 78* (1), 11–16.

Jennings, P. (1997, February 27). *ABC World News Tonight.* American Broadcasting Corporation.

Lawton, M. (1995, October 25). Students fall short in NAEP geography test. *Education Week* [online]. Available Internet: http://www.edweek.org.

McQuaid, E. P. (1989, January). A story at risk: The rising tide of mediocre education coverage. *Phi Delta Kappan, 70* (5), K1–K8.

Moloney, W. J. (1995, October 17). Statement on NAEP 1994 geography results [Press Statement], pp. 1–2.

NAEP shows most students lack geographic skills. (1995, October 18). *Education Daily, 29* (226), 1, 3–4.

National Academy of Education. (1996). *Quality and utility: The 1994 Trial State Assessment in reading.* Stanford, CA: Author.

National Academy of Education. (1997). *Assessment in transition: Monitoring the nation's educational progress.* Stanford, CA: Author.

Plate, T. (1996, November 26). California prospect: In schools, "freedom" brings mediocrity. *The Los Angeles Times* [online]. Available Internet: http://www.latimes.com/.

Riley, R. W. (1995, October 17). Statement of U.S. Secretary of Education, Richard W. Riley: 1994 NAEP Geography: A First Look [Press Statement], pp. 1–3.

Rose, M. (1997, January 30). Saving public education. *The Nation* [online]. Available Internet: http://www.thenation.com/.

Shanker, A. (1996, December 1). Where we stand: A commonsense approach [Paid advertisement]. *The New York Times*, p. E7.

U.S. schools in crisis; so what else is new? (1996, November 22). *The Chicago Sun-Times*, p. 39.

Van Moorlehem, T. (1996, November 21). U.S. students need . . . smarter schools. *Detroit Free Press* [online]. Available Internet: http://www.freep.com/.

Walsh, M. (1994, February 16). Are newspapers missing the beat? *Education Week* [online]. Available Internet: http://www.edweek.org/.

Who's top? (1997). *The Economist* [online]. Available Internet: http://www.economist.com.

Wolf, R. (1997, February 11). Transcript: Setting standards. *Online newshour: Measuring education.* Available Internet: http://www.pbs.org/newshour/.

CHAPTER 7

Reading and the Media

DOROTHY S. STRICKLAND

BODYBAG JOURNALISM! The first time I encountered this term I was listening to radio broadcast journalist Charles Osgood on WCBS, who was referring to the tendency of local television stations to focus most of their attention on fires, murders, rapes, and other tragedies. According to Osgood, a group called the Rocky Mountain Media Watch actually generated a Mayhem Index, which monitored the percentage of news devoted to this type of material. On a particular evening, one local television station was reported to have an index of 73%. Apparently, disasters are easy to cover, and they generate good visuals. Protesters say that this is bad journalism, but no one disputes the fact that mayhem gets attention.

Similarly, in their book *The Spiral of Cynicism: The Press and the Public Good*, Coppella and Jamieson (1997) complain about the media coverage of political campaigns. They suggest that the media tend to focus on attacks, not advocacy, and that they deliberately look for areas of breakdown, rather than of agreement, among political candidates. These concerns interest me because they are consistent with what I discovered to be the prevailing opinion among reading educators about the media's treatment of reading and literacy education. Educators criticize the media for inaccurate or biased reports of plunging test scores and rising illiteracy, saying that such reporting serves more to alarm the public than to inform it. Most noneducators agree that the media provide a dismal picture of reading achievement in our country.

Noneducators, however, are less convinced that this view is distorted, incorrect, or incomplete. Even those who say they mistrust the media are convinced that, unlike in the good old days, there is less teaching or learn-

Imaging Education: The Media and Schools in America. Copyright © 1998 by Teachers College, Columbia University. All rights reserved. ISBN 0-8077-3734-8 (pbk), ISBN 0-8077-3735-6 (cloth). Prior to photocopying items for classroom use, please contact the Copyright Clearance Center, Customer Service, 222 Rosewood Dr., Danvers, MA 01923, USA, tel. (508) 750-8400.

ing of reading going on today, particularly in the public schools. Ironically, such broad generalizations do not reflect the public's experience with its own local schools. Each year, the Phi Delta Kappa/Gallup poll shows that the public gives much higher grades to local schools, about which they are more familiar, than to schools in general, where their opinion is much more likely to be swayed by the media (Elam, Rose, & Gallup, 1996).

The public's perception of the schools and of reading instruction is influenced not only by what is reported in the media but by the *way* in which it is reported. To an overwhelming degree, classroom teachers, administrators, teacher educators, and researchers whom I encounter say that they want the media to reflect accurately what is happening in the schools regarding reading. They say that they want the public to have access to the truth about teaching methods in current use and about reading achievement. They complain, though, that the news about reading is one-sided and invariably slanted toward the negative.

One of the biggest concerns of educators is that the media tend to turn every discussion or issue into a controversy. Some say that even the most complex issues are reduced to simplistic arguments that ignore nuances. The controversy in 1997 over Ebonics, an issue directly related to literacy education and one that touched on racial issues, as well, is often cited as an example of how the media may have misled the public with superficial and inaccurate reporting. Joel Pett's cartoon, reprinted here, expresses precisely the way that many educators felt during the Ebonics debates, whether or not they agreed with the Oakland School Board's approach to a serious literacy problem.

Indeed, as I talked to individuals and collected material for this chapter, I found an abundance of negative articles, many focusing on extreme positions on various issues related to the teaching of reading. I found some examples that have an approving tone, as well, and some in which the media simply attempted to report information about reading instruction in a dispassionate, objective manner. If it is true that the media tend to focus on what gets the public's attention and that they use journalistic methods that cause people to take notice, then it is equally true that these are the stories that reading educators and the general public are most likely to read, view, or listen to. These are also the stories that are apt to remain most vivid in everyone's memory. Of course, it is not good news that alarms people; negative news is more provocative. Shocking revelations get discussed at the watercooler. Stories that point to problems regarding our children's ability to read and write cause us to sit up and take notice.

Even when the media are reporting a positive announcement related to reading, the negative implications may overwhelm the good news. For example, in announcing his reading initiative, America's Reading Chal-

Pett Peeves   **by Joel Pett**

Reprinted with permission from *Phi Delta Kappan*, March 1997.

lenge (August 27, 1996), President Clinton advanced some promising proposals and emphasized the importance of literacy in the lives of children
and adults. In an effort to capture the public's attention and justify the
expenditure of $2.75 billion to support these initiatives, the proposals were
couched in the context of claims about the dismal state of reading achievement in the United States. The president and his advisors faced the same
problem that researchers and grant writers continually face when they
generate proposals for funding. It does not help to paint a picture that is
only marginally gloomy when you are requesting funds for research or
development projects. One is obliged to portray existing conditions as extremely grim, and certain to become even grimmer if one's proposal is rejected. The point, of course, is that in cases such as these, the media is no
more likely to stress the negative than are those who furnish the information and opinions that they report.

   This chapter will focus on key events and issues that have drawn media
attention to reading instruction and achievement. Enduring issues such as
teaching methodologies, reading achievement, testing, and adult literacy
will be framed within a historical context. Throughout, certain questions
guide the discussion: What has the media reported about reading? Do the

reports reflect reality, at least as far as I know it? What harm (or good) have those reports done? How have they affected the public's perception of the schools and the public's perceptions of educators and policy makers? What has been the impact on the kind and amount of support given to schools? Before trying to answer these questions, however, it is important to take a look at the circumstances and conditions that have brought us to where we are today.

HISTORICAL PERSPECTIVES AND INFLUENCES

During the Colonial period, an alphabetic spelling system was used to teach reading. Learning to read was almost totally an oral process. Instruction was directed toward a single purpose, the reading of religious and moral books; only a limited number of people were actually taught to read. In the early 1800s, Horace Mann introduced the whole word method of teaching reading. He stressed memorizing entire words before analyzing letters and letter patterns. His approach emphasized silent reading and reading for comprehension. A phonics method was introduced in the latter half of the 19th century. Children were taught individual letter-sound relationships and how to blend them to decipher words. Teachers became dissatisfied with this method because too much attention was placed on word analysis and too little was given to comprehension. The approach was temporarily abandoned around 1910, and replaced with the new "look-and-say" method. It, too, proved unsatisfactory to many teachers. Children were expected to learn every word as a sight word, making progress slow and laborious.

About 1920, the silent reading method emerged as the official reading program in many schools. This method urged the total abandonment of all oral methods of instruction and testing. Widespread administration of standardized tests called the public's attention to the vast individual differences among children in reading achievement. It also inspired teachers to try out new instructional methods to better accommodate individual differences. Research during this era gave rise to the extremely popular method that followed—the basal reading method, which was launched throughout the United States in the early 1930s. The Dick and Jane readers (and others like them), as these basal programs would come to be known, would become the staple of reading instruction methodology in this country for several decades to come.

The basal method prevailed over other methods until the early 1960s, when there was a return to phonics. Schools wanted more organized skill development programs with some attention to reading in the content subjects. Specialized phonics programs were introduced into many schools to augment the basal program. The return to phonics was also partly inspired by media reports of illiteracy among the military of World War II and by the birth of the atomic age.

Media reports during the 1950s and 1960s continued to express fear of the possibility of an illiterate population unable to face the challenge of an era of Sputnik and the emerging space age. Concern was expressed for our threatened democracy. Interest in reading instruction soared during this period with laypeople and the media criticizing the schools' methods. One of the most vocal proponents of phonics was Rudolph Flesch, whose book *Why Johnny Can't Read* (1955) hailed phonics as the cure for what he perceived as widespread and growing illiteracy. Educators searched for ways to improve reading instruction. The range of reading achievement among students continued to baffle educators and the public. Although many children were not learning to read as well as expected, others were reaching new heights of proficiency. Numerous research studies were conducted to determine why some children, particularly poor and minority children, were not succeeding.

During this period, numerous studies were launched to test the superiority of one approach to reading instruction over another. Unfortunately, no strong conclusion could be drawn from these studies. No one approach was so distinctly better than others in all situations and in all respects that it could be considered the best method or used exclusively (Bond & Dykstra, 1967).

The publication of *Learning to Read: The Great Debate* (Chall, 1983) brought considerable attention to the phonics debate. Jeanne Chall examined the existing research literature for evidence on the best way to approach beginning reading. She concluded that "a code emphasis tends to produce better overall reading achievement by the beginning of fourth grade than a meaning emphasis" (p. 137). Chall's conclusions regarding beginning instruction were challenged by many (e.g., Rutherford, 1968), raising questions about the validity of the research studies on which she based her conclusions and the arbitrary nature of her classification system into code- and meaning-emphasis categories. Although Chall did not suggest that her findings be used to endorse systematic phonics approaches, her work has been highly influential in support of those who would endorse a heavy emphasis on phonics in beginning reading.

Changes in methodology abounded during the 1960s and early 1970s. Some were minor; others important. All were attempts to solve the nation's "reading problem." In the 1970s and 1980s, basal reading programs became elaborate language/reading methods systems with a wide array of core and optional components. Many states turned to competency testing of students and teachers to guard against the perceived incompetencies of both. Researchers, educators, and publishers of reading materials continued to address an ever expanding set of new and complex challenges, as schools faced an increasingly diverse population and a society in which the schools were called upon to take on more and more responsibility. Little did they know that something was about to happen that would arouse the media as never before.

It was in April of 1983 that the Reagan White House released its critical report on the status of American Schools, *A Nation at Risk* (National Commission on Excellence in Education). Americans were not accustomed to having their schools criticized. This was the first time that a report on elementary and secondary schools was sponsored by the secretary of education, prepared by a prestigious committee, and endorsed by the president.

Although it was the most widely distributed and the best known report, *A Nation at Risk* was not the only one that was generated during this time period. At least eight major reports critical of the public schools were issued during the 1980s. To a greater or lesser extent, all of them addressed issues related to reading and literacy achievement. The fallout from these reports, including the discussion and critiques in the media, has had lasting effects on the public's perception of how well children are reading. Even when statements in the reports have proved contradictory or incorrect, disparagement of the schools and of the teaching of reading have remained constant. Not all the effects on the schools were negative, however. Constructive criticism and response to some reports took the form of school partnerships for literacy with the business community and the upgrading of technological opportunities for learning to read. Efforts such as these continue into the 1990s.

During the 1990s, the reading systems published by a few major publishing companies—fewer than eight by this time—continued to dominate the materials and methodology used to teach reading. Although these expanded basals differed somewhat, virtually all had changed in similar ways. The inclusion of authentic literature with the original text relatively unaltered was a major departure. Another important difference was the expansion of reading programs to include an integrated approach to instruction in all the language arts: listening, speaking, reading, and writing. Some even included spelling.

The reexamination and reshaping of educational practice was inspired and affirmed, if not spearheaded, by the whole language movement. A theoretical perspective and professional movement that has roots in the progressive philosophies of education of the 1930s, whole language began to have a significant impact during the 1980s as teachers sought to have a greater say about curriculum and sought to teach reading in ways that they felt reflected more meaningful and "authentic" educational experiences for children. It is not surprising that the major controversy about reading today is focused on the debates on whole language versus phonics.

THE GREAT DEBATES CONTINUE

A look at media coverage of reading during the latter half of the 1990s reveals that the debate between whole language and phonics dominates. In some ways, this is a continuation of previous debates between phonics and other approaches to the teaching of reading. Over the years, the call for phonics has continually reemerged as the answer to problems, perceived or real, associated with reading achievement and instruction. Most would agree, however, that the current debate is much more volatile and public than any in the past. This is due in part to the media's unprecedented and sustained attention, making this debate an excellent focal point for an examination of the media and reading.

Attacks on whole language have raged throughout the United States; nowhere, however, have they been more evident than in the state of California, where the phonics versus whole language debates, which often play themselves out in the media, have been most extreme. More than three quarters of the media reports reviewed for this chapter contain references to California and its reading woes. Such headlines as "California Leads Revival of Teaching by Phonics" (New York Times, May 22, 1996) and "State Poised to Lead U.S. in Reading Reform" (Los Angeles Times, May 9, 1996) are very common. Transcripts of television and radio talk shows that focus on literacy invariably include numerous references to California and its problems with reading achievement.

During the 1980s, California, like many states and school districts throughout the country, turned to more holistic, literature-based instructional practices to address some of the literacy problems of concern. This was in keeping with the influences present at the time, which have already been discussed. In 1987, the California Language Arts Framework, a guide for curriculum, was revised to incorporate what was then the current best thinking of the day. The Framework was widely distributed throughout the country and became the subject of numerous educational forums and discussions. No doubt the great flair and fanfare with which California does everything makes the nation keep close watch on its activities. As Richard C. Anderson, professor and reading researcher at the University of Illinois, stated, "California has always had a disproportionate influence in literacy, no matter what direction it was pointed in. In the 1980s, California led the country in responding to the message—that many kids were bored with drills, hated reading and could not discuss the meaning of stories. To fix things, the state's reading experts declared that repetitive exercises would be discouraged in favor of the best children's literature" (*Los Angeles Times*, May 9, 1996). Less than a decade later, California was again making headlines, this time for its move in a very different direction.

When reading test scores placed California's students last in the nation, tied with Louisiana and just above Guam, Delaine Eastin, California's chief state school officer, declared a crisis and appointed a task force to advise her on how to improve reading achievement. The task force recommended that basic skills such as phonics be balanced with opportunities to read and discuss compelling literature, as favored by advocates of the whole language philosophy. Governor Pete Wilson offered to spend $127 million on textbooks and teacher training with the proviso that such skills as phonics and spelling be stressed. The reform called for phonics-based texts for every kindergartner, phonics training for primary-grade teachers, and a requirement that all new teachers demonstrate that they are competent to teach phonics and to diagnose students' reading difficulties.

Producers of phonics-based materials have taken advantage of the media to publicize their products. Radio and television "infomercials" have been the means by which a few publishers of reading materials have presented their programs to the public. Most excoriate the public schools and current methods of teaching reading, while advocating phonics and the purchase of their materials. Hooked on Phonics is the best known of these, since it was arguably the most famous of the reading programs sold via television and radio. During the early 1990s, it was virtually impossible to listen to the radio without encountering the catchy slogan "Hooked on Phonics works for me." The extensive amount of advertising made the product highly recognizable. Testimonials from people who claimed to have used the product themselves or with their children painted a very convincing picture of reading success. Hooked on Phonics was obviously addressing a need on the part of the American public. It was built on and fed into the public's belief that our children are not being taught to read.

In discussing Hooked on Phonics on ABC's *Nightline* (October 18, 1995), Ted Koppel commented that "someone was spending a great deal of money pushing some sort of program that would teach children how to read. You don't spend that kind of money unless the market for such a product is sufficiently great to warrant the expenditure." He concluded, "A lot of our schools are not teaching a lot of our children how to read." The makers of Hooked on Phonics were forced into bankruptcy when their sales plummeted after being cited by the Federal Trade Commission for false advertising. Coverage of the rise, fall, and potential reemergence of Hooked on Phonics and of its creator, John Shanahan, by *Forbes* magazine (Darlin, June 17, 1996, p. 47) emphasizes the financial issues surrounding the debate. With phonics making a big comeback, *Forbes* predicted that the company's revenues would reach $14 million in 1997. Shanahan predicted $30 million.

The return to phonics could have far-reaching implications for publishers of instructional materials on reading. Texas has also pushed for an emphasis on phonics and basic skills. Texas and California are the largest consumers of reading programs and ancillary materials. Their actions affect the entire national textbook market and thus influence how reading is taught in every state. It is little wonder that publications and news broadcasts that deal with economic issues would follow this debate with interest.

For the most part, media coverage of the California debacle placed a heavy emphasis on the dreadful state of reading education and, in turn, on the need for phonics as a response to this sad condition. ABC's *20/20* (October 13, 1995) included a segment featuring John Stossel, a harsh critic of whole language, without a counter representative from the other side. Compared with the critics of whole language, those who speak in its defense or who express skepticism about its being the single cause of California's literacy problems are relatively mute.

Repeated attacks on one side of the argument may make it appear that the criticism is more widespread than it actually is. Nonprofit groups on the phonics side of the issue devote countless hours and endless campaigns to promoting their view. It is not my purpose here to argue for or against phonics or whole language but to note that those in favor of the arguments posed by the phonics advocates seem to have more media presence. Even unsubstantiated and outrageous attacks on individuals and on the International Reading Association, an organization to which virtually all of the reading educators and researchers on all sides of the issues belong, appear to go unchallenged.

An attempt to promote voices from more than one side of the issue was an interview on National Public Radio's *All Things Considered* (May 14, 1996), involving Bill Honig, former state superintendent of California, under whom the literature-based Language Arts Framework was developed (Honig has since become a strong advocate for a return to basics); California first-grade teacher Laura Grannon, who attempts to blend whole language with specific instruction in phonics; and Regie Routman, educator and author of numerous books about whole language. Routman expressed concern over two huge misconceptions about whole language: that "classrooms are not organized and that exposing kids to good literature means depriving them of phonics." Although a strong advocate for phonics,

Honig admitted that "it's wrong to blame California's low reading scores solely on whole language. We have the largest class sizes in the country. We have been flat on funding. We have other social conditions. We have second language issues. So, all of that, obviously, makes it more difficult to teach youngsters to read."

In a much discussed article, "The Great Debate Revisited" (1994), Art Levine discussed the pros and cons of "meaning first vs. phonics first debate." Although whole language enthusiasts will disagree with his conclusions, Levine does demonstrate an effort to get at some of the more complex issues surrounding the debate. More reasoned and less volatile thinking was also evidenced in an editorial in the *Los Angeles Times* (May 9, 1996), which argued:

> But in embracing traditional reading methods, Wilson and education officials ought to remember that no one method—whether phonics or something else—will work for all children. Phonics should be used along with whole-language techniques, which can be of value in a well-rounded program capable of teaching all young Californians to read.

Several explanations may account for the fact that the strong phonics advocates get more attention from the media than do those who take a more moderate or strong whole language approach. Those who promote phonics see themselves as championing a cause to save America's children from illiteracy. Casting themselves as crusaders in a battle against the status quo, they are highly aggressive in getting their argument out to the public. They tend to address very complex issues with simple, easily digested arguments and answers. This is very compelling for a journalist working within the constraints of a sound bite or a short article. Those on the whole language side, and those in the vast majority somewhere in between the two extremes on these issues, tend to be more measured in their responses. Their answers to questions are likely to be more complex, and they are inclined to make suggestions that are multifaceted and thus less easy to capture with a simple, unidimensional message.

In an effort to clarify some of the issues that surround the debate, the International Reading Association, which represents over 70,000 reading educators with a variety of points of view, put out a statement on *The Role of Phonics in the Teaching of Reading* (1997). Aimed at the general public as well as at educators, the statement affirms that phonics is an important aspect of beginning reading instruction, that classroom teachers value and teach phonics as a part of reading, and that phonics is best taught within the framework of a total language and arts program.

READING ACHIEVEMENT, TESTS, AND MEDIA REPORTS

As with most of the controversy around reading, California's reading wars were fueled by reports of declining test scores. Achievement test scores and what is made of them have proved to be the single most volatile and contentious aspect of media attention to reading. In addition to taking note of the National Assessment for Educational Progress (NAEP), the national barometer of achievement in reading and math, today's media report the results of state and local assessments. Districts and schools are ranked and compared with each other so that the public may scrutinize the quality of education, as well as the real estate values that test scores are thought to influence. Yet, virtually any educator will tell you that the test scores alone only give part of the picture and that what is construed as a decline or rise in scores may be misleading.

An analysis of the test scores that form the basis of the California controversy calls into question certain assertions about the decline in test scores since the 1987 adoption of the literature-based Language Arts Framework. Writing in response to a commentary by Edward Fry in *Reading Today* (December 1995/January 1996) in which Fry blames whole language, in part, for California's reading woes, Jeff McQuillan (1996/1997) allows that California ranks near the bottom nationally in reading achievement. But, McQuillan argues, "there is no evidence that the situation has gotten any worse in the past 10 years" (p. 33). He points out that California ranks 49th in books per pupil, 50th in librarians per pupil, 39th in books per capita, 31st in number of books at home, and 9th in the number of children living in poverty. He states, moreover, "There is no indication in the NAEP data that whole language lowers reading test scores. If the self-reports of teachers who claim to be using whole language are accurate, then the 1992 and 1994 NAEP results are a resounding vindication of literature-based instruction."

McQuillan's conclusions are corroborated by the statements of Secretary of Education Riley on national television and reported by the press immediately after the NAEP results were reported. "Riley said the report found that fourth graders whose teachers placed heavy emphasis on literature-based reading instruction had higher average proficiency than those who received little or no such emphasis" (*Star Ledger*, September 16, 1993).

McQuillan's sentiments are echoed in a letter to the editor of the *Los Angeles Times* (R. Moore, May 17, 1996): "Reading scores that are 'second to Guam' didn't happen overnight, or because we're suddenly teaching whole language instead of phonics. California's curriculum framework has always included, and still includes, phonics. The low reading scores predate the introduction of whole language. . . . California has the worst school libraries in the nation. We would have to hire 2,000 school librarians just to be second worst."

Use of the NAEP to show declining test scores is indeed a questionable activity. The 1994 NAEP results reveal little change in the reading proficiency of students at the 4th-, 8th-, and 12th-grade levels. Causing concern is that just 25% of 4th graders, 28% of 8th graders, and 34% of 12th graders reached the level of proficient, which indicates solid academic performance. Whereas it can certainly be argued that we need to do better, it is incorrect to say that overall reading ability is in decline. Nevertheless, there were significant declines in certain states (California was not among them), a result that needs careful attention (*Reading Today*, June/July, 1995).

Media reports of widespread illiteracy among elementary and high school students and declining SAT scores have had a negative impact on teachers and teaching. In many areas of the country, the alleged inadequate preparation of students coupled with increased federal and state appropriations for education have aroused the indignation of the public to the point of their demanding that teachers justify their output (students' qualifications) in terms of the input (public monies). Outcome measures on standardized tests often become the sole determiner of a school's or a teacher's competence. This presents a major contradiction for teachers of literacy at all levels.

At a time when teachers are asked to expend energy on such instructional reforms as the composing process and response to literature, the public is calling for more tests, particularly those that are norm referenced and identify particular skills. In education, test scores represent the bottom line. As a result, many teachers feel obliged to teach reading and writing in a way most expedient for success on tests rather than a way consistent with the reforms in the profession. This occurs even when teachers know that in the past this kind of teaching has not led to the desired improvement. Public pressure, inspired in part by the media, causes many teachers to return to the teaching of phonics and grammar through rote drills and the memorization of rules rather than through procedures that teach these skills through meaningful use. In the graduate university courses that I teach, the students—teachers themselves—often tell me that they return to such methods not because they are effective, but because they provide visible evidence of coverage of *the basics*, a key issue when test scores are disappointing.

Of course, the news from test results is not all bad. The 1992 report of the International Evaluation of Educational Achievement (IEA) study of reading literacy reveals that 9- and 14-year-olds are reading well. Results of our 9-year-olds were just below those of Finland, whose students scored highest of all the participating countries. Ironically, the lack of success with attempts to improve reading through testing has engendered more, not fewer, tests and an increased attention to test scores in the press. In fact, many believe that the media have led the way in turning the public's attention toward new targets for testing—the teachers. "The newspapers and magazines that had reported students' low test scores began to say that Johnny couldn't read and Jenny couldn't write because teachers couldn't teach, and that teachers couldn't teach because they couldn't read or write much better than could Johnny or Jenny" (Chaplin, 1986, p. 118).

Many states now issue annual "report cards" comparing districts and schools within a district on test results in specific areas of instruction. These, too, illustrate the impact that media coverage can have on schools and on the teaching of reading. Typical of the reaction to such a school report card was that of a resident of Scarsdale, New York, one of the state's top-rated school districts. The disappointed resident wrote to the local newspaper: "Where, as in Scarsdale, you pay premium property taxes, you are entitled to premium test scores" (*New York Times*, February 23, 1997). One principal in Scarsdale was reported to have held seven meetings with parents and an eighth with real estate agents, who were concerned that mediocre scores would make it difficult to sell houses.

Attempts by superintendents to challenge the accuracy of the reports were aimed as much at the way test scores were reported in the press as they were on changes in the methods of testing in the past. For example, superintendents objected to the *New York Times*'s ranking of schools by using selections from the state-issued report cards and an adjustment of reading scores to reflect differences in community income. It will come as no surprise that many Scarsdale parents are calling for more homework, a return to the basics, and explicit phonics.

MOVING FORWARD

Public discussion about reading instruction is commonly conducted within a framework of hotly contested arguments. Many reading educators believe that the media are to blame. Educators complain that journalists rarely communicate with reading educators, educational researchers, and policy makers beyond an immediate story under consideration. The media focus most of their attention on specific reports about reading, usually research reports that get attention because of their prestige or close ties to policy. Reports such as those based on the NAEP are considered reliable. This is understandable. But, too often, little attention is given to the details underlying complicated findings.

As someone who is frequently called by the media to comment on various issues related to reading, I am often dismayed by the mere slice of a 30-minute conversation that gets reported in a news article, not to mention the incongruous context in which it is placed. I am aware of the constraints under which journalists work. They deal with deadlines. In today's media market, they also are often required to entertain as well as inform their audiences, whether they be readers, viewers, or listeners. Thus, they have a bias toward the new, the different, and the controversial. Journalists say that too often research on reading merely confirms common sense, which is fine, but not news. Stories get covered because they are easy and accessible. Many local newspapers use reprint services to publish stories first published in major publications such as the *New York Times* and the *Wall Street Journal*. This usually means that the most controversial and volatile reports will be circulated widely.

It has been suggested that many people have an opinion about reading instruction simply because they know how to read. It may be that journalists have the impression that they know a great deal about literacy education because they are highly literate themselves. Actually, this may give them a false sense of "logic" about what is or is not appropriate in literacy education and may color their reporting. Journalists who specialize in writing about education and develop experience in that area are apt to be more sensitive to the issues surrounding a story.

Although it is apparent that journalists and educators disagree on many issues, they share a responsibility and a desire for making the public debate about educational issues truly informative and honest. There is no reason that the two groups need to be adversaries in this process. The media play an important role in influencing public policy about reading. They are particularly effective in influencing parents, taxpayers, and politicians. Each group is interested not only in literacy but in getting its money's worth from the schools. The public needs journalists who will work with educators to provide the most accurate and balanced education coverage possible.

Meanwhile, reading educators and researchers might raise the level of debate by writing in the language and style of journalists or at least by communicating in a manner that the ordinary citizen can understand. Public information services in college departments of literacy education and in school districts should assist reporters in localizing national trends. The producers of research reports on reading might benefit from the help of those in the public relations field in getting across the message that they want to put forth to the public. Opportunities for reading educators and journalists to talk with one another in seminars designed for that purpose or in less formal ways might help to build trust. Individual teachers and groups of educators might use the Op-Ed pages of their local newspapers to share their views about issues related to reading and the media coverage of them.

Reading educators are among many groups in our society who recognize the key role that the media play in the public's perception of them and what they do. My hope is that the media will work with reading educators to portray issues involving reading in a way that reveals their complexity and that inspires constructive critique and debate.

BIBLIOGRAPHY

Berliner, D. & Biddle, B. (1995). *The manufactured crisis*. Reading, MA: Addison-Wesley.

Bond, G. & Dykstra, R. (1967). The cooperative research program in first grade reading instruction. *Reading Research Quarterly, 2*, 5–142.

Chall, J. (1983). *Learning to read: The great debate*. New York: McGraw-Hill.

Chaplin, M. (1986). The political issues since 1960. In M. Farmer (Ed.), *Consensus and dissent* (pp. 113–126). Champaign-Urbana, IL: National Council of Teachers of English.

Coppella, J. & Jamieson, K. H. (1997). *The spiral of cynicism: The press and the public good*. New York: Oxford University Press.

Elam, S. M., Rose, L. C., Gallup, A. M. (1996). The 28th annual Phi Delta Kappa/Gallup poll of the public's attitudes toward the public schools. *Phi Delta Kappan, 78*, 41–59

Flesch, R. (1955). *Why Johnny can't read*. New York: Harper.

Kirsch, I. S., Jungeblut, A., Jenkins, L., & Kolstad, A. (1993). The National Adult Literacy Survey. Princeton, NJ: Educational Testing Service.

Levine, A. (December, 1994). The great debate revisited. *Atlantic Monthly.*

McQuillan, J. (December 1996/January 1997). Whole language not to blame in California. *Reading Today, 14*, p.33.

National Commission on Excellence in Education. (1983). *A nation at risk: The imperative for educational reform*. Washington, DC: U.S. Department of Education.

The role of phonics in the teaching of reading. (1997). Newark, DE: The International Reading Association.

Rutherford, W. (1968). Learning to read: A critique. *Elementary School Journal, 69*, 72–83.

Second looks at the U.S. adult literacy survey. (December 1993/January 1994). *Reading Today*, 10.

School Desegregation, Press Coverage, and Public Perceptions

LEONARD B. STEVENS

In the 1970s, school desegregation migrated from the Deep South to the North. It was accompanied by violence, most notably in Boston, but also in other places, such as Pontiac, Michigan. This frightening bit of history was not lost on a place like Cleveland, Ohio, where a post-Boston trial over segregated city schools played out, slowly and bitterly, in an old federal courthouse. Media coverage was heavy. After the court declared that desegregation would occur, it took 3 years to develop a plan and exhaust the posttrial litigation steps. With the history of Boston still fresh, school desegregation in Cleveland was anticipated with very deep public anxiety, even fear. When desegregation began, it was witnessed by squads of national reporters, who encamped in Cleveland to report the racial violence that was regarded as inevitable.

A LOCAL STORY

Education has been, par excellence, America's instrument of social progress and reform.
—Lawrence A. Cremin, *The Genius of American Education*

Cleveland is a big, proud, ethnic American city on the south shore of Lake Erie, settled by land developers who set out from Connecticut. The settlement's expansion was force-fed by a handy convergence of railroads, waterways and iron ore. The early population was augmented by Eastern

Imaging Education: The Media and Schools in America. Copyright © 1998 by Teachers College, Columbia University. All rights reserved. ISBN 0-8077-3734-8 (pbk), ISBN 0-8077-3735-6 (cloth). Prior to photocopying items for classroom use, please contact the Copyright Clearance Center, Customer Service, 222 Rosewood Dr., Danvers, MA 01923, USA, tel. (508) 750-8400.

European immigrants and African Americans from the agrarian South, who worked the steel industry. In the 1970s and 1980s, the city and its environs were devastated by the economics of big steel and the out-migration of manufacturing jobs. Here, school desegregation began on Monday, September 10, 1979, one week after Labor Day, following a wrenching legal battle that continues even now. Press coverage of school desegregation saturated the Black and White communities in the city and its surrounding suburbs.

In 1979 and 1980, the 2 years in which the 100-plus schools of Cleveland were desegregated in three successive semesters, I worked in Cleveland as the school monitor for the U.S. district court, and in so doing performed 82 press interviews. (I served from 1978 to 1988 as director of the Office on School Monitoring and Community Relations, an agency created by federal court order "to observe, assess and report on the progress of the desegregation of the Cleveland Public Schools." The agency is still operative at this writing, and is 19 years old.) Actually, I did considerably more interviews, probably double or even triple these 82, counting all the impromptu telephone calls and spontaneous face-to-face discussions. The 82 represent only the scheduled interviews recorded in my calendar. The point is that press coverage of school desegregation in Cleveland was intense and unrelenting.

The headlines in the city's two daily newspapers summarized the atmosphere and personalized the issues by referring to personalities involved in the hot controversy. In the headlines that follow, *Battisti* refers to the then–chief judge of the federal court in Cleveland who presided over the school case and ultimately ordered the desegregation of the city's schools, and *Mottl* refers to then–U.S. representative Ron Mottl, a local congressperson who early on staked out a high-profile antibusing stand:

BATTISTI GIVES SCHOOLS PICK OF 3 PLANS TO DESEGREGATE, TELLS THEM TO
    CHOOSE 1
FALL TERM TO BRING BUSING FOR 6,000
SCHOOLS OPPOSE BUS-BUYING REQUEST
STATE DEFERS FUNDS ON CITY SCHOOL BUSES
OHIO SCHOOL GROUPS ASK TO JOIN IN ANTI-BATTISTI SUIT
MOTTL FORCES A VOTE ON ANTIBUSING BILL
33% PLAN TO DISOBEY BATTISTI'S BUS ORDER
DESEGREGATION GETS THE BLAME

In the 13 months (July 1978 through July 1979) immediately preceding the start of desegregation, a span of 396 days, Cleveland's two daily newspapers published 1,339 stories on the impending desegregation of the city schools, an average of more than three stories a day. Press coverage was so incessant that the monitoring office I ran employed a full-time press secretary. The media demands on the monitoring office, of course, were heightened by the fact that the judge presiding over the school desegregation case was not available to reporters, as is typical with federal judges, except to the extent that court hearings that he held were open to the public and the press.

To examine the vocabulary used by the local daily press to describe school desegregation issues, the articles and their headlines were analyzed (for this chapter) for word choice. Figure 8.1 shows the subjective and objective terms for desegregation-related topics that were counted in this analysis. In the case of newspaper story text, the review focused on the first three or four paragraphs of each article and counted the frequency of use of these terms. The purpose of the review was to get a statistical idea of how often during the 13-month period when the desegregation issue had extraordinary visibility local readers were exposed to the terms in question, and also the comparative use of subjective (emotion-laden) terms

FIGURE 8.1. Subjective and Objective Terms for Desegregation-Related Topics Used in Word Frequency Analysis of News Items and Headlines

Subjective Terms	Objective Terms
Racial balance, quotas	Desegregation, integration
[Rigid, statistical]	[Flexible, lawful]
Reassignment	Assignment, deployment
[Arbitrary change]	[New pattern]
Busing, forced busing	Transportation, bus service
[Mandatory, arbitrary]	[Pupil service]
Interruption, reduction, elimination	Equality, fairness
[Problem, threat]	[Change with a purpose]
Closings, safety	Economy, improvement, cost-effectiveness
[Inconvenience, problem]	[Rational change]
Costs, prohibitive costs	Redistribution, equality
[Burdensome, difficult]	[Rational change]
Lower standards, lower pupil performance	Fairness, equity, nondiscrimination
[Threat to quality]	[Better distribution of quality]

Note: Terms in brackets are connotations.

versus objective (descriptive) terms. (The review was carried out by Sandra L. Moore pursuant to methods that I designed.)

A total of between 400 and 500 articles contained one or more of the terms. It was not uncommon for a single article to use both subjective and objective terms. Where the same word was used two or more times in one article, the review recorded a count of 1. Where two or more different words were used in an article, the review recorded the total number of uses. Thus, the total count is conservative. The terms in the articles that were reviewed were used a total of 899 times. Of the 899 uses, 561 were of objective terms, and 338 were of subjective terms. In other words, although the reporters who wrote the stories used descriptive terms more often than they used emotion-laden terms, they nonetheless made extensive use of the emotional terms.

The headline writers (who in big-city daily newspapers are not the reporters who write the stories) were much more inclined to use the subjective terms. A total of 298 headlines were found that used either the subjective or the objective terms. Of the 298 headlines, there were 152 uses of descriptive terms, and 146 uses of emotion-laden terms. In other words, the headlines, printed in larger and bolder type than newsprint, and presumably getting greater attention from readers, used the emotional words of school desegregation about as often as they used the descriptive vocabulary. Furthermore, in terms of gauging the impact of headlines, one must bear in mind that sometimes readers do not venture beyond the headlines. In sum, local readers in Cleveland in this relatively brief period were exposed to emotion-laden descriptors of school desegregation with regularity. Put another way, it would have been difficult if not impossible for a local reader of the two newspapers during this period to have avoided the emotional terms in the course of routine newspaper reading about school desegregation.

Two years later, in the summer of 1981, just after the final phase of desegregation had been implemented, the monitoring office that I headed commissioned an opinion poll to measure community perceptions of the desegregation program. Desegregation was a young and troubled program. Violence had been averted, but the school district had botched the program in numerous administrative ways, including ways affecting bus service for the children attending the newly desegregated schools. The poll was conducted by a local polling firm. A total of 475 parents of pupils enrolled in the city schools were interviewed by telephone. The parent sample was stratified by residential zone, and was racially representative of the school district's pupil population.

The poll (Decision Research Corp., 1981) found little outright support for desegregation, except among Black parents; and a deep unwillingness even to accept it, especially among White parents (see Table 8.1). It found a considerable amount of belief among Black parents that desegregation eventually would improve the schools, and deep disbelief in this premise by White parents. It found a perception among many Black and White parents alike that the schools had gotten worse over the preceding 5-year period. It found biracial belief that desegregation had worsened discipline problems in the schools, with this particular belief especially strong among White parents.

People acquire their perceptions of schools from various sources. These sources cannot be identified with surgical precision, and the totality of public opinion cannot be attributed to any one particular source, least of all media coverage. Yet, how can one fail to connect the opinions of school desegregation articulated by parents and the extensive use of subjective, emotion-laden terms by the daily print media in Cleveland in their coverage of school desegregation, especially in the vocabulary of headlines, but also in the leading paragraphs of news stories? It would be unreasonable to assume an absence of connection. Undoubtedly, the media contributed something of substance to the public's opinions, which then were measured by a poll.

TABLE 8.1. Community Perceptions of Public School Desegregation, Cleveland, Ohio, 1981

Perception of Desegregation	Black Parents (%)	White Parents (%)
Attitude toward desegregation		
Support desegregation	24	5
Cannot accept desegregation	17	49
Desegregation will improve school quality in the long run		
Agree	44	7
Disagree	43	86
Quality of public schools today compared to 5 years ago		
Below average today	42	55
Below average 5 years ago	17	9
Discipline problems have increased as a result of segregation		
Agree	54	78
Disagree	33	13

Source: Decision Research Corporation, 1981.

Indeed, if a poll of parents in Cleveland in the early period of school desegregation had found broad support for desegregation, a widely held perception of desegregation as an instrument of school improvement, a generally positive view of the schools, and a sense that the schools were increasingly orderly and well controlled (as indicated by diminishing concern for pupil behavior and discipline), such findings would have unearthed parent perceptions that contradicted a good deal of what the parents had been reading in the daily press, and the language describing it. During the years immediately preceding desegregation in Cleveland, one local civic leader, Daniel R. Elliott Jr., used to remark periodically that one headline with one incendiary word could wipe out 2 or 3 months of painstaking work by an entire team of community peacekeepers seeking to calm parents' anxieties and to bring them practical information. His observation was based purely on an instinctive sense of the local scene, but it seemed, then and now, close to the mark.

ATTITUDES NATIONALLY

Perhaps the most destructive personal harm of segregation [in schools] is this: It may teach Black children to view themselves as inferior by virtue of their race, and White children to view themselves as superior because of their race. Either outcome will be recognized by parents as grave distortions of a child's character.
— Meyer Weinberg, Testimony before the Subcommittee
on Civil and Constitutional Rights

School desegregation is characterized by paradox, one dimension of which deals with public attitudes toward the issue. While desegregation generally is regarded as strongly unpopular—even the NAACP, a civil rights organization whose name is synonymous with school desegregation, now has internal debates on the matter (Holmes, 1997; see also Watson, 1997)—opinion polls often show support for desegregation at levels that can only be seen in this context as surprising. The 1981 Cleveland poll cited above, for example, found nearly one out of five of all the respondents (18%) in support of desegregation at a time when the program not only generated community-wide fear of race-related violence but also exhibited such profound administrative flaws that the federal court found it necessary to temporarily remove operational control of the program from local school officials and turn it over to a court-appointed administrator.

Historically and nationally, the pattern of public attitudes toward school desegregation looks like this:

• Twelve years before the U.S. Supreme Court's *Brown* decision, which prohibited de jure racially segregated schools, and during a time when racially separate schools were still constitutionally legal, just 2% of the residents of the Deep South held the opinion that Black and White students should attend school together. In the North, 40% of the public supported school desegregation. This is 1942 poll data (Vergon, 1994). In brief, support for desegregated schools prior to *Brown* was limited, and in the all-important South, where segregated schools were most pronounced, it was all but nonexistent.

• Two years after the *Brown* ruling, 49% of the nation supported the idea of desegregated schools. This is 1956 poll data (Vergon, 1994). In brief, support for desegregated schools grew from the latter stage of the pre-*Brown* era to the time of *Brown*, even though no school desegregation had actually taken place yet as a result of *Brown*. Nor, ironically, did desegregation come quickly to the school district of Linda Brown, the Black schoolgirl who attended the segregated Monroe School in Topeka, Kansas, and whose surname labels the *Brown* lawsuit. Her school, built in 1926 with a stone front that announces its name above the front door, still stands, although it is vacant and all but abandoned. In 1994, 40 years after *Brown*, a federal district judge in Topeka adopted a desegregation plan for what is now called Unified School District 501. The plan, now being implemented, is to produce what Linda Brown's family had sought when she was a child.

• Twenty years later, in the mid-1970s, following extensive and heavily litigated school desegregation across the South, extension of school desegregation to the North, and a landmark Supreme Court decision in a Charlotte, North Carolina, case that explicitly authorized the use of school busing to accomplish desegregation of schools, a 1976 Harris poll found 78% of Americans opposed to "busing to schools outside their neighborhoods to achieve desegregation" and just 14% in support of it (Harris, 1976, 1987; see also Snider, 1987). (Although Harris's original report of the 1976 polling data [Harris, 1976] referred to 81% opposition, in a subsequent publication [Harris, 1987], he referred to 78% opposition in 1976. I have assumed the later figure to be the accurate one.) In brief, the single most controversial method of desegregating schools, mandatory reassignment of pupils to schools far enough from home so as to require a bus ride— "busing" in the shorthand vocabulary of the media—enjoyed little support in the minds of Americans at the time when busing was becoming a new American experience.

• Ten years later, in 1986, after a period of widespread desegregation in school districts in all regions of the nation, Harris (1987), to his surprise, found that opposition to school desegregation had receded to 53% (from 78% 10 years earlier), and support for desegregation had risen to 41% (up from 14% 10 years earlier). Harris called the 10-year attitudinal sea change "one of the most dramatic turnarounds in recent history." Moreover, of those families whose children had participated in school busing for desegregation, 71% said that the experience had been "very satisfactory." White families were satisfied at a level of 73%, and Black families at a level of 64%. (When comparing these particular Black-White numbers, it is useful to know that in school desegregation programs, Black pupils often bear a disproportionate share of the transportation burden.) Support for "busing of school children to achieve racial balance" (41% overall) was especially strong among younger adults. Those aged 25 to 29 favored desegregation at a level of 51%, and those aged 18 to 24 favored it at a level of 60%. The 1986 Harris poll findings (Harris, 1987) are reinforced by a Phi Delta Kappa/Gallup poll of public attitudes toward the public schools. Assessing public opinion as to the "biggest problems confronting the public schools," this poll found concern for "integration/busing" diminishing from 1981 to 1986. By comparison, public concern for "use of drugs" rose during this time frame (Gallup, 1986). It is reasonable to assume that as support for school desegregation gained, desegregation would be less likely to be cited as a problem. In brief, as school desegregation programs attained widespread impact nationwide, support for desegregation grew, even as conventional wisdom (in the Congress in 1981, the largest source of federal funding for school desegregation was abolished) held that school desegregation was altogether unpopular.

• In the 1990s, attitudes toward school desegregation have remained roughly unchanged since the mid-1980s. Charles Vergon, a veteran student of school desegregation, has concluded: "Public opinion, nationally constituted, seems to be far more supportive of school integration than are many in formal and informal leadership positions both within and outside government" (Vergon, 1994, p. 496). He cites a 1991 *Boston Globe* poll that asked whether respondents would support busing if it were the only way to integrate schools and if their own children would be involved: 41% of the White respondents, 60% of the Hispanic respondents, and 76% of the Black respondents said yes. He also cites a 1994 *USA Today* poll that found 52% of Whites and 84% of Blacks who "indicated that they wanted more done to integrate the schools" (Vergon, 1994; see also Edmonds, 1994).

Gary Orfield, an authority on desegregation trends, cites a local survey in Louisville, Kentucky, done in the early 1990s by the *Louisville Courier-Journal* as "one of the most interesting local surveys of the 1990s" on the topic of school desegregation. A county-wide school desegregation program was put into place in Louisville as a result of litigation in the 1970s. At that time, more than 90% of Whites and about 40% of Blacks were opposed to it. In the recent survey, of parents whose children were bused,

53% of White parents and 81% of Black parents said that the experience was satisfactory—and 36% of the overall community opposed the idea of ending the desegregation program (Orfield, 1995; see also McDonald and Scott, 1991; and McConahay and Hawley, 1979).

In brief, during the current period when considerable attention is focused on the closing of existing court-supervised school desegregation programs and when efforts to launch new desegregation initiatives are rare, it would be incorrect to assume that poll data support the abandonment of school desegregation policy, notwithstanding the knee-jerk negative reaction typically engendered by mention of the term busing.

COVERING SCHOOL DESEGREGATION

Race . . . tangles a snarl of ideas that no one can sort out.
                        —Theodore H. White, *The Making of the President*

When reporters and editors involve themselves in school desegregation, they tackle an issue that is both paradoxical and complex. The paradoxical character of school desegregation stems from the fact that the issue is related to race, and race is America's enduring dilemma. For example:

• The basis for most school desegregation required by the Federal courts is the equal protection clause of the Fourteenth Amendment to the United States Constitution. Thus, to desegregate illegally segregated schools is to operationalize the Fourteenth Amendment, a democratic act by textbook definition. Yet communities, Cleveland among them, on the occasion of school desegregation, typically perceive something undemocratic at work when the Fourteenth Amendment places at risk neighborhood schools that ironically have no constitutional protection.
• Americans want their children's schools to be integrated (90% of White Americans said this as early as 1982), yet balk at use of the instrument—the courts—that has caused most school integration to date (47% in 1992 would leave the courts out of the matter even if the result would be segregated schools) (Vergon, 1994).
• Equality is a cornerstone of the American way. But equal-treatment issues inextricably connected to school desegregation (such as placements in gifted programs, identifications for disability programs, classroom groupings, pupil discipline, pupil achievement, high school graduation

rates) are matters loaded with contentiousness and unending rationalizations for longstanding racial disproportions.

• Overt racial discrimination is universally rejected in modern America. But local control of public schools is an anthem in American political science with a melody capable of drowning out contemporary vestiges of educational discrimination that, while real, have been inevitably grayed-out by time and therefore require effort to discern.

For reporters and editors, the end result is a dilemma of their own, for the public officials and private citizens who speak about school desegregation often do so in ways that manifest the paradoxes. Thus does accurate quoting of news sources reinforce contradictions and myths about school desegregation, and thus does simple reporting of what was said permit opportunities for explication of the issue by the media to fall by the wayside. The complexity of school desegregation stems from the fact that most of this has been accomplished not as a result of policy choice by state and local school authorities, but as a result of their default as policy makers and the subsequent intervention of the judicial system in response to complaints of institutional discrimination. To cover school desegregation as a reporter, therefore, is to grapple with a social policy enveloped by a family tree of not-so-simple constitutional law that in turn is rooted in a history of race in the United States.

Well over 1,000 local school districts have experienced racial desegregation of their schools. (In all, there are about 15,000 local school districts in the United States. Not long ago, there were many more. Consolidation of small districts has reduced the number from the total of more than 100,000 that existed in 1946.) In one 4-year period, 1968 to 1972, 498 school districts implemented desegregation plans, and 496 others negotiated desegregation plans with federal officials for subsequent implementation; meanwhile, between 1965 and 1975, another 200 districts began desegregation programs on the initiative of local school authorities (Vergon, 1994).

School desegregation began in the South, where state constitutions and state and local policies separated pupils on the basis of their race by law. There, the image of school desegregation was one of law enforcement, captured most poignantly perhaps by Norman Rockwell, the illustrator, in a well-known portrait of a little Black girl in a neat white dress escorted by faceless U.S. marshals along a sidewalk strewn with racial graffiti and the smashed remains of a tomato hurled against a wall in racial rage. In the 1970s, as desegregation moved northward, Denver, Colorado, was the first school district in the North to experience court-ordered desegregation. It was soon joined by others.

In the North, racial segregation of pupils had not been embedded in laws, as in the southern states, although some northern states (Ohio among them) had enacted segregated schooling laws. Rather, school zoning, policies on where to situate new schools, and a host of other practices had been piggybacked on housing patterns to yield racially identifiable, if not altogether racially separate, schools. Indeed, the practices of school districts in the North came to form a monotonous list of segregative acts. When U.S. district judge Frank J. Battisti of Cleveland found that city's schools unconstitutionally segregated by race in 1976, the methods that had been used by the school district to accomplish segregation fell neatly onto the list of illegal practices: school zoning, school construction, grade organization of schools, special transfers, pupil transportation, underuse and overuse of schools, rental of private buildings, linkage to segregated housing, portable classrooms, optional attendance zones, teacher assignments, school closings, building conversions, and changes to the boundaries of the school district. Were I a newspaper reporter again, as I was in my first life a long time ago, I'd need to know something in general about school desegregation law before I could write about it without being trapped by my own assumptions and the statements of sources. For starters, I'd need to know at minimum the following principles, which, in this brief and nonlawyerly summary, have been among the leading rules of school desegregation, as enunciated by the U.S. Supreme Court, since 1954:

• School districts are not bound by the U.S. Constitution to desegregate any schools even if all their schools are one-race schools—provided they did not cause the segregation. For segregation to be unconstitutional, the segregation must be the intentional product of governmental policy, on the local or state level, or both. Knowing this, reporters will be less apt to quote without explanation the claims of antidesegregation advocates that government and civil rights lawyers are bent on racially balancing every school in America just because they happen to believe it's proper social policy.
• School districts ordered by federal courts to desegregate their schools are lawbreakers. This does not include school districts that operate under court supervision exclusively as a consequence of settlement agreements that usually do not include an admission of intentional segregation by the school district. The reference here is to districts that have been found liable by a court for intentional segregation. Cleveland is illustrative. The school district and the state of Ohio were found guilty of violating the Constitution as a result of a trial at which they defended themselves and lost. Such school districts are required by law to remedy their constitutional violations—specifically, to desegregate the schools that they illegally segregated. Knowing this, reporters can describe in context the ensu-

ing school desegregation process, including its burdens, costs, pains, and problems, as a normal legal step with a legitimate foundation—without falling into the imprecise vocabulary of "forced" desegregation that leads readers and listeners to believe that a "judicial tyranny" has imposed itself on "innocent" local officials who are now "victims" of an event in "social engineering."

• A desegregating school district is not required to desegregate each and every school in its system, or to make the racial composition of all of its desegregated schools exactly alike. Numbers, the law teaches, are "a starting point" but not "an inflexible requirement" (*North Carolina State Board of Education v. Swann*, 1971). Knowing this, reporters will be able to recognize the vocabulary of "quotas" for what it is: misleading hyperbole which is, not incidentally, incendiary.

• School districts with ongoing desegregation programs are not obliged, annually and forever, to adjust pupils' school assignments so as to fit schools to prescribed racial standards. The natural ebb and flow of demographic change inside communities is recognized by school desegregation law as a reality. In essence, the law does not require schools to keep up with demographics, so long as school authorities don't manipulate demographics, directly or indirectly. Knowing this, reporters will be able to cover school desegregation as a program with its feet in the real world, and not as (1) a penalty that (2) is grounded in a theoretical world which (3) makes life impossible for school authorities who (unlike judges) have to deal with practicalities.

• Courts are not intended to supervise school districts in perpetuity. The federal courts "from the very first" have seen their involvement in school desegregation as "a temporary measure" (*Board of Education v. Dowell*, 1991). Knowing this, reporters can—and should—ask the ultimate school desegregation question of local school officials: Exactly what are you doing today, while under court supervision, to prepare this school system for the inevitable day in the future when there is no court to instruct you as to what to do and what not to do?

• A school district with a court-supervised desegregation program is required to make the program actually work, not just say it made an effort that failed. In brief, a desegregation program "is to be judged by its effectiveness" (*North Carolina State Board of Education v. Swann*, 1971). Knowing this, reporters can give short shrift to any verbiage from school systems as to how hard they worked at desegregation, how much they spent and how many obstacles they encountered—and focus their writing instead on the legal bottom line, which is the results.

• School desegregation involves more than the racial mix of schools and classrooms. Indeed, it involves education. Commonly, school desegregation embraces magnet schools, curriculum content, after-school activities, teacher training, parent involvement, pupil discipline, programs for both gifted and disabled pupils, services for non-English-speaking pupils, high school completion rates, even the choice of principals for schools. Knowing this, reporters can cover school desegregation as a program with multiple dimensions, and not as a "busing" event that detracts from the normal school task of education.

• Community attitudes cannot deter school desegregation. The reason is simple: Constitutional rights are at stake. This principle tends to be well-known in the abstract, but it tends to get lost as desegregation programs age. Then, "what the community thinks" comes to the fore. Knowing this, reporters will be able to listen knowingly when they hear school boards or school superintendents speaking of changing a desegregation program because of factors they perceive as either desirable or unacceptable to "the community."

The simple reality is that reporters and editors who know too little about the legal context of school desegregation leave themselves at risk, despite their intentions to be evenhanded and their proficiency in being accurate, of being contributors to the heat of school desegregation while adding little light to the subject. In other words, to cover this issue with excellence, it's not enough to be accurate; it is necessary, in addition, to place statements and actions in the appropriate factual context.

LESSONS

> Today, education is perhaps the most important function of state and local governments. . . . In these days, it is doubtful that any child may reasonably be expected to succeed in life if he is denied the opportunity of an education. Such an opportunity, where the state has undertaken to provide it, is a right which must be made available to all on equal terms.
> —*Brown v. Board of Education*

School desegregation, indeed all race-related school issues, would be better understood if certain lessons were to be applied. Among the lessons are these:

• Reporters, editors and news directors who deal with desegregating school systems should be well-informed about the basic history of school desegregation and the legal requirements that apply to it. School desegregation lawyers speak of "*Brown* and its progeny," the school desegregation cases since 1954 that in the aggregate set forth the legal rules of school desegregation. Not all the cases are of equal importance. But the key ones form the basic history lesson that needs to be known by those who write about the subject, and those who influence it as a result of their editorial and reporter-deployment choices. (When I wrote about school desegregation as a young reporter, I had not even read *Brown*. There is no reason for contemporary reporters to be so poorly prepared.)

• Media coverage of school desegregation should include close analysis of school desegregation results, and the likely causes of success and failure of desegregation programs. Often, school desegregation falls short of the mark not because the goal was wrongheaded, the plan was poorly constructed, or uncontrollable factors intervened, but rather because people in the desegregating school system, or those overseeing it, performed incompetently or halfheartedly. This is no small item.

• Poll takers should get themselves up-to-date about the present and emerging shape of school desegregation so as to bring polling instruments and poll analysis into line with contemporary standards. Gone is the school desegregation era when pupils were either Black or White and nothing else, when *busing* signified a mandatory change of school, when planners trod lightly around the "tipping point" of racial composition, and when desegregation was limited to changing a school's pupil enrollment and faculty assignment to conform to racial standards. The era has arrived when desegregation programs engage Latino and Asian pupils as well as African American and Anglo children (and thus desegregation implicates language-of-instruction issues), when bus rides are sought by parents in districts where magnet schools and schools of choice are offered, when tipping point theory is irrelevant in desegregating districts where the majority of pupils consists of children of color, and when the typical desegregation program incorporates school-improvement initiatives. Yet, often the questions put to the public by the poll takers have not kept pace with the changes. The old questions frequently continue to be asked in the same old way. As a result, "[m]ost of the information we get [from polls] about public attitudes . . . taps reaction to an outdated set of alternatives" (Orfield, 1995).

• Opinion polls should be analyzed—closely and skeptically—by reporters who cover school desegregation, with attention paid to the polling instrument as well as to the poll results. What questions were asked? How were they phrased? What language was used in the questions? In short, was the poll skewed by loaded questions? Nowadays, polling in relation to school desegregation is done not only to measure attitudes about school desegregation in general, but also about potential community support for particular desegregation methods, including magnet schools, specialty programs, and schools of choice. Polls, in other words, have become part of the desegregation planning equation. In brief, the educational opportunities that families and children have in desegregating school systems would be well-served by an informed press that looks critically at polls put forward as support for, or opposition to, particular programs.

CONCLUSION

The ideology of equality has done some good. . . . But most of its effects are bad.
—Richard J. Herrnstein and Charles Murray, *The Bell Curve*

[I]t is irrelevant whether a government's racial classifications are drawn by those who wish to oppress a race or by those who have a sincere desire to help those thought to be disadvantaged. . . . In each instance, it is racial discrimination, plain and simple.
—Justice Clarence Thomas, Concurring opinion
in *Adarand Constructors v. Peña*

In short, our time is not one receptive to racial remedies.
—Andrew Hacker, *Two Nations*

Ultimately, of course, the results of school desegregation depend on the schools, not on media coverage of the issue. At the same time, school desegregation takes place in a community climate, which in turn affects the work of school desegregation. Media coverage of desegregation surely contributes to every community's political climate. In this connection, reporters and editors have had more than 40 years of input to the perceptions that Americans presently hold of school desegregation. The media, like it or not, are more than observers and recorders of school desegregation. In addition, the media are inescapable participants in the sense that they contribute to the public's perceptions, which in turn help to define the limits and the targets of school desegregation policy.

School desegregation is not over and done with, not given the respective places of race and schools in America. Race will not disappear from this uniquely diverse American society; and the public schools are irretrievably linked to this society's economic pulse. In the future as in the past, what reporters and editors say about race-related school issues, and how they say it, will indeed count. The media will measure up to its institutional casting as a fourth estate to the extent that insight-added reporting helps community perceptions become more thoughtful and less emotional at the perilous intersection of race and education.

BIBLIOGRAPHY

Adarand Constructors v. Peña, 515 U.S. 200 (1995) (Thomas, J., concurring).

Board of Education of Oklahoma City Public Schools v. Robert L. Dowell, 498 U.S. 237 (1991).

Brown v. Board of Education, 347 U.S. 483 (1954).

Cremin, Lawrence A. *The Genius of American Education*, New York: Vintage, 1965

Decision Research Corp., "A Survey of Attitudes of Parents with Childen Enrolled in the Cleveland Public Schools," Author, August 1981.

Edmonds, P., "Only Real Difference: How Best to Desegregate," *USA Today*, May 12, 1994.

Gallup, Alec M. "The 18th Annual Gallup Poll of the Public's Attitudes Toward the Public Schools," *Phi Delta Kappan*, September 1986.

Hacker, Andrew. *Two Nations: Black and White, Separate, Hostile, Unequal.* New York: Scribner, 1992.

Harris, Louis, "Poll: Most Are Still Anti-Busing, But . . . ," *New York Post*, July 8, 1976.

Harris, Louis, "Number Opposed to Busing for Racial Purposes Drops 25 Points over a 10-Year Period," *The Harris Survey*, January 5, 1987.

Herrnstein, Richard J., & Murray, Charles. *The Bell Curve: Intelligence and Class Structure in American Life*, New York: Free Press, 1994.

Holmes, Steven A., "At NAACP, Talk of a Shift on Integration: Desegregation Policies Face Growing Dissent," *The New York Times*, June 23, 1997.

McConahay, John B. and Hawley, Willis D., "Reaction to Busing in Louisville: Summary of Adult Opinions in 1976 and 1977," Duke University Center for Policy Analysis, 1979.

McDonald, Stan and Wade, Scott, "Whites Divided over Plan to End Forced Busing," *Louisville Courier-Journal*, October 27, 1991.

North Carolina State Board of Education v. James E. Swann, 402 U.S. 43 (1971).

Orfield, Gary, "Public Opinion and School Desegregation," *Teachers College Record*, vol. 96, no. 4, summer 1995.

Snider, William, "Opposition to Busing Declines, Poll Finds," *Education Week*, January 21, 1987.

Vergon, Charles B., "*Brown* at the Threshold of the 21st Century: Enduring or Withering Legacy?" *Journal of Negro Education*, vol. 63, no. 3, 1994.

Watson, Denton L., "Saving the NAACP's Soul," *The New York Times*, June 25, 1997.

Weinberg, Meyer, Testimony before the Subcommittee on Civil and Constitutional Rights, U.S. House of Representatives, 1981.

White, Theodore H. *The Making of the President 1968: A Narrative History of American Politics in Action*, New York: Atheneum, 1969.

The Media's Narrow Approach to Higher Education Coverage

THE COST of going to college should be an important story by anyone's measure; it has more immediate ramifications for readers and viewers than have many other educational topics. Why, though, should coverage concentrate on a relative handful of high-cost institutions? In Chapter 9, Rochelle L. Stanfield raises questions about articles on tuition that every editor ought to be asking his or her reporters. If writers on the business pages covered retailing the way that education writers cover college tuitions, readers would get the impression that Tiffany and Bergdorf Goodman represented the entire gamut of retailing in the United States.

Similarly, articles on admissions dwell on a small number of highly selective institutions, creating a sense that the intense competition for spots in the freshman classes at such prestigious redoubts as Princeton and Duke represents the situation throughout higher education. This, too, is journalism by omission. Richard W. Moll and B. Ann Wright have built their careers in the admissions offices of colleges. They know the terrain and are positioned to critique the coverage. As they point out in Chapter 10, the drama would be lacking if stories on admissions made it clear that most undergraduate applicants get into their first-choice institutions. The intense competition highlighted by the media has little relevance to the experience of most people who get admitted to college in this country.

The college guides, with their ratings, are the final ingredient in this stew of exaggerations. One of the more preposterous gambits of this special segment of the media has to do with the numerical ratings that the guides ascribe to colleges. Bathed in statistics to lend a scientific patina to the rankings, the guides want readers to believe that it really means something to be number 5 instead of number 8. Such an approach is closer to alchemy than science and serves as a surrogate for genuine journalistic inquiry into the quality of higher education. According to Don Hossler in Chapter 11, the guidebook-ratings enterprise, although it may influence the small portion of students interested in the most expensive, most competitive institutions, may have little connection to the vast majority of college applicants.

The Media and Public Perceptions of Tuition Costs

ROCHELLE L. STANFIELD

THE COST of going to college catapulted up to third place in the list of Americans' biggest worries during the mid-1990s. As public opinion polls documented a rising concern among average families who feared that they would not be able to afford college for their children, politicians of both parties seized on that anxiety as a winning issue in the 1996 election campaigns. The media reported on each aspect of the developing story: the price tag for higher education, the public's anxiety about it, especially as reflected in the poll results, and the political reaction. To do so was an obvious journalistic task. But did the media go further than merely report on a national phenomenon? Did the media, in effect, provoke public fear?

Asking these questions presupposes that American families worried needlessly about college costs. Advocates for the poor chorus a loud "No!" But spokesmen for higher education institutions and organizations insist that that was the case, and point to public misperceptions about the cost of college—misperceptions that the media helped perpetuate. Participants in national surveys and focus groups on higher education consistently overestimated the tuition at public and private colleges and universities. Even though the price of higher education continued to escalate in 1996, it remained a lot lower than the public believed. In addition, federal, state, and institutional aid further reduced the cost of college to within the budget of average American families.

That was not quite the picture painted by the media. An analysis of how newspapers, newsmagazines, and to a lesser extent, radio and televi-

Imaging Education: The Media and Schools in America. Copyright © 1998 by Teachers College, Columbia University. All rights reserved. ISBN 0-8077-3734-8 (pbk), ISBN 0-8077-3735-6 (cloth). Prior to photocopying items for classroom use, please contact the Copyright Clearance Center, Customer Service, 222 Rosewood Dr., Danvers, MA 01923, USA, tel. (508) 750-8400.

sion covered the story of college costs shows that the media played some role in, at least, fanning the flames of anxiety. They did so primarily by emphasizing the cost at a small number of high-priced schools and by downplaying the ubiquity of financial aid. A Yale University or Stanford University may post a sticker price well in excess of $30,000 a year for tuition, fees, and room and board, for example, but only a minority actually pay that amount. The overwhelming majority of students at high-cost and moderately priced institutions alike use a combination of federal, state, and university grants and loans to substantially lower actual out-of-pocket expenses.

A handful of in-depth analyses in 1996—a series in the *Philadelphia Inquirer*, for example, a *Newsweek* cover story, and the *U.S. News & World Report*'s annual college issue—played to public discontent by trumpeting the high sticker prices and burying the financial aid explanations. The overwhelming majority of stories involved the passive coverage of political speeches and news conferences mounted by government agencies, foundations, and interest groups that study trends in higher education and often have their own agenda to promote. In these cases, the press was just the messenger. The message, however, was the same: College costs too much.

A messenger with a monopoly on the sources of information wields tremendous influence on public opinion. But with a subject such as higher education, which touches so many individuals directly, the media provide only one piece of the multidimensional base on which the public forms its opinions. Unlike foreign policy, for example, where most people must rely heavily on the media, information about tuition costs is more likely to derive from personal experience; the bill comes in the mail. And almost everyone knows somebody whose family receives such a bill. In addition, financial advisers, college aid consultants, and other professionals carry the word to middle-income families. Even television commercials get into the act. An ad for John Hancock Insurance, for example, urges parents to talk to their insurance agent to be sure their daughter would be able to afford the six-figure price tag for college no matter what happened.

Apparently, no major polling organization asked people how they formed their opinions about how much it costs to go to college. Participants in focus groups on higher education commissioned by the American Council on Education and conducted in 1993 and 1996, however, cited both personal experience and media coverage to back up their sometimes erroneous opinions about the cost of college.

Did the media therefore influence the public's perception of how much it costs to go to college? Undoubtedly. Was the perception skewed? Somewhat. Were the media to blame? Partly. But the media had a lot of help. Indeed, probably the media's greatest shortcomings here, as so often is the case, lay in accepting at face value the message supplied by others and then in portraying with bold strokes of black and white a subtle reality that has many shades of gray.

The reasons for passivity on the part of the press are many. It is easier and faster simply to report what others proclaim. In this case, the message that the sky is falling was much more dramatic and newsy than stories containing all the "yes, but's . . ." of cheaper college alternatives and financial aid. To some extent, an attempt to portray college as not that expensive, after all, required proving a negative. The sticker price was posted and could be simply stated. To dig out all the mitigating factors that reduced the sticker price relied on anecdotal evidence that was much harder to find and to quantify.

CONTEXT: FACTS AND AGENDAS

The widespread public perception of rising college costs did, in fact, match the basic media message and reflect an essential fact of life: The cost of attending college continued to increase much faster than average household income in the mid-1990s. The College Board's annual survey of colleges reported in September 1996 that tuition for the school year that began that fall had increased by 5% at private colleges and universities and 6% at public institutions. Room and board rose 4 to 6%. This was nearly twice the 3% rate of inflation. However, the rate of increase had slowed, as higher education spokespeople were quick to point out; 1996 was the 4th year in a row that tuition costs had gone up by about 5%. During the 1980s, by contrast, college costs rose in most years by 7 to 11%, according to calculations from Education Department statistics.

That the increase had stabilized might have provided relief to the spokespeople for higher education, but it was small comfort to the average family whose household income had been creeping up at an even slower pace. Between 1980 and 1995, tuition at public 4-year colleges and universities—the institutions attended by two thirds of the students in schools that grant a bachelor's degree—rose by 234%, the U.S. General Accounting Office reported in August 1996. During that 15-year period, median household income had gone up only 82% and the cost of living, 74%.

Seen in that context, public anxiety over college costs was natural. Never has it been more important to attend college. The gap in earning potential between high school and college graduates keeps widening, while household incomes fail to keep pace with college costs. Making this situation seem even worse, most of the parents of college-aged children in the mid-1990s had themselves gone to college in the early 1970s, a period of very slow growth in college costs and when tuitions were more stable.

Nonetheless, the reality of the mid-1990s was that the actual price tag still was not that steep for most middle-income families. Almost 56% of full-time undergraduates at 4-year institutions paid no more than $3,999 in tuition during the school year that started in fall 1996, the College Board reported (1996). Community college tuition averaged $1,394 that year. The numbers provided fodder for everyone with a point to make—the higher education establishment, politicians, policy advocates, and the media. Each constituency approached the subject with a different point in mind. Rising college costs confronted higher education with a serious threat, the political/policy community with an opportunity to argue for changes, and the media with a good story. The higher education camp and the political/policy forces each tried to sell the media on its formulation of the story. For the most part, the media bought the latter's version, to the dismay of the higher education establishment.

The American public has given the nation's higher education system—unlike elementary and secondary education—extremely high marks for several decades. Only on the issue of cost have most Americans been critical. But college and university officials viewed that criticism with alarm, fearing that the price tag rebellion might lead to greater dissatisfaction with other aspects of higher education, such as management efficiency or personnel policies of the institutions. "Higher education essentially has ridden a very long wave of public goodwill, the belief that it is valuable and that people don't need to ask a lot of questions," David Merkowitz, former director of public affairs for the American Council on Education (ACE), summed up the situation. "But over the last decade, increasingly people are asking questions, especially opinion leaders. And the price spiral has created more concern."

So organizations such as ACE, the American Association of Universities, the American Association of State Colleges and Universities, and the National Association of Independent Colleges and Universities tried to spin the story their way: Cost increases are moderating; even at these higher prices, postsecondary education is still a bargain; financial aid makes a college education possible for just about any willing student.

Meanwhile, politicians tried to capitalize on the growing alarm. As the election campaign heated up, President Clinton used anxiety over college costs to promote his education agenda and to propose a middle-class tax cut. "Now, it is clear that America has the best higher education system in the world, and that it is a key to a successful future in the 21st century. It is also clear that because of cost and other factors, not all Americans have access to higher education," he said in a commencement address at Princeton University on June 4, 1996, when he proposed tuition tax credits and tax deductions.

Other Democrats jumped on the bandwagon. "Unless we make our higher education more affordable, education will be a luxury only the wealthy can afford and working families will be forced to make tough choices between making mortgage payments and funding their kids' college education," Representative Martin Frost, a Texas Democrat, said the following day in praising the Clinton proposal. Advocacy groups were close on the heels of the politicians. In September, for example, the Center for the Study of Opportunity in Higher Education, the research arm of the Washington-based National Council of Educational Opportunity Associations, and the College Board released a report titled "College Opportunities and the Poor" that proclaimed: "College is becoming less affordable . . . we are losing ground in the effort to equalize college opportunities and have been for most of the past 15 years" (p. 6).

The media picked up the hand-wringing of the politicians and advocacy groups and all but ignored the explanations of the higher education establishment. This media treatment thus confirmed the opinions about the exorbitant cost of higher education that the public had been developing from personal experience and anecdotal evidence.

THE MEDIA RESPONSE

Each branch of the diverse media covers higher education to a different degree and in its own way. The national print press—the news weeklies and such widely-read daily newspapers as the *New York Times,* the *Wall Street Journal,* and the *Washington Post*—report on higher education regularly and in some depth. Most of them have assigned reporters to the higher education beat. Several of the news weeklies also publish college guides, either as a special issue (*U.S. News & World Report*) or a separate publication (*Newsweek*). The television magazine shows might have a back-to-school item that deplores the rising cost of college, but generally they limit their coverage of higher education to such scandals as improprieties that have been disclosed in university research. Such regional daily newspapers with a reputation for investigative reporting as the *Philadelphia Inquirer* also do major pieces on higher education glitches. For the most part, however, the dailies and radio news simply report what the politicians, foundations, organizations, and the educational institutions themselves hand out about tuitions.

In a separate category are the specialized media, both print and broadcast. A variety of newspapers, magazines, and newsletters are devoted specifically to higher education. Their coverage is intense, but only indirectly relevant to the shaping of general public attitudes toward college costs. To the extent that education reporters in the general media and community leaders and opinion molders read such publications as the *Chronicle of Higher Education* or *Education Week,* for example, they add to the information base that eventually gets filtered through to the public. Such house organs as that of the Association of Governing Boards, *Trusteeship* magazine, provide an outlet for the higher education community to talk to itself. The financial media, on the other hand, closely cover the cost of higher education and tend to be read by a broader segment of the public, especially the community and opinion leaders.

In 1996, the single piece that probably provoked the most anger and fear within the higher education community was *Newsweek*'s cover story on April 29. Stark type, superimposed on a figure in cap and gown, announced: "$1,000 a Week, The Scary Cost of College." Inside, the kicker—the smaller type accompanying the main headline—noted that "elite colleges carry a $1,000–a-week price tag" and "epic sticker shock shakes the foundations of higher education."

The point of the story, which was timed to coincide with the acceptance, rejection, and financial-aid letters that colleges and universities typically send to applicants in April, was Now that you got in, how are your parents going to pay the bills? It focused, not unexpectedly, on the high-priced schools. The lead paragraphs described the Strick family in Syracuse, New York, whose sons would be attending Brandeis University, where tuition and room and board would be $28,827 for the year, and Bates College in Maine, with a $27,415 sticker price. The third paragraph, however, carried this disclaimer:

> It [the $1,000 a week] is also, of course, a price paid by only a relative handful of affluent familes whose children attend prestige schools—the Ivies and 30 or 40 big-name institutions like MIT, Stanford and Duke. The *average* cost of a year at a private college or university is significantly less ($17,631) and the average cost of attending a public four-year college or university is lower still: $6,823.

The piece also spelled out some of the intricacies of financial aid, described how private schools often discount tuition, and asked, "Is an Ivy League degree worth $1,000 a week?" The answer: "The evidence, it seems, is mixed."

Like many stories of this type, this *Newsweek* piece totally ignored community colleges, by far the cheapest alternative—with average annual tuitions of less than $1,500—for the first 2 years of higher education. Although President Clinton has tried to publicize community colleges and upgrade their image, in the mainstream media they mostly remain second-class institutions in the media. One reason is their split personality, their divided mission between providing the first 2 years toward a bachelor's degree and short-term technical and job training courses. Another explanation has to do with the large portion of remedial courses offered by community colleges, lowering their prestige even further in the estimation of the well-educated editors and reporters at magazines such as *Newsweek* or *Time*. A spokesperson for the American Association of Community Colleges complained that just to have community colleges included in *Money* magazine's September 1996 college guide, the association had to pay for an ad. The overall impression left by such stories as the *Newsweek* piece was that sending children to college is a family budget breaker. Higher education spokespeople considered that a grossly unfair distortion. Journalists defended it as a legitimate cut at one slice of the higher education story and thus fair game.

A few weeks before the *Newsweek* article, the *Philadelphia Inquirer* ran a five-part series from March 31 to April 4, 1996, that used the high cost of college to make a different point: "An *Inquirer* investigation has found that the reason for the massive leap in college costs was not a result of schools spending to educate students. In fact, the percentage spent on instruction has dipped," the March 31 story began. "Prices rose because the market would bear it," the piece continued a few paragraphs later. The real culprits, the *Inquirer* insisted, were the administrators:

> Since 1975, administration in higher education grew at more than four times the rate of student enrollment. . . . Administrators, research faculty, better rooms, more racquetball courts—none had anything to do with the quality of undergraduate education. Yet they helped push prices sky-high.

These and other stories on rising college costs in *Time* and the *Washington Post* sounded alarm bells at higher education organizations such as ACE. Terry W. Hartle, ACE vice president for governmental relations, took to his own branch of the media, the education trade press, to rouse college officials to counterattack. In the July/August 1996 edition of *Trusteeship*, Hartle urged college and university governing boards to "explain better the actual (rather than perceived) cost of attending their institution, and help raise the level of awareness among the general public about the economic realities of higher education." Hartle listed five reasons for the increase in college costs, number one being the rapid growth of scientific knowledge that has forced colleges to hire "more specialized staff and faculty" and invest "in their professional development." He ended with a dig at the media. College and university officials, he wrote, may "believe the media will write balanced stories that describe why college costs are increasing and what officials are doing to hold down prices. As recent news articles demonstrate, this [is] not a safe assumption."

Did the media take heed and moderate coverage? Only a little bit. *U.S. News & World Report* headlined the lead story (Elfin, 1996) in its 1997 annual college guide on September 16 "The High Cost of Higher Education," with the kicker "College exacts a painful toll on family finances." But the story began, not entirely tongue-in-cheek, with the economic dilemma facing college presidents. "The trouble is," it explained in the third paragraph, "that higher education remains a labor-intensive service industry made up of thousands of stubbornly independent and mutually jealous units that must each support expensive and vastly underused facilities."

The story gave, if somewhat grudgingly, the higher education side: "For their part, the colleges blame spiraling tuition on an assortment of off-campus scapegoats—congressional budget cutters, stingy state legislatures, government regulators and parents who demand ever more costly student health and recreational services." But it then bit back: "Rarely mentioned are the on-campus causes of the tuition crisis: declining teaching loads, nonproductive research, ballooning financial aid programs, bloated administrative hierarchies, 'celebrity' salaries for professional stars and inflated course offerings." Unfair? That probably depends on the reader's perspective.

Higher education spokespeople criticized the *U.S. News* guide as elitist and contended that it fostered an exaggerated public perception of college costs. But the bias was subtle. A piece on choosing the right college urged applicants to consider their career goals, comfort level in different settings, grade point average and test scores, financial situation, and other aspects of college education, not just the prestige in the name. That sounds pretty straightforward. However, the advice came from counselors at two prestigious suburban Washington high schools, Bethesda-Chevy Chase, a public school, and Holton-Arms, a private school whose tuition exceeds that of most colleges. Does the source color the information?

The *U.S. News* guide then ranked colleges and universities based on a survey of 1,422 schools. It divided the institutions into four categories: national universities, national liberal arts colleges, regional universities, and regional liberal arts colleges. That would seem a fair way not to pit Harvard University against the University of St. Thomas in Minnesota. But then came the subtle tilt: The guide listed all 229 national universities and 160 national colleges with their pricey annual costs. It listed only the 15 top universities and 10 top colleges in each of four regions and did not include their, generally lower, price tags.

Money magazine published its 1997 college guide the same month, but took a very different approach. Headlined "Your Best College Buys Now," the package ranked schools by *Money*'s 16 criteria for value-for-money. The top 10 schools included expensive and exclusive California Institute of Technology ($18,216 a year in tuition and fees) and little-known and inexpensive Truman State University in Kirksville, Missouri ($3,108 for Missouri residents; $5,516 for out-of-state students). However, the lead story commented: "Yet even that amount would be a stretch for most families." The *Money* package listed tuition, room and board, and "average discounted cost" for all 1,115 colleges in its survey.

While readers were mulling over the two distinct perspectives on college costs presented by *U.S. News* and *Money*, the College Board released its annual survey. "1996–97 Increase in College Costs Averages Five Percent; Student Financial Aid at Record High," said the headline on the September 25 press release, which began:

> In two studies released today, the College Board reported that college tuition and fees for 1996–97 continued to climb at almost the same rate as last year, and that financial aid was available to students at a record level—more than $50 billion.

Across the country on September 26, most of the major dailies reported this news in unadorned fashion. "College costs are rising an average of 5% this year, but financial aid is available at a record level of $50.3 billion— much of it in unsubsidized loans, a survey out Wednesday says," reported *USA Today*. Cox News Service wrote: "Although tuition costs increased again this year, sending a child to college isn't as expensive as most parents fear." The *Chicago Tribune*'s Washington bureau said: "The rise in college tuition costs is slowing but remains higher than inflation, prompting more students to turn to the federal government for help, according to a study released Wednesday." The *Washington Post* put a slightly negative spin on its piece, which opened: "The cost of college, one of the American public's top concerns, has gone up again."

Broadcast news coverage paralleled that of the dailies. Typical was Channel 2 News in Portland, Oregon, which somewhat cryptically reported: "New survey shows cost of attending college is rising. College Board Survey says 4 year public college tuition up about 6 per cent for undergrads and at 4 year private colleges students pay about 5 per cent more. Room and board costs up as well."

MEDIA BIAS—OR BALANCE?

Are the media biased in their reporting of college costs and does their slant mislead the public into overestimating the amount needed for a postsecondary education? Or, are higher education spokespeople overreacting to basically balanced coverage, and have they been, in fact, saved by media inattention from much more potentially damaging revelations of institutional mismanagement that led to skyrocketing costs? The answers are not neatly packaged. The best response probably would be some of each. The twin journalistic tendency to dramatize a story by emphasizing the shocking elements, such as the price of Ivy League schools, and to overlook or underreport the subtler features, such as college aid and tuition discounting, leaves the public with a skewed perception of the intricacies of the higher education financial equation. Ironically, the very tactics that guarantee that a story will make an impression can mean that the impression is not an accurate one.

Spokespeople for higher education organizations typically make two basic points when they criticize media coverage of college costs: The emphasis on Ivy League and other high-priced institutions reflects journalistic elitism, particularly among newsweekly and national daily reporters and editors; and that emphasis causes the public's misperception of costs, documented by polls and focus groups who asked participants to estimate tuition at various types of institutions.

Journalists are more highly educated than their readers. In 1992, 82% of American journalists had college degrees, more than triple the proportion of the general public, according to a comprehensive study of journalists. For newsmagazines, the number was even higher: 95%. Nearly one fifth of the newsmagazine journalists had attended an Ivy League college, compared to about 3 to 4% of daily and wire service reporters, and even smaller proportions of broadcast journalists (Weaver and Wilhoit, 1996).

Merkowitz of the American Council on Education had the facts on his side when he voiced this common complaint:

> Why do people in the media focus on such a narrow set of institutions, primarily the elite privates and state flagships? Because that's where most of them went to school and that's where their kids are going to school.

D. H. Weaver, a journalism professor at Indiana University, agreed. He said:

> They (reporters and editors) are in a different class, less likely to represent working class people or lower middle class people. I think

that has an effect on what they choose to write about and how they choose to cover different things.

But Stephen Hess, a senior fellow at the Brookings Institution in Washington, who has written several books about Washington's media elite, did not concur. "It probably doesn't make any difference because journalists are professionals now. They have standards and they're fighting against whatever biases they might have," he said in an interview. Regardless of their education level or where they went to college, most journalists would agree that reporting on sky-high college costs makes a better story than discussing all the nuances of paying for a college education.

This discontent by higher education with the media boils down to the contention that as a result of biased reporting, the general public thinks colleges and universities charge more than they do. For proof, spokespeople point to polls and focus groups commissioned in recent years by ACE and similar organizations. Asked to estimate the tuition at public universities, participants in six focus groups conducted in March 1996, for example, guessed $6,130, slightly more than double the $2,982 figure at the time. Similarly, they pegged private research universities at $19,590, nearly $5,100 above the actual $14,510 average. Ironically, the participants' guesses were about what the College Board figured that total cost, including room and board, would be at those institutions that school year: $6,823 at a public university, $17,631 at a private university. The estimates were supposed to exclude room and board, but does a bill-paying parent mentally apportion the two costs?

James Harvey, a higher education consultant in Washington, D.C., who conducted an early set of focus groups for ACE, did not think so. "University spokesmen like to draw a very fine line between tuition, fees, and room and board. I don't think most people think like that," he said in an interview. He further disagreed that public perceptions, whether distorted or valid, were based entirely on media reports:

> People [also] get their impression of college costs [from] what it actually costs them to send their kids to school. I think these [university] administrators have their heads in the sand. People actually have to write checks to send their kids to school. They're going into debt. Their kids are going into debt. It's not just the headlines that are driving this.

A study comparing public perceptions of California higher education in 1993 and 1996 provides a small reality check on how knowledgeable the public actually is about the cost of college. In 1993, the California economy remained stuck in the recession that had abated over most of the nation 2 years earlier. But tuition at state colleges and universities had continued to rise dramatically. Californians interviewed for the study expressed extreme concern about access to higher education. Three years later, the economy had picked up while tuition had been frozen. The report concluded:

> Still convinced of the importance of a college education, Californians today are less anxious about a young person's opportunity to get one. . . . Survey data, of course, do not explain definitively why anxiety has lessened, but the stabilization of tuition and fees must be partly responsible. (Immerwahr, 1997, p. 8)

If college costs across the country were to stabilize in a similar way, perhaps the public would react much like their counterparts in California, regardless of which institutions the media profiled or the particular adjectives the media used to describe tuition costs.

BIBLIOGRAPHY

College Board. (1996) *The College Board Annual Survey of Colleges, 1996* and *Trends in Student Aid: 1986 to 1996*. New York: Author.

Elfin, M., et al. (September 16, 1996) "Best Colleges: What School is Right for You? 1997 Annual Guide." *U.S. News & World Report*.

Gladieux, L. (1996). *College Opportunities and the Poor: Getting National Policies Back on Track*. Washington, DC: College Board, and the Center for the Study of Opportunity in Higher Education.

Hartle, T. W. (1996a, July/August). "In Tuition Matters: The Bottom Line Counts." *Trusteeship*. Association of Governing Boards. Washington, DC.

Hartle, T. W. (1996b, October). "In Tuition Matters: The Bottom Line Counts, Part Two." *Trusteeship*. Association of Governing Boards. Washington, DC.

Harvey, J., et al. (1994). *First Impressions and Second Thoughts: Public Support for Higher Education*. Washington, DC: American Council on Education.

Harvey, J., and Immerwahr, J. (1995a). *The Fragile Coalition: Public Support for Higher Education in the 1990s*. Washington, DC: American Council on Education.

Harvey, J., and Immerwahr, J. (1995b). *Goodwill and Growing Worry: Public Perceptions of American Higher Education*. Washington, DC: American Council on Education.

Heller, K., and Eng, L. (1996). "Higher Education: How High the Price?" Five-part series, March 30–April 4. *The Philadelphia Inquirer*.

Hess, S. (1996). *News amd Newsmaking*. Washington, DC: Brookings Institution.

Immerwahr, J. (1997). *Enduring Values, Changing Concerns: What Californians Expect from Their Higher Education System. A Report from the California Higher Education Center*. New York: Public Agenda Foundation.

Immerwahr, J., with Boese, J. (1995). *Preserving the Higher Education Legacy: A Conversation with California Leaders. A Report from the California Higher Education Center.* New York: Public Agenda Foundation.

Immerwahr, J., with Farkas, S. (1993). *The Closing Gateway: Californians Consider Their Higher Education System. A report from The California Higher Education Policy Center.* New York: Public Agenda Foundation.

KRC Research and Consulting. (1996). "Public Perceptions of the Cost of Higher Education," prepared for The Higher Education Associations. (unpublished document) New York.

Larson, E. (March 17, 1997). "Why College Costs Too Much." *Time.*

Morganthau, T., and Nayyar, S. (April 29, 1996). "Those Scary College Costs." *Newsweek.*

U.S. Department of Education. (1997). *Digest of Education Statistics, 1996.* Washington, DC: Author.

U.S. General Accounting Office. (1996). *Higher Education: Tuition Increasing Faster Than Household Income and Public Colleges' Costs.* (GAO/HEHS-96-154) Washington, DC: Author.

Weaver, D. H., and Wilhoit, G. C. (1991). *The American Journalist, A portrait of US. News People and Their Work* (second edition). Bloomington: Indiana University Press.

Weaver, D. H., and Wilhoit, G. C. (1996). *The American Journalist in the 1990s. US News People at the End of an Era.* Mahwah, N.J.: Lawrence Erlbaum Association.

"Your Best College Buys Now: Key Facts You Need on 1,115 Four-Year Colleges." (1996, September). *Money.*

What College Selectivity Looks Like to the Public

RICHARD W. MOLL AND B. ANN WRIGHT

AS THE AUTHOR of *Playing the Selective College Admissions Game,* one of us was waiting nervously some years ago in the greenroom of a network television studio to be called for a segment on the morning program. Unfortunately, the directors had not provided a list of questions that might be asked on camera, as had happened in previous interviews. So, when Dick Moll was summoned to the set, and interrupted the interviewer from seriously perusing her *New York Times* while the local news was being broadcast, she looked up and let him have it: "Look, Mr. 'Mole,' I haven't read your book. I'll ask you whatever the prompter tells me to ask you. . . . Every parent watching us today wants to imagine their kid at Harvard, and the interview with you will probably be the most popular piece on this morning's show as a result. So whatever I ask you, just be elitist. Yes, just be elitist— they'll all love it, and you will sell books." Big smile as she turned to the camera, and we were on, live.

THE UNDUE EMPHASIS ON A FEW INSTITUTIONS

The media themselves, particularly national newspapers and magazines, have been following the television interviewer's quiet but firm advice for years, and have now unnecessarily brought the story of who-gets-in to the level of crisis, and worse, disturbing misrepresentation. Presupposing that every parent wants his or her kid at Harvard or one of perhaps two

Imaging Education: The Media and Schools in America. Copyright © 1998 by Teachers College, Columbia University. All rights reserved. ISBN 0-8077-3734-8 (pbk), ISBN 0-8077-3735-6 (cloth). Prior to photocopying items for classroom use, please contact the Copyright Clearance Center, Customer Service, 222 Rosewood Dr., Danvers, MA 01923, USA, tel. (508) 750-8400.

dozen high profile colleges—or, more cynically, that a compelling and sensational case can be made over and over again regarding the trauma of getting into, and paying for, about 20 "top" colleges—article after article on admission and financial aid seems to be limited to the Ivy League schools and a few of their boutique first cousins: Duke, Stanford, MIT and Cal Tech, Georgetown, Amherst and Williams, and a handful of others. The implication is that the superselectivity and superhigh tuitions of these schools are the norm. So, as kids and parents read only about out-of-reach institutions, they quite naturally (and mistakenly) infer that getting into any college, and paying for it, will be cause for frenzy.

Reporters stalking and reporting on a handful of highly selective colleges have created serious anxiety that has incrementally escalated at the family dinner table and in high school corridors. Of course, there has always been anxiety about "getting in." But demographic swings in the number and gender of traditional-age college entrants, an added squeeze through the front gates prompted by the string of Ivyish colleges that went coed in the early 1970s (thus doubling their applicant pools), the escalation of cost and accompanying reports of the high gamesmanship required to get financial aid, and the stampede toward early decision programs have all legitimately added intensity. But the media add fuel to the fire by concentrating on the far upper extremes. As a result, high school kids with college aspirations are not having much fun any more.

"Crash: As the scramble to get into a selective college grows tougher, is it any wonder that high school seniors are feeling more and more overwhelmed?" asked the *Boston Globe Magazine*'s cover story on a Sunday in late March of 1997. The article was typical of the press's spring ritual (late March to early April is when the most selective colleges announce their decisions) of dramatizing something related to college admissions, almost always featuring only the superselectives. This article appeared on the newsstand alongside an issue of *Time* that featured a cover with a varsity letter sweater inscribed "How Colleges Are Gouging U," a case study of the questionable pricing at the Ivy League's University of Pennsylvania.

The *Globe* article profiled students of several Boston-area high schools, focusing on Boston Latin School and Brookline High School and the trauma of being admitted to the "right" college. For example:

> With more colleges inviting students to apply early, junior year has become what senior year once was, and senior year has become a frenetic blur. "One of my teachers said that senior year is like Newark Airport," said one of the students. "No one wants to be there, but they have to go through it to get where they're going."

The article referred—surprise!—to the pressures related to getting into only three Massachusetts institutions: Harvard ("Applications to Harvard have soared by more than 50 percent over the last five years."), Wellesley ("Applications have increased by more than a third in four years"), and the always intimidating MIT. There is no mention of other colleges throughout New England with considerably easier access, demanding programs, and strong reputations. Typically and equally misrepresentative, the article concentrated only on the high schools' very top students who are realistic in trying for Ivy. But what about the other 80% of the students from these schools that send over 90% of the seniors on to college? Are we to infer that everyone is stressed out?

Similarly, an early spring issue of *Newsweek* in 1997 headlined a student-written article, "Is This What Life's All About?" The 16-year-old author, a high school student in Virginia, drags us through her impossible schedule from getting up early and "looking into the mirror and seeing puffy eyes" to usually missing breakfast, to the 45-minute commute to school, to "flying" from one class to the next, "using spare time to finish homework," and then on to practice, club, or volunteer organizations, to finally getting home around 8 P.M.—"I wolf down dinner, usually microwaved soup or cold cereal by myself, as my family has already eaten"—to "start four hours of homework." She continues:

> This cycle continues week after week, broken only by weekends full of homework and chores. . . . Why do we do this to ourselves? We're not addicted to stress and not all of us are overachievers. The numerous teens who push themselves academically have their own personal justifications, but nearly every high-school student who works into the early morning hours is after one thing: acceptance to a "good" college. . . . Pressure to attend a prestigious university comes from everywhere. School administrators, guidance counselors and parents make it seem as if my life will be over unless I get into a good college.

She sounds like the prototype for a 1996 article in the *Washington Post* titled "Competition for Admission to Elite Colleges Tests the Limits of Students." It says:

> This year, many top universities, including Harvard, Princeton, Columbia, Brown and the University of Pennsylvania, received the highest number of applications and handed out the lowest number of acceptances in their history. The University of Virginia and Georgetown University also had a record number of applicants. . . . With these longer odds, students know that perfect grades and test scores are no guarantee of admission. So many Washington area students are pushing themselves in every conceivable way to

reach their dream college, students and educators say. They are loading their schedules with college-level courses that can push their average above the traditional 4.0 peak, sometimes taking extra classes during lunch hour or before the regular school day starts. They're squeezing in sports, music or volunteer work, believing that selective colleges will expect such activities.

One professional caught in the middle of this frenetic, well-publicized race is the overworked, underpaid guidance counselor or college advisor. At college-conscious public high schools and at all preparatory schools, there is increasing parental pressure on the counselor to see that students have a wide array of attractive college choices, with a big name or two at the top of the list. A consequence of parental demand for "improved college admissions results" is rampant grade inflation throughout the nation's secondary schools, public and private. But still, the counselor bears the brunt of the responsibility for college placement.

Bobbie Swain, the director of college guidance at Poly Prep Country Day School in Brooklyn, New York, decided the media were getting so carried away, and her constituency so flustered that she had better, in self-defense, send a memo to her students and parents to put the college admissions ordeal in perspective. She wrote:

> Recent articles have focused attention on the intensity of the college search as some parents and students seek a recipe for getting into the Ivy League and other colleges with instant name recognition. The media have discussed the stiffness of the competition at these schools, highlighting students with exceptional credentials who did not make it into one or more of these institutions. . . . But effective college planning is based on the reality of what a student has become by senior year. Thus, a student who has had only modest academic success should not expect that a school counselor or even a hired consultant can simply wage some kind of ad campaign to "sell" the student to an extremely competitive university if there are no other compelling factors or forces at work to bring that application into some kind of special review. The counselor at an independent school or any high school understands that all students are not destined for the same kinds of places, and there are lots of success stories from colleges of all types, some covered in thick traditional ivy, and some with different and equally viable flora.

Meanwhile, the admissions officers at the Elite are probably not upset with all the hoopla (but do Williams and Duke need any more applications?). However, even the most selective colleges have spent nearly 3 decades now attempting to convince the historically "nontraditional" high school prospects—those who can't pay the full freight, those who are not Caucasian, those who attend average secondary schools—that they should try for Ivy because Ivy has democratized and is looking for a "classful of differences." Then, along come the media to frighten off the masses. "The media could be a help, but instead, they're now scaring people away," says Jane Reynolds, dean of admission at Amherst College.

REINFORCING NOTIONS OF ELITISM

Enough talk for the moment of colleges frightening the applicants and making their high school careers miserable as a consequence. What is happening out there in admissions? Granted, a few colleges are painfully hard to crack, but what about the hundreds of others, many with recognizeable names? And do most kids make dozens of applications to find a suitable place? The College Board has the statistics and the answers. Students applying as freshmen in the fall of 1995 to 4-year public institutions (including "public ivy" universities such as the University of Virginia, UC Berkeley, Michigan at Ann Arbor, and William and Mary) filed an average of only 3.3 applications. In turn, the publics combined admitted 70% of their applicants. At private colleges, applicants made an average of 4.3 applications, and the colleges admitted 64% of those applying. Further, the College Board reports that only 37% of the 4-year institutions admitted fewer than three quarters of their applicants in 1984. By 1995, there was little change: 38 percent. Perhaps most surprising, given the headlines we're accustomed to reading, is that only 8% of the 4-year institutions admitted fewer than half of their applicants in 1984, and that percentage remained stable in 1995.

In other words, a hefty 53% of the colleges and universities in America traditionally admit 75 to 99% of their applicants to the freshman class, and 11% have open admissions. This is hardly the crunch that the media have consistently featured in headlines the past few years! "Admissions Boom at Top Colleges" (*New York Times*), "Better Students Find the Choice Colleges Are Rejecting Them" (*New York Times*), "Competition for College Feeds Elitism" (*Washington Post*), "Frustration is the Price of Admission" (*Los Angeles Life*). In fact, the newsletter of the National Association for College Admission Counseling reported in May 1997 that 70% of the institutions answering their end-of-year admissions survey still had freshman openings for the fall semester, and 83% reported openings for transfers!

The endless media concentration on the most elite colleges, overlooking the sane competition to gain admission to the majority of America's good colleges and universities, finds eager sympathizers—and ready manipulators. Note what the revered columnist Russell Baker wryly wrote on May 21, 1996, in his *New York Times* column titled "The College Night-

mare." He accepts no responsibility on behalf of his paper and its competition for the "getting in" hysteria. Instead, he blames the admissions
officers:

> News from the education front is often the most depressing stuff in the paper,
> but the present flurry of stories about college admissions is enough to make
> patriots fear for the future of the nation. . . . For whatever reason, an aston-
> ishing number of Americans who do not have the wealth of the Indies are
> now urging their children to strive for the most expensive education money
> can buy. It is a waste of breath to point out that Abraham Lincoln educated
> himself, that Andrew Carnegie's school was a cotton mill or that H. L.
> Mencken had only a high school diploma. . . . Because competition for fancy
> colleges is so intense, high school students apparently devote much of their
> youth to the labor of creating impressive applications for admissions offic-
> ers. . . . It makes you shudder to think what we are doing to people who will
> be running the country 25 years hence. Think of it: 15-year-olds with con-
> sultants attached to get them into the best of all possible colleges. . . . These
> stories about high school strivers shaping their lives to measure up for col-
> lege admissions ought to make admissions officers ashamed of themselves.
> In addition to training for the SATs, eager beavers spend their youth com-
> piling records of achievement in arts, sports and community service in the
> hope that admissions officers will cry "Amazing!" and put the financial
> screws to their parents. . . . It doesn't seem to have a lot to do with being
> young. Sounds more like premature middle age, doesn't it?

The admissions officers do have views on all this, but assuming guilt
is not high on the list. Some admissions directors of "the elite," which seems
to be the media's chosen phrase for the 8% or so of the colleges and universities that admit fewer than half of their applicants, feel left out because
only the superelite become the featured few in print. For example, in 1997
there was a slight downturn in applications at most of the Ivy League
schools, and as expected, the top national papers had a field day. Even the
most visible educational trade newspaper, the *Chronicle of Higher Education*, left the impression that most highly selective colleges were down in
applications by their headline "Elite Private Colleges See a Drop in Applications" and by featuring Harvard, Yale, Dartmouth, and Rice. But Vassar
(one of the elite 8% admitting fewer than 50% of its applicants), where
coeducation has finally jelled, had a 30% increase in early decision applications and a 16% increase in regular applications, and was not mentioned.
Columbia, the only Ivy institution with an increase in 1997, was mentioned
midway through the *Chronicle*'s article, but very briefly. Part of the problem here has to do not just with the reporting on admissions, but with the
reporting generally. The media tend to ignore all but the most elite institu-

tions in almost all respects. Dozens of superb, selective institutions are irked that they find it hard to "get news" because the media give so much attention to the favored few. Witness these examples:

• The College of New Jersey (public), which until June of 1996 had been known as Trenton State College, tells a droll tale of how it finally won a bit of publicity at the time of the name change. Jesse Rosenblum, associate vice president of college relations, reports: "It seems that Princeton University was founded as The College of New Jersey in the 1700s, but relinquished the name in 1896 in favor of Princeton. (Princeton had no copyright or trademark protection of its original name and had not used it extensively in the past 100 years or even before.) . . . At the time of our name change, I called the *New York Times* and offered the story to them. There was no interest. It was only several weeks later, when Princeton sued the college in State Superior Court that the *Times* covered the story of Princeton's suing for unfair competition. . . . The suit was eventually settled out of court." It took the Princeton angle to make the name change newsworthy.
• In the early summer of 1988, Richard Skelton, assistant vice president for enrollment planning at Bucknell University, took a call from the mother of a young man who had not applied to Bucknell. She was asking Bucknell to admit her son, who had been denied admission at Princeton and Brown but had been wait-listed at Duke and Virginia. She was incredulous that he discouraged the possibility of a late application, not to mention immediate admission. "I took time to inform her that Bucknell had received 7,250 applications for 880 spaces in the class, and that we had more than 450 students on a ranked waiting list, should slots open during the summer," Skelton said. He elaborated: "She insisted that we place her son at the top of the waiting list; I firmly said that was not possible. To say that she was miffed is an understatement. She then asked where Bucknell was located and if anyone at the *New York Times* had ever heard of it. It was obvious that what mattered most was whether or not the top media had heard of Bucknell, not the quality of the faculty, the curricular dimensions, or the richness of the Bucknell experience. I ended the conversation by saying that we were in central Pennsylvania and that 7,250 applicants had heard of it, thank you."
• For at least a decade, said Geoffrey Gould, admissions director at the State University of New York at Binghamton, parents have called him "in shock" to ask that he correct the "mistake" made on their child's application. "How," they ask, "could Binghamton have placed Johnny or Cindy on the waiting list, when he had been admitted to Johns Hopkins and she to Barnard?" . . . The message is clear: Binghamton must be in error because private colleges are obviously more selective than public universities—at

least in the minds of inhabitants of the Northeast. Gould said: "How, I have asked, do they divine that impression? Over and over they cite the press as their source of indisputable truth. The fact that we had 11 applications for every space for a particular program (albeit fewer for some other programs) can make us very, very selective for some applicants, but not for all. Their inability to differentiate is understandable, but mutually frustrating. . . . Rarely does the press seek to provide a sophisticated understanding of admission issues and process, although recently *USA Today* has done the best job of trying to create some depth of understanding. Their toll-free Admission and Financial Aid Hotlines seek to provide professional expertise from both the public and private sectors for parents and students thirsty for reliable information about the dicey business of college choice."

• A few years ago, Kathleen Killion had to argue with a guidebook editor's proposed lowering of the "selectivity" rating for New College of Florida, where Killion was admissions director. Because the institution was admitting more than 55% of its applicants, the editor assumed that selectivity at New College was in decline. "Our quality indicators—GPA, SATs, class rank and difficulty of high school curriculum—were up over previous years, and were consistently among the highest in the nation," Killion said. "Although we have been favored of late by the national media, I must say that the media's confusion regarding 'competitiveness' versus quality puts pressure on me to increase applicant numbers without regard to applicant appropriateness. If I reject more students, the media will tell the world that New College is measurably more selective, when actually it means only that more students not suited to New College have spent $20 and a lot of time filling out the application. Artificially bolstering applicant numbers doesn't really make us any more or less difficult to get into than we were before, but everybody thinks New College has changed for the better. That's a disservice to everyone!"

THE MEDIA'S SPIN ON SELECTIVITY

The colleges that are not in the media's Fab Few know that those in that lofty group will become even more selective by means of their constant exposure. Institutions that achieve high rankings and get headlines muster even more prestige, therefore more applications and a higher yield on their accepted applicants. Unfortunately, the desire for more public visibility and prestige tempts many colleges to report their admissions data selectively. The admissions director at New College is joined by a crowd of other admissions officers concerned about superficially altering class statistics to gain greater public notice and respect. But few are as embarrassed by the exercise as she. In fact, quite a few admissions officers have found their own ways to move up in the rankings and into the headlines.

Consider the reporting of SATs, for example. Aside from, What percentage of their candidates do they admit? the most frequently asked question to popularly determine selectivity is, What are their SATs? And this is where colleges have considerable leeway. Reporting institutional SATs is probably the most egregious aspect of college self-profiling. When a questionnaire asks for the SATs of a class, there are multiple ways of answering the question: the mean SATs of all entering freshmen; the median SATs of all entering freshmen; the mean or median SATs of all applicants; the mean or median SATs of all admitted students; the mean or median SATs of students with "special admits" removed. Anyone understanding these groups will recognize that there will be considerable differences in the numbers that are derived, category by category. The results are more than apples and oranges, more like kiwi and kohlrabi. And yet the media compare colleges as if self-reported SAT scores (compiled in a myriad of ways) are the absolute verities of life.

To further complicate matters, some colleges exclude students from their statistics in order to present a so-called selective profile that leaves out the group now referred to in the admissions profession as Not in Profile Students ("NIPS"). Deirdre Carmody of the *New York Times* first made notice of this phenomenon in a November 1987 article titled "Colleges' SAT Lists Can Be Creative Works." She listed the groups whose "scores are not included in the class profile because they would pull down the class average." These include children of alumni, recruited athletes, disadvantaged minorities, foreign students, and sometimes "others" who simply have embarrassingly low SAT scores. Clearly, the results of SAT reporting can have spectacular effects on the perceived quality of a college. Admissions officers have made attempts to monitor the situation and find agreement on a firm, uniform method of reporting admissions-related statistics— SATs, average grades, and class rank of candidates, for instance. But colleges will flaunt their independence in imaginative reporting until a wide consensus is reached and put in place.

As we have seen, newspaper and magazine reports on colleges have a major effect on individual colleges' reputations. But it is perhaps television, with its hard-hitting sound bites and vivid pictures, that is most effective in presenting the audience with memorable impressions. With all its potential for encouraging the public by informing them of higher education's advantages, including a huge wage premium over a high school education, too often the media focus on another type of extreme—the bizarre and unexpected. An example is the annual handwringing about the terrible job market for college graduates. Although the 1997 employment opportunities for new graduates are the best in years, the networks have continued to suggest otherwise.

Witness a spring 1997 human interest story on a network nightly news show, the subject being the tough job market for college graduates. The reporter began by showing a recent Smith College graduate looking through a dumpster (for food? for shelter?), while the background statements indicated that even graduates of prestigious colleges could not always find jobs. The segment continued for a full 3 minutes. The embarrassed alumna, a recent graduate, called Smith the next day to report that the dumpster sequence had been entirely staged by the news segment's producer to dramatize (sensationalize?) the young woman's plight, whereas other information that she had provided about her subsequent graduate school and employment experience was ignored in the piece. She had no intention of suggesting that she was desperate and destitute, as she knew that graduates often take a few months to find an appropriate position. Shouldn't we expect that journalistic ethics include avoiding manufactured scenes that mislead the audience simply because the reporters wish to illustrate the theme of the week? Producers defend these actions as illustrating possible outcomes; watching parents, however, will remember this harrowing scene as the potential fate of their own Ivy-aspiring children.

Going hand in hand with misrepresentations about selectivity and outcomes are the misrepresentations related to the cost of attending college, as discussed in Chapter 9. They are fueled by the same articles that create nervousness about "getting in" by limiting the discussion to the most inaccessible institutions, the Ivy League and its extended small family. Donald Stewart, president of the College Board, says: "Focusing too much on the highest-priced institutions overstates the problem and unduly alarms the public. . . . For most Americans, the fact remains that college is still accessible, especially in light of the financial aid currently available."

Why do all segments of the media continue to lavish attention on elite colleges, with their high costs and impossibly selective admission standards? It's a question worth pondering, when one considers that of the 3,500 colleges in this country, the overwhelming media attention focuses on no more than two dozen institutions. One theory is that the media know that Americans are tremendously status conscious, with advertising and brand recognition a major aspect of capitalism. Just as Kodak is in all photography stories, whereas Big Blue, Intel, and Microsoft have a hold on technology pieces, "HYP" (as Harvard/Yale/Princeton are commonly known) is the acronym for prestige and high visibility in the world of education. The media focus on the elite colleges has reinforced the old maxim You get what you pay for, so that much of the public equates the price of the elites with high value. What is known as the Chivas Regal effect works for those top schools. In fact, there is real reluctance by colleges as well as corporations to cut prices, since the received wisdom is that falling out of the top circle of those that charge the highest tuitions would raise suspicions of a drop in quality. "What's wrong with brand X or Elite U. that they had to cut prices? They must be hurting." Who can afford such risks?

Of course, high tuition has its downside, even for colleges of the highest reputation. Increasingly, the media have plugged financial aid negotiation as a panacea for high costs. An example comes from an April 1997 morning network television talk show interview on the subject of bargaining with colleges for financial aid. The financial aid advisor, employed by a well-known guidebook publisher, opined that shopping for college is like buying a used car; thus the financial aid award given with the offer of admission is only a sticker price, an initial offering to be negotiated. Upon receiving an award letter, the response from the parents to the college should be "That's not enough," with information about competitive offers thrown in if possible. Following this 8:15 A.M. segment, several calls came to the Smith and Vassar financial aid offices before noon, using these exact words and strategies. Such calls happen with such frequency these days that negotiations from families have become known in financial aid offices as "dialing for dollars." Now, we might believe that consumerism in this country supports good advice for finding the best deal, but it hardly suggests haggling with an educational institution that has made its most generous offer of financial aid to thousands of students.

On another front, the much discussed subject of college rankings has become tangled with costs, marketing, reputation, and public perception of value. As indicated in Chapter 11 in this book on ratings and rankings, we know that these media evaluations have a major impact on public perceptions. The annual *U.S. News Best Colleges* guide (known among admissions officers as the "swimsuit" issue) is at once the most controversial and the most carefully researched and quantitative of all such publications. Many high school and college counselors detest the rankings because they feel that they interfere with counseling and the goal of a good fit for individual students. Editors answer with words about serving the public and the "public's right to know." But much as colleges dislike being judged, there is clearly a market for such evaluations. Families love them because of the simplicity of the single vertical column that says college number 5 is better than number 6. Never mind that these colleges may be separated by .1% in the overall quantitative ratings, or that the rankings have changed because of a different weighting system used in the most recent year.

Thus, when a college falls from number 10 to number 12, as happened to Smith recently, or from number 1 to number 3 (the fate of Harvard), phone lines are clogged with alumni/ae and families wanting to know what has caused the college to decline so severely in one year, when in fact there has been no change in the institution, only a change in the numerical weighting of SATs versus retention versus endowment versus alumni giving versus other factors. The most disturbing aspect of this phenomenon is that families really don't and can't possibly know the value of an education at a specific college, since this does not become apparent for many years after graduation. In his paper "Why Can't a College Be More Like a Firm?" Gordon Winston asks of the differences in the marketing of profits versus nonprofits. He suggests that the purchase of a college education is much more like buying a cancer cure than a car or house, since the tendency is to play it safe and buy the best you can afford.

In addition, since the so-called wage premium available to college graduates is now a matter of public knowledge, increasingly we read of elaborate theories that the distribution of wealth in this country is based largely on skills and education. There may even be some subtle return to the belief in college as an elaborate finishing school, a preparation for life in the upper-middle to upper classes, where students learn not just Shakespeare and Freud, Kerouac and Keynes, but also how to rub shoulders effectively with the privileged. Andrew Hacker, in his book *Money: Who Has How Much and Why* (1997), suggests that professors and administrators are as much role models as teachers and leaders. "The years at college and graduate school pay off because they burnish students' personalities," he writes. "The time spent on a campus imparts cues and clues on how to conduct oneself in corporate cultures and professional settings" (pp. 231–232). Thus, the substance of a student's education might matter less than the style and the ambiance at the college and in the classroom. Given all this, is it any wonder that families are vulnerable to the hierarchies created by the media, which leads directly to the Chivas Regal effect: Families who want status and the best education for their children are convinced they must buy the best name-brand college education available to them.

But what about the equally pricey not-so-well-knowns? These are the colleges that, lacking visibility and therefore positive image, are scrambling for students, worrying about net tuition revenue, and offering fire-sale prices to fill the beds. For the upcoming boom of students arriving with high hopes but little money for escalating costs, these colleges and universities offer hope. But do Americans learn about them in the media? No, we read about a tiny fraction of the universe of higher education, the almost-impossible-to-reach segment. As a result, parents and high school students are left yearning for a piece of the best, the elite, despite the exhorbitant price. Why else would people hire consultants, prepare to mortgage all they have, call in every chit from every contact they know, as they pray for an offer of admission from Olde Ivy?

Largely because the media keeps hyping Olde Ivy.

BIBLIOGRAPHY

Hacker, A. (1997). *Money: Who Has How Much and Why*. New York: Simon & Schuster.

Moll, R. M. (1994). *Playing the Selective College Admissions Game*. New York: Viking Penguin.

Everybody Wants to Be Number One:
The Effects of the Media's College Rankings

DON HOSSLER

RANKING INSTITUTIONS of higher education has become a major preoccupation of publishers, educational observers, and higher education administrators and faculty. It seems that hardly a month goes by without a new ranking of colleges and universities or at least a newspaper article about rankings appearing in print somewhere in the United States. Variations of these rankings have existed for some time now. More than a decade ago, David Webster (1984) wrote an article in *Change* magazine titled, "Who is Jack Gourman and Why is He Saying All Those Things About My College?" The *Gourman Report,* created by Jack Gourman, ranked the quality of undergraduate majors in colleges and universities throughout the United States. Today, years later, we could paraphrase Webster and ask the question, What are these publications and why is everyone paying so much attention to them? This certainly is a medium of high visibility. The publications with rankings represent a shift away from objectivity. Such journals as *U.S. News & World Report* and *Money* magazine rank colleges and universities in numerical order. Such others as *Birnbach's New and Improved College Guide* provide subjective descriptions of colleges and universities.

Unlike these newer publications that rank or rate colleges and universities, traditional college guidebooks have been published for decades, but they still do not attempt to rank or rate colleges and universities. Instead, they provide encyclopedic information about topics such as student enrollment, academic program offerings, social and physical environment, and, often, the financial health of colleges and universities. The purpose of guide-

Imaging Education: The Media and Schools in America. Copyright © 1998 by Teachers College, Columbia University. All rights reserved. ISBN 0-8077-3734-8 (pbk), ISBN 0-8077-3735-6 (cloth). Prior to photocopying items for classroom use, please contact the Copyright Clearance Center, Customer Service, 222 Rosewood Dr., Danvers, MA 01923, USA, tel. (508) 750-8400.

books has been to help students to learn more about institutions that they are considering attending.

Although some guidebooks focus on graduate and professional schools, most concentrate on the undergraduate degree. What they *do* rate—although they do not rank it—is the academic competitiveness or selectivity of the institution. Peterson's guides, for example, rate 4-year colleges as most difficult, very difficult, moderately difficult, minimally difficult, or noncompetitive. Ratings of academic selectivity are not intended to be overall rankings of institutional quality, although many readers take them to be this. Measures of selectivity are intended to help students understand how difficult admission might be and to provide a rough indicator of the number of academically talented students who enroll at given campus. Guidebooks, however, do not offer subjective descriptions or recommendations about the quality of social life or the types of professors found at a specific college or university.

Efforts to rate or rank the quality 4-year colleges and universities numerically can be traced at least to 1910, when the noted psychologist William Cattell published his first article ranking the quality of academic programs (see Webster, 1986). Efforts to rank institutions used to focus on graduate programs. Since the early 1980s, however, the visibility and importance of publications carrying undergraduate ratings and rankings has increased dramatically, producing some tension between higher education and the media. *U.S. News & World Report* and *Money* magazine were among the first to publish special issues of popular magazines that attempted to provide useful guidance information to potential college students and to rank most 4-year institutions in the United States. These publications rated all colleges and universities on the basis of their undergraduate programs—not their graduate programs. In addition to publications that focus broadly on undergraduate programs, other more specialized rankings are now published annually. For example, *Business Week* conducts ranking studies of business schools (both undergraduate and MBA programs) and publishes them each fall.

Some of the new publications of undergraduate and graduate school rankings appear to be money makers. In particular, *Money Magazine's Best Buys* and *U.S. News & World Report's* ranking of top undergraduate institutions and graduate programs in many fields of study seem to sell briskly. McDonough, Antonio, Walpole, and Perez (1997) report that the most recent special issue of *U.S. News & World Report's America's Best Colleges* sold more than 2.4 million copies. In addition, it sold approximately 700,000 copies of its college guide, which it marketed separately. Recently, *Time* magazine and *Newsweek* have launched their own special issues focused on college admission. Both attempt to take advantage of the success of college rankings publications; neither of these, however, provides rankings. Examining interviews with several publishers of magazines that produce college guidebooks and rankings, McDonough et al. (1997) estimate that total revenue from the various news magazines that publish college rankings and guidebooks will reach almost $16 million a year in sales alone. Additional revenue is derived from advertising. Rating colleges and universities has indeed become big business.

When publications ranking colleges first appeared, many faculty members, university administrators, and observers of higher education did not pay much attention to them. As the circulation and media coverage of such publications as *Money Magazine's Best College Buys* grew, however, interest from the higher education community also increased. Higher education professionals initially focused on the impact of these new ratings on the college enrollment decisions of students. High school guidance counselors, college admissions officers, and other higher education administrators pondered the effects that the publications would have on how students selected a college and on overall student enrollments (Hossler & Foley, 1995; Hossler & Litten, 1993; *Studentpoll*, 1995).

As the popularity of these publications grew, critics began to focus on the process by which the information they provided was derived. A series of articles in the *Wall Street Journal* by Steve Stecklow (1995a, 1995b) described systematic reporting of inaccurate information for college guidebooks, rankings, and financial reports. Stecklow documented the many rumors about the inaccuracies of institutional data that had circulated in the admissions profession for many years. In an earlier article, Pollock (1992) reported significant discrepancies between information about colleges appearing in different guidebooks. In addition, Pollock questioned the accuracy of information provided to the publishers of guidebooks and rankings. Concerns about the accuracy of institutional information provide the rationale for examining the impact of guidebooks and rankings on higher education institutions.

In this chapter, I consider the impact of guidebooks and ratings on students, parents, and institutions of higher education. The effects on these different audiences are not mutually exclusive concerns. If college administrators and faculty believed that the publications had little impact on the enrollment decisions of potential college students, administrators would have little reason to present institutional data in a way that would result in their campuses being ranked more highly. The next section of this chapter begins with a brief overview of relevant theories used to investigate the effects of mass media on society. These theories provide a unifying framework for evaluating the impact of college guidebooks and rankings on students, parents, and institutions of higher education. This is followed by an examination of the effects of college guidebooks and rankings on students and parents. I then turn my attention to an analysis of the effects of guidebooks and rankings on higher education institutions themselves.

There is, however, a paucity of research on the impact of guidebooks and ratings. Recently, some high-quality studies of the effects of guidebooks and rankings have started to appear, but they remain few in number. In the section of this chapter where I examine the impact of guidebooks and rankings on college enrollment decisions, I draw heavily on this small set of studies. Whereas research on the effects of guidebooks on the enrollment decisions of students is limited, there are no empirical studies of the effects of guidebooks and rankings on colleges and universities. In preparation for this chapter, I phoned senior enrollment managers, admissions officers, and institutional researchers to gather information. I conducted a lengthy telephone interview with Al Sanoff, the managing editor of *U.S. News & World Report's America's Best Colleges*. I also circulated a request for comments and information on a national list-serve for enrollment managers. In addition, an electronic database search was conducted. As a result of the limited number of studies on the impact of publications on students or institutions, my observations are presented as more of an essay than a piece of empirical research.

THEORETICAL LEADS FROM MASS MEDIA RESEARCH

Three relevant theoretical perspectives pertain to the role of the media: agenda setting, accumulation of minimal effects, and social expectations. Two of these perspectives overlap.

Agenda setting refers to the role that the mass media play in emphasizing certain topics or issues, so that, as a result, the public perceives these issues as important (DeFleur & Dennis, 1996; Dominick, 1996). Bernard Cohen, in his book *The Press and Foreign Policy*, notes that the media are not always successful in telling people what to think; they are more successful in telling people what to think *about* (Cohen, quoted in Dominick, 1996, p. 543). With agenda setting as a conceptual framework, it is possible that the high visibility these guidebooks have achieved may cause students and parents to think about the importance of institutional quality and the attributes of quality in new and more focused ways.

The theory of the accumulation of minimal effects holds that issues on which the media focus repeatedly and consistently over long periods cause individuals to become increasingly aware of the messages that are transmitted (DeFleur & Dennis, 1996). Over time, the public develops a growing comprehension of the topic. As this process continues, individual meanings, attitudes, and beliefs come to guide the reactions of people. Thus, minor changes in individuals accumulate slowly, and significant shifts in attitudes and behaviors evolve over time. In the case of guidebooks and rankings, this theory implies that the growing number and circulation of these publications may have a cumulative effect on students and parents.

Finally, social expectation theory presents a more complex view of the impact of media on society. DeFleur and Dennis (1996) specify that groups function as social organizations that develop group norms and specialized roles; these help create social controls that function as group norms that all members are expected to follow (DeFleur & Dennis, 1996; Dominick, 1996). Knowledge of norms, roles, and social rank can be acquired through incidental exposure to media. Even if the portrayals are inaccurate, they may still influence beliefs and norms. Social expectation theory, like minimal effects theory, raises the possibility that over time publications with rankings could shape the norms and beliefs of students and their families. Rankings and college attributes that become associated with highly ranked colleges and universities could affect the college expectations of students and parents. These theories provide a framework for examining current and potential effects of college guidebooks and rankings on students, parents, and higher education institutions.

THE IMPACT OF GUIDEBOOKS AND RANKINGS
ON ENROLLMENT DECISIONS

Larry Litten (1986) and Phillip Kotler and Karen Fox (1985) were among the first scholars to explore empirically the relationships between marketing concepts and student college choice. According to Litten (1986), the decision-making process for choosing a college—like that for selecting a physician or joining a club—contains the seeds of risk and uncertainty. For most high school students in the United States, college selection is their first noncompulsory educational decision, a decision for which they have had no previous practice. The benefits of higher education are intangible, and not immediate. Adding to the confusion, the decision also involves entering unfamiliar surroundings, maybe even moving away from home and leaving friends. Experts say consumers look for ways to make sure they are choosing correctly when making an intangible purchase. The more intangible, risky, and expensive the decision, the more likely potential purchasers are to seek out additional information.

But ratings and rankings may not have the wide influence that their publishers would like to imagine. Two comprehensive reviews of research on student college choice (Hossler, Braxton, & Coopersmith, 1989; Paulsen,

1990) indicate that older students, in particular, do not consider a large number of colleges and universities. For them, the decision to attend college and of where to attend are often the same. This is because they usually select the nearest and lowest-cost institution. Younger, traditional-age students who plan to live at home and commute to a nearby college or university make their decisions in similar fashion. Both groups gather very little comparative information about the institutions they are considering.

Galotti and Mark (1994) examined the effort and focus of the decisions of high school juniors and seniors in Minnesota. They found that students devoted the greatest amounts of time and energy to the college decision-making process during the second semester of their junior year and the first semester of their senior year. This is consistent with other research (Hamrick & Hossler, 1996). This is the time period during which published ratings and guidebooks are apt to have their greatest impact on those students who *do* rely on these materials.

Longitudinal studies conducted by Galotti and Kozberg (1996) and Galotti and Mark (1994) included measures of the kind of information that students consulted and how much they used those sources. They got their information most frequently (in rank order) from parents, friends and classmates, students presently attending or soon to be attending colleges of interest, college brochures, and materials in high school guidance or career centers. College guidebooks were in the midrange of sources consulted, but were one of the more frequently used print media sources of information. These results suggest that guidebooks may not exert high levels of influence over students' decisions. Institutions of higher education are limited in the extent to which they can sway parents, peers, and teachers. These observations cannot answer a more fundamental question, namely, the extent to which guides and rating books indirectly affect what parents, teachers, and peers say to students when they are consulted for information.

Two recent works look specifically at the impact of guidebooks and rankings upon the college enrollment decisions of students. McDonough and her colleagues (1997) use a national data set, the Cooperative Institutional Research Program's (CIRP) 1995 Freshman Survey, to examine how much entering first-year students used guidebooks and rankings in their college choice decisions and how influential these publications were in the decision-making process. Hossler and Foley's (1995) work, using insights gained from reviewing previous research and interviewing admissions officers, looks at a similar set of questions. Overall, there is remarkable overlap in their findings. Indeed, McDonough and her coauthors (1997) base their analyses on a set of questions raised by Hossler and Foley (1995).

Hossler and Foley found that rankings and guidebooks do not affect the college decisions of low-income and first-generation college students, nontraditional students, and students who live at home and commute to school. McDonough and her colleagues (1997), using multivariate techniques to analyze a national data set, had similar findings. Hossler and Foley (1995) also suggested that rankings and guidebooks had, at best, a small effect upon the enrollment decisions of students who were considering local and regional public in-state colleges and universities. McDonough et al. (1997) reported similar findings. They found that rankings in national magazines did not have as large an impact on the enrollment decisions of students who entered public colleges and universities. There are some important differences, however, in the findings of these two studies for high-ability students and students with higher levels of parental income. McDonough et al. (1997) found that as student ability, parental income, and parental education increased, students were more likely to report that they thought rankings in national magazines were important in shaping their opinions about colleges. The authors conclude that students with the characteristics of applicants who would be likely to apply and enroll in highly competitive private colleges and universities were those most likely to rely upon college rankings as they make their decisions.

McDonough's (1994) research on the use of independent college counselors provides some insights into why some upper-middle-class families, more so than middle-class or low-income families, might rely more heavily on such sources as guidebooks and ratings. In her research on the use of independent college counselors, McDonough states, "Students have socially constructed themselves as college applicants needing professional assistance to stay competitive in the college access contest and have managed to create the conditions of a growth industry" (p. 444). In other words, parents have convinced themselves and their children that the only way to maintain higher social status and incomes is to attend more elite colleges and that private counselors help them to get into these schools. These same observations may explain why a small group of students and parents have started to place more emphasis on guidebooks and ratings.

The upshot of this limited research is that guidebooks and ratings have little or no impact on the college enrollment decisions of a large portion of high school students. Guidebooks and rankings appear to exert some influence on high-ability students from upper-middle-class and upper-class families, especially those most likely to attend highly selective institutions. Of course, these conclusions beg the question of how much college counselors, parents, and others might be influenced by ratings and guidebooks, and, in turn, influence students' decisions. Unfortunately, no research is available on this topic. But the impact of rankings and guidebooks could be more influential for more selective private colleges that seek to enroll large numbers of high ability students. Thus, there is reason to question why—as they affect so few students—guidebooks and ratings have received so much interest in recent years.

THE IMPACT OF GUIDEBOOKS AND RANKINGS ON INSTITUTIONAL ADMINISTRATORS

As already mentioned, media coverage in the *Wall Street Journal* as recently as 1995 documented the use of false data that was reported to rankings and guidebooks by colleges and universities (Stecklow, 1995a). *Wall Street Journal* reporter Steve Stecklow pointed out that inaccurate and misleading data are not uncommon in guidebooks. He noted examples of college administrators who have failed to report SAT scores or the high school rank of students admitted into special programs for underachieving students. He found that some institutions inflated their financial health. Stecklow uncovered evidence that some campus administrators intentionally provided incorrect or misleading information as part of their marketing strategies. In an earlier study, Charles Pollock (1992) found inconsistencies in the information reported in different guidebooks about the same college or university. He speculated that many institutions were neither careful nor consistent in how they reported institutional information to guidebook publishers. Pollock admonished high school guidance counselors, students, and parents to be careful in attaching too much importance to information found in guidebooks.

College and university administrators have not been silent about the rise of college rankings. Many senior college administrators and admissions personnel have raised serious questions about the validity of efforts to rank colleges or individual academic programs. This is clearly an area of contention between the media and institutions of higher education. Gerhard Casper (1997), president of the Stanford University, wrote a letter to *U.S. News & World Report* in which he stated, "I hope I have the standing to persuade you that much about these rankings—particularly their specious formulas and spurious precision—is utterly misleading."

The focus on the accuracy of information provided by institutions of higher education and the public criticisms of guidebooks and rankings by college administrators demonstrate that the level of awareness and concern about rankings and guidebooks in the higher education community is rising. As a group, college and university administrators display a love-hate attitude toward college rankings. For marketing purposes, many colleges and universities publicize their rankings when they are high and ignore them when they are low. As one director of admissions from a large public flagship institution stated: "We curse them as misguided and false when our college turns out bad. We quote them in our publications and college day programs as overdue praise from outside our walls when we turn out good."

This love-hate relationship is understandable. Even though researchers have greatly expanded our understanding of the college choice process and how colleges and universities can intervene to influence this process, the fact remains that researchers can still not accurately predict which colleges students will choose. Many admissions officers are still not sure which of their marketing and recruitment activities really make a difference and which have little or no impact. In the midst of these doubts, guidebooks and ratings can serve as another source of *uncertainty reduction,* something more tangible for senior campus administrators and admissions officers to point to in an effort to explain their success or failure in attracting the right number of students with a desirable set of academic and nonacademic attributes. Thus, college ratings can become something to which to attribute enrollment successes and failures.

College administrators and faculty, on the other hand, realize that measuring institutional quality is difficult. Hossler and Litten (1993) note that many guides and rating books make evaluative statements about campuses without providing any information as to how they secured data for their statements. This is not the case with such publications as *U.S. News & World Report's America's Best Colleges* or *Money Magazine's Best College Buys,* but it is true for other widely used rankings and guidebooks. For rankings publications, however, Hossler and Litten point out a more vexing problem. Absolute rankings accentuate relatively small differences among institutions. Fractions of percentage points may separate a public university ranked 7th from a university ranked 10th. Even the statistical difference between an institution ranked 7th and one ranked 27th may be small, yet students and parents may believe that there are large distinctions between these institutions.

As the visibility and attention given to college rankings has increased, the number of observers within and outside of the academy who are questioning how colleges and universities are responding to these publications has also grown. There is clear evidence of inaccurate or false information being provided to publishers of guidebooks and rankings and this, too, warrants further examination. Insights based on telephone conversations and E-mail interactions suggest that few colleges and universities intentionally falsify information. Approximately 20% of the responses I received to the information-gathering phone calls and E-mail for this section indicated that some campuses paid much attention to rankings. Many of these responses were not unethical or devious. For example, one campus reported that it was now giving weight to ACT scores in awarding its prestigious academic scholarships. Admittedly, the campus administrators with whom I was in contact do not constitute a random sample. The campuses intentionally misrepresenting institutional data were undoubtedly less likely to respond in a candid and open fashion to my queries. Although no compelling evidence of widespread falsification of institutional data materialized from this study, visible sources of pressure on campus administrators are apparent. Descriptions of these pressures and other themes that emerged from phone interviews and E-mail exchanges are presented in the rest of this section.

THE PRESSURES ON INSTITUTIONS

The most consistent responses suggest that few institutions put pressure on campus administrators or faculty to raise their institutional image. During my phone conversations and E-mail exchanges, I most frequently received information from admissions and institutional research administrators. They reported that the most recurrent source of pressure to enhance a campus's ranking appears to come from alumni. As one director of admissions at a medium-size private university wrote in an E-mail response:

> Each fall, the letters from puzzled, alarmed, and angry alumni begin to cross my desk. Of course, the size of the alumni association is dramatically larger than the size of the faculty and administration, so perhaps their "response rate" is actually quite low; however, for sheer numbers, they seem to be the most concerned. On the campus itself, there is no pressure.

Two or three responding administrators indicated that the president and the trustees paid close attention to rankings, but these responses were unusual. The conversations and E-mail notes I received indicated that most faculty are pretty sophisticated about rankings and that they do not take them too seriously. In keeping with the observation that external audiences such as alumni are often concerned about rankings, a small number of respondents said that vice presidents of institutional relations or directors of alumni affairs were most concerned about the ratings of their campuses. Along with admissions personnel, administrators concerned with public relations are likely to be more sensitive to the perceived impact of media such as college rankings. Thus, some institutions do face pressure when it comes to rankings. A senior, highly regarded vice president of enrollment management at one private university said that he was experiencing more "inducements" from senior campus administrators "to make our situation look better." The director of admissions at an elite university on the East Coast reported that a senior campus administrator made a personal visit to the editors of *U.S. News & World Report* after the campus dropped significantly in the rankings. A senior vice president at a regional public university disclosed that the president was "fixated on rankings" and that there was great pressure on everyone within the university to take all steps possible to increase the standing of the university.

These examples, however, were the exceptions. The most common concern reported by directors of institutional research and admissions officers was not about the pressure they are experiencing from alumni, trustees, faculty or the president. Rather, they were concerned with the time required to complete the growing number of information forms being requested by the publishers of guidebooks. A director of institutional research said that compiling the data to complete these surveys was taking increasingly more staff time with no additional staff resources. One problem, which may be a more frequent cause of inaccurate and conflicting information in ranking and guidebooks, is that many schools lack the databases, personnel, or both to complete each survey accurately and thoroughly. In the past it has not been uncommon for the task of completing a guidebook survey to be assigned to an assistant director of admissions who, in an effort to *get the damn thing done,* might estimate some figures just to get the survey in the mail.

This suggests a complex set of attitudes about guidebooks and rankings. Most college administrators are unwilling to ignore them. A few seem willing to falsify information to present their campuses in a favorable light. The majority feel compelled to provide information and expend staff time and resources to do so. There is also growing concern about the time required to provide this information. To remedy many of these problems, the American Association of Collegiate Registrars and Admissions Officers (AACRAO) is spearheading a movement to create a common data form for all guidebook publishers. The discussions even include the interesting possibility of charging a fee to publishers for completing their survey forms. There is a sense that publishers are making a great deal of money from these guidebooks and rankings and therefore it is only fair that they pay the growing costs of providing information. Professional associations such as that for college registrars have been trying to create such a form since the 1980s; however, there is a renewed interest in this goal.

Institutions vary in respect to the impact of rankings and guidebooks on institutions. Large public flagship institutions were most likely to report that rankings have little impact. Directors of institutional research or admissions directors were most likely to state that the guidebooks are generating little or no discussion on their campuses. One respondent from a public flagship institution said, "We pay attention to rankings but have not made any real or cosmetic changes in response to them." Interestingly, a small number of administrators said that rankings of graduate programs were generating more discussion. As part of their ranking efforts, *Business Week* magazine mails surveys to alumni and currently enrolled students at all business schools. One administrator reported that the dean of the business school had sent out letters to alumni and students enrolled in their MBA program that subtly encouraged them to rate their alma mater more favorably in order to boost the program's rankings.

At another research university, an institutional research oficer confided concerns that one of the academic units was touting the rankings it had received in the *Gourman Report*. This ranking report has been strongly criticized for its lack of validity (Webster, 1984). The director of institutional research at another university disclosed that someone had completed the *U.S. News & World Report* data sheet in a casual manner and provided estimates of graduate student GRE scores. The director noted that this school does not routinely store students' GRE scores; rather, these data are maintained by each department. She noted that she had not completed the questionnaire and was uncertain as to how the school had estimated its scores. She suspected that they had "rounded up."

Like public flagship universities, 4-year campuses that attract large numbers of commuting and nontraditional students are also not too concerned about rankings. Administrators at both public and private institutions share the same perspective. The vice president at one private university wrote in an E-mail note: "My institution has historically catered to working adults and part-time students. . . . College rankings, therefore, have not been much of an issue here."

The responses from public regional universities, however, imply that senior administrators are more likely to be concerned about where they are ranked. One enrollment dean at a regional state university reported that the president and other senior administrators are using the rankings as a target. He said that there was considerable effort to increase the quality of students, to increase merit-based financial aid, and to improve faculty salaries and other institutional expenditures that are used to calculate institutional rankings. Another administrator at a regional institution confided that his campus now gives more attention to student class rank for all merit scholarships because this is one of the variables included in calculating institutional rank in several publications that rank institutions. Finally, another vice president for student life at a regional campus concluded: "The president is totally preoccupied with rankings."

Several small and medium size private colleges similarly offered comments that indicate that there is more pressure on their campuses to respond to "how they place" in rankings and guidebooks. A vice president for enrollment management at a medium-size private university reported that there was pressure on her campus to report the math SAT scores of international students, but to withhold the verbal scores in order to improve the average SAT scores of entering students. The director of institutional research at a small liberal arts college said:

> The rankings have had subtle effects that have influenced some agendas. . . . The social science faculty believe that the failure to achieve distinction in the guides that rank/rate colleges is the result of a failure of the admissions and public relations offices to complete surveys with *"enthusiasm."*

The director of institutional research at another small private university divulged that the director of admissions who completed a survey omitted the grade point averages, class rank, and SAT scores of all students who were admitted conditionally in a special program for underachieving high school graduates. It is not surprising that some less visible regional private and public colleges and universities take guidebooks and rankings more seriously. These institutions constantly struggle for visibility and respect from their academic colleagues and from the general public.

Undoubtedly, this chapter would be more intriguing if I had found consistent evidence of wide-scale misrepresentation of information for ratings and guidebooks. It appears that, instead, there may be some pressure at a few institutions to withhold or falsify information to enhance their rankings. For many campuses, rankings and guidebooks have little or no impact on administrators or faculty. Public relations and admissions personnel use rankings when their campuses are ranked highly and ignore them when their institutions are ranked low.

A more pervasive effect of guidebooks on many institutional administrators and faculty is their influence on institutional priorities. Some of the criteria used in many ranking formulas include faculty salaries, improved retention rates, and library holdings. The use of rankings as benchmarks to improve salaries or library holdings would hardly be described as insidious on most college and university campuses. However, much like the problems associated with "teaching to the test" that occurs sometimes in public elementary and secondary schools, too much emphasis on rankings as benchmarks can lead to decisions that may enhance campus rankings but diminish the educational objectives of the institution. There are creative tensions inherent in the use of rankings as benchmarks. They can be helpful in achieving institutional goals, but they should never become ends unto themselves.

SUMMING UP

The rapid rise of rankings and guidebooks as yardsticks for measuring quality in higher education has caught many college and university administrators by surprise. The competitive nature of American higher education and a strong consumer-oriented relationship between students and institutions have created an environment that has facilitated the success of college ratings and guidebooks. Some publishers, *U.S. News & World Report* and *Money* magazine, for example, have found a strong market niche with their guidebooks and rankings. Clearly, they are providing a service for some segments of the American population.

As the sales of such publications have grown, the attention of more and more college administrators has been drawn to them and especially to their numerical ranking. At the moment, evidence from a variety of sources suggests that the impact of guidebooks on students and institutions is not as pronounced as the popular press might suggest. The limited available evidence suggests that the matriculation decisions of only a relatively small proportion of potential college students are strongly influenced by guidebooks and rankings. Similarly, guidebooks and rankings do not exert a strong influence on large numbers of college and university administrators.

In the context of all of the important issues that should influence students, parents, and institutional administrators, this is the way things should be. Despite the criticisms that have been leveled at publishers, they say it has never been their goal to exert a strong influence on students or institutions. In an interview, Al Sanoff, the managing editor of *U.S. News & World Report's America's Best Colleges*, said: "Not that many colleges and universities say what we do influences their behavior nor do we think what we do should influence them. . . . Nobody anticipated the success of our publication. We hit the right zeitgeist."

It is more difficult, however, to be certain about the long-term impact of guidebooks and rankings on institutions. Their high visibility is still a very recent phenomenon. It is not yet possible to determine their long-term impact as an important source of information. If they continue to garner high levels of visibility, then both the agenda-setting theory and social expectation theory would suggest that rankings will exert more influence over the college matriculation decisions of students and the advisory role that parents play (DeFleur & Dennis, 1996; Dominick, 1996). Even if the impact on the college choice decisions of students is less strongly influenced by rankings, the theory of the accumulation of minimal effects could eventually have a strong impact on the college choices students make (DeFleur & Dennis, 1996; Dominick, 1996). If the influence of college guidebooks and rankings on students and their parents increases, their impact on college and university administrators will also grow. Greater impact may increase the probability that more institutions will falsify data to enhance their rankings.

College and university administrators should be thoughtful as they ponder their own attitudes and how they direct admissions officers, institutional researchers, and others to respond to requests for information and the substance of guidebooks and rankings. Some administrators have manipulated admissions standards to raise their rankings (Hunter, 1995). In my research and consultation activities, I have had a number of opportunities to interact with faculty and campus level administrators about rankings. On several occasions, I have been surprised at the level of cynicism expressed about guidebooks and the information provided in them. Good scholars who would never "fudge" data for their own research often express attitudes that would make it easy for midlevel administrators to justify manipulating information to achieve desirable results. Rankings whose reliability, validity, and value have been routinely questioned by scholars have been used in institutional press releases if they make a campus look better. Presidents, academic administrators, and faculty who tout their rankings in guidebooks of questionable validity only enhance the possibility of unethical reporting of data. Such actions are eventually discovered and ultimately diminish the credibility of all institutions of higher education.

There is still much we don't know about the impact of rankings and guidebooks on prospective students and institutions of higher education. Clearly, college rankings, as a form of media, are having an impact on colleges and universities. Their effect on the college enrollment decisions of students and parents is less certain. Eventually, if college administrators conclude that rankings have little impact on the decisions of students, their influence on colleges and universities will wane. These findings lead to several potential questions that do not lend themselves to strong research designs or, therefore, to answers. Nevertheless, the topic will be an engaging one to follow for the next few years.

BIBLIOGRAPHY

Casper, G. (1997, January 5). Fighting the rankings of a college guide. *New York Times Education Life,* Section 4A, p. 17.

DeFleur, M. L., & Dennis, E. E. (1996). *Understanding mass communication.* Boston: Houghton Mifflin.

Dominick, J. R. (1996). *The dynamics of mass communication.* New York: McGraw-Hill.

Galotti, K. M., & Kozberg, S. F. (1996). Adolescents' experience of a life-framing decision. *Journal of Youth and Adolescence, 25,* 3–16.

Galotti, K. M., & Mark, M. C. (1994). How do high school students structure an important life decision? A short-term longitudinal study of the college decision-making process. *Research in Higher Education, 35,* 589–607.

Hamrick, F. A., & Hossler, D. (1996). The use of diverse information gathering methods in the postsecondary decision-making process. *Review of Higher Education, 19,* 179–198.

Hossler, D. (1991, November). Choosing colleges: A summary of a four-year study of college choice. Paper presented at the American Association of Collegiate Registrars and Admissions Officers Enrollment Management Conference, Atlanta.

Hossler, D., Braxton, J., & Coopersmith, G. (1989). Understanding student college choice. In J. Smart (Ed.), *Higher education: Handbook of theory and research, Vol. 5.* New York: Agathon.

Hossler, D., & Foley, E. (1995). In D. Walleri and M. K. Moss (Eds.), *New Directions in Institutional Research, No. 88: Evaluating and responding to college guidebooks and rankings.* San Francisco: Jossey-Bass.

Hossler, D., & Litten, L. H. (1993). *Mapping the higher education landscape.* New York: College Board.

Hossler, D., Schmit, J., Vesper, N., & Bouse, G. (1992). Final report: A longitudinal study of the postsecondary plans and activities of Indiana high school students and their parents. Report to the Lilly Endowment, Indiana University-Bloomington.

Hunter, B. (1995). College guidebooks: Background and development. In D. Walleri and M. K. Moss (Eds.), *New Directions in Institutional Research, No. 88: Evaluating and responding to college guidebooks and rankings.* San Francisco: Jossey-Bass.

Kotler, P., & Fox, K. (1985). *Strategic marketing for educational institutions.* Englewood Cliffs, NJ: Prentice-Hall.

Litten, L. H. (1986). Perspectives on pricing. In D. Hossler (Ed.), *New Directions in Higher Education, No. 53: Managing college enrollments.* San Francisco: Jossey-Bass.

McDonough, P. M. (1994). Buying and selling higher education: The social construction of the college applicant. *Journal of Higher Education, 65,* 427–446.

McDonough, P. M., Antonio, A. L., Walpole, M. B., & Perez, L. (1997). College rankings: Who uses them and with what impact. Paper presented at the Annual Meeting of the American Educational Research Association, Chicago, IL, March.

Paulsen, M. B. (1990). *College choice: Understanding student enrollment behavior.* (ASHE-ERIC Higher Education Report No. 6.) Washington, DC: Association for the Study of Higher Education.

Pollock, C. R. (1992). College guidebooks—users beware. *Journal of College Admissions, 135,* 21–28.

Schmit, J. (1991). An empirical look at the search stage of the student college choice model. Dissertation, Indiana University.

Stecklow, S. (1995a, April 5th). Colleges inflate SATs and graduation rates in popular guidebooks. *Wall Street Journal*, pp. A1, A4, A8.

Stecklow, S. (1995b, October 12). Universities face trouble for enhancing guide data. *Wall Street Journal*, p. B2.

Studentpoll. (1995, Fall). *1*(1).

Webster, David S. (1984, November/December). Who is Jack Gourman and why is he saying all those things about my college? *Change* magazine, pp. 14–20.

Webster, David S. (1986). *Academic quality rankings of American colleges and universities*. Springfield, IL: Charles C. Thomas.

Images of Education
in the Visual Media

In CHAPTER 12, Amy Stuart Wells and Todd W. Serman wonder why anyone who has seen Hollywood's version of an urban school, a favorite film subject, would ever want to work in one. The film world depicts schools as one big war zone, an approach that the authors say dates back more than 40 years, to the 1955 release of *Blackboard Jungle.* And even private schools come off as undesirable in the movies, often portrayed as places of oppression. Think about *Dead Poets Society.* The sole redeeming feature of the typical school, as detailed in a succession of films, is the lone, heroic teacher. Wells and Serman point to Samuel L. Jackson's Trevor Garfield in *187* to illustrate this genre. School administrators usually fare no better. "Hollywood principals regularly make disparaging remarks about students and their lack of intelligence or promise," say Wells and Serman.

Television, in its own special way, also fails to fulfill its potential in the news coverage of education. The problem is not so much negativity, often the charge against the print media, as it is the absence of education as a topic of coverage. "The real drama of the learning experience that touches every student somehow still eludes the incredibly versatile medium," writes George R. Kaplan in Chapter 13. He maintains that even with a multitude of cable outlets that crave programming, education still gets hardly a tumble. Kaplan says that the culprit is the bottom line, the profit-driven mentality that determines what gets on the tube and what does not. But he concedes that viewers do not flock to quality news coverage of education even on those unusual occasions when it is available.

This attitude by television's tastemakers also seems to prevail when it comes to the entertainment side of the business. In Chapter 14, John Leonard reviews the list of education-related shows that have fallen victim, usually rather swiftly, to ratings. For every *Gunsmoke* that kept Matt and Kitty hungering after each other for a couple of decades, there is a clutch of teacher series, such as the four that debuted in the fall of 1996 only to be canceled by the following summer. "There is no good reason why they shouldn't be celebrated on prime-time television, that honor roll and rap sheet of culture, at least as much as doctors, lawyers, cops, and cowboys," Leonard writes of teachers as subjects for series. He says that the content of an ongoing drama set at a school or a college might be uplifting to the audience. *Dangerous Minds,* a series that died quickly, Leonard asserts "was at least nostalgic for the bygone era when all of us had cherished teachers," and the short-lived *Christy* was "based on an idea as old as the Republic; . . . you can't afford to waste a single child."

CHAPTER 12

Education Against All Odds:
What Films Teach Us About Schools

AMY STUART WELLS AND TODD W. SERMAN

IF MOVIES were our primary source of information on the state of American education, teacher shortages in urban public schools would skyrocket. Quite simply, any teacher lacking the physical strength to throw gang bangers against walls or through windows would not apply. Movies tell us that suburban public schools have fewer gangs and less violence than their urban counterparts, but they are virtually run by bored, anti-intellectual adolescents majoring in sex, drugs, and delinquency. Of course, the alternative to public schools, according to Hollywood, is not so great either. The elite private prep schools with their ivy-covered walls and high-status curriculum are oppressive institutions full of snobby and obnoxious brats. Their main purpose appears to be beating the life out of children who thought education was about questioning and exploring ideas and not simply about maintaining tradition and upper-class solidarity.

Conscientious and caring parents (who are few and far between in movieland) would not dream of sending their children to any of the above. No wonder home schooling is on the rise. The only hope, in the celluloid world of education, is the heroic teacher—that superhuman agent of change, able to help promising students overcome all adversity, including poverty, gangs, peer pressure, and unreasonable parents. But they do not stop there. Our Hollywood teacher heroes frequently take on the entire corrupt educational "system," which generally encompasses a mass of self-interested school administrators, school board members or trustees, teachers, unions, and lawyers, as well as the rules and regulations they create.

Imaging Education: The Media and Schools in America. Copyright © 1998 by Teachers College, Columbia University. All rights reserved. ISBN 0-8077-3734-8 (pbk), ISBN 0-8077-3735-6 (cloth). Prior to photocopying items for classroom use, please contact the Copyright Clearance Center, Customer Service, 222 Rosewood Dr., Danvers, MA 01923, USA, tel. (508) 750-8400.

The basic plot of courageous teacher battling the system to save his or her students (or a subset of them) from a life of destitution has endured on the silver screen for more than 50 years. From Bette Davis as Miss Moffat in *The Corn Is Green* (1945) to Samuel L. Jackson as Mr. Garfield in *187* (1997), teachers in the movies have fought against all odds to educate their students. Despite this familiar plot, the school setting in which it unfolds has changed fairly dramatically over the years. The stakes are now higher for students, parents, and educators, as violence and death have become more frequent visitors to the classrooms and corridors of schools. We set out in this chapter to document these changes over time and to discuss the role of films in painting images of schools—images that moviegoers young and old carry with them when they go to school each day, decide whether to pursue a career in education, choose a school for their children, or vote on the next school bond issue.

Our goal was to learn how Hollywood has portrayed both public and private K–12 schools in major feature films. We wanted to examine the images of schools, students, and educators presented in widely distributed films over the past 6 decades to consider what possible lessons audiences may have gleaned from them. According to author bell hooks (1996), "cinema assumes a pedagogical role in the lives of many people" (p. 2). Films teach their audiences about both the real experiences of real people and imagined experiences of imaginary people. As hooks (1996) notes, films give us a "reimagined, reinvented version of the real" (p. 1) that may look somewhat familiar, but is actually a universe away the world of the real. She argues that the hint of the real meshed with the totally unreal is what makes movies so compelling.

We set out to study the "reimagined and reinvented" version of the real world of schools on videotapes and film reels. We soon realized that there are hundreds of movies with scenes inside schools and classrooms and that we needed to narrow what we meant by films about education. We were not, for instance, looking simply for movies about youth culture that use schools as a backdrop, a convenient location where adolescents interact. Such "youth culture" films as *Clueless* (1995), *The Breakfast Club* (1985), *Carrie* (1976) and *Heathers* (1989) come to mind as movies about adolescent rites of passage that happen in and around school, but are not necessarily shaped by educators in any meaningful way. These movies often include educators as characters, but they are generally minor roles and the interaction between the students and the educators is not central to the film. Of course, the distinctions between youth culture films and films about schools and education are blurry at best, and thus we included *Fast Times at Ridgemont High* (1982) in our sample, even though it is arguably as much about coming of age in suburbia as it is about the role the school plays in that process.

Also, all of the films we analyzed were about elementary or secondary schools and not about higher education. Although there are some powerful movies about life and learning on college campuses, including *Teacher's Pet* (1958), *School Daze* (1988) and *Higher Learning* (1995), these films and the issues they raise were beyond the scope of our study. Thus, we sought movies that presented images of K–12 schools and their impact on students. Also, because we wanted to look at popular feature films— those most enduring and broadly distributed—we used availability as one selection criteria, figuring that the most popular films would be the most readily available. The most popular classic films, such as *Good-bye, Mr. Chips* (1939) and *To Sir With Love* (1967), were readily available at the nearby video store. And most of the major films on education from the last 15 years, even those that were not blockbuster hits, such as *Class of 1999* (1990), were still available at one video store or another.

We found other films in the University of California–Los Angeles Film and Television Archive, which specializes in films from the 1940s and 1950s. Searching by computer in the archive led us to some movies we might otherwise have missed, such as *Bright Road* (1953), about an all-Black school in the South, with Harry Belafonte, and *A Child Is Waiting* (1963), about a school for students with mental disabilities starring Judy Garland and Burt Lancaster. Also, while we tried to restrict our sample to films about American schools, there were a handful of films about schools in the United Kingdom that are widely known on this side of the Atlantic, namely, *Good-bye, Mr. Chips* (1939), *The Corn Is Green* (1945), *The Belles of St. Trinidad's* (1954), *To Sir With Love* (1967), *Another Country* (1984), and *The Browning Version* (1994). We included these films in our analysis, given our goal of studying movies that have helped shape images of education among people in the United States.

And finally, we realize that several of the films we watched were made more than once and thus have at least two versions with different casts. When more than one version existed for films such as *The Corn Is Green*, *Good-bye, Mr. Chips*, and *The Browning Version*, we sometimes watched both versions, sometimes chose the one with a better reputation, and sometimes rented the version most readily available. Altogether, we watched 36 films (listed at the end of the chapter) and realized that though our list of movies is comprehensive, it is not exhaustive. Still, as far as we know, this is the most thorough study of films on education yet undertaken.

WHAT WE LEARNED ABOUT EDUCATION
AT THE MOVIES—TEACHERS AS HEROES

Clearly, the most central theme that emerges in film after film about schools is that of the idealistic and heroic teacher, fighting against all odds to save the deserving students through inspiration and motivation. This teacher-as-savior theme plays itself out in both poor public and wealthy private schools—from Garfield High School in the barrio of East Los Angeles to Welton Preparatory School in the New England countryside. In *Stand and Deliver* (1988), East Los Angeles teacher Jamie Escalante (played by Edward James Olmos) guides poor Latino students at Garfield through the most difficult high school math curriculum and exam, past a parade of teachers, administrators, and testing service cops who had not believed it possible. In *Dead Poets Society* (1989), teacher John Keating (Robin Williams) dares Waspy and wealthy prep school students at Welton to find their own voices even as their parents and educators try to stifle them.

Sometimes our heroes win, proving to others who have doubted them that they are right, that their students can learn, can succeed, can engage in the educational process. This was certainly the case for Escalante in *Stand and Deliver* (1988) when his students passed the Advanced Placement calculus exam, not once, but twice. But it was also true for other heroic teachers such as Miss Moffat in *The Corn Is Green* (1945), when poor Morgan Evans is offered a scholarship to go to Oxford University or for teacher Jane Richards in *Bright Road* (1953), when she final breaks through and reaches young C. T., an insightful but deeply troubled student. Similarly, teacher Louann Johnson (played by Michelle Pfeiffer) in *Dangerous Minds* (1995), takes a group of rowdy and disrespectful students and transforms them into young scholars eager to analyze poetry. As one of the students, who is saved by Johnson from dropping out of high school and the college prep track to attend an alternative program for pregnant teens, tells her teacher, "we see you as being our light."

Other times the victory is more pyrrhic, clouded by major setbacks and hard lessons. For instance, John Keating in *Dead Poets Society* (1989), lost his job, lost one of his best students to suicide, and lost faith in the other students, at least temporarily, when they betrayed him and contributed to his demise at the hands of the headmaster. Still, in the final scene of the movie, several of the boys defy the headmaster by standing on their desks to honor Keating and his unconventional teaching methods and romantic worldview. Although it is not clear what its implications are for the students as the headmaster yells at them to sit down, the symbolic act clearly pleases Keating as he leaves his classroom and the school for the last time (Cohen, 1996).

Similarly, in *Conrack* (1974), Pat Conrad, the White teacher on the all-Black island of Yamacraw in South Carolina, is fired in the end for taking his students across the river on Halloween to trick-or-treat in a White neighborhood. In the short time he was at the tiny, one-room Yamacraw Elementary School, he had become a popular teacher and had succeeded in turning his students on to music, history, geography, and much more. These accomplishments only made his sudden departure all the more tragic for the poor, Black students who had not been taught to read or write by their previous teachers. In *Mr. Holland's Opus* (1995), veteran music teacher Glenn Holland, played by Richard Dreyfuss, is laid off when the board of education cuts the music program at the high school. Hundreds of his former students show up for a farewell surprise performance of his *American Symphony,* and he is told by one of his first students, who has since gone on to become governor, that "there is not a life in this room that you have not touched." Still, Glenn is out of a job, and he fails to change the board of education members' minds about their decision to cut music out of the curriculum. He tells them that they have become "lazy" in accepting the budget crisis, but to no avail—even though some of these school board members are his former students as well.

Perhaps the most tragic heroic teacher of all is Trevor Garfield, a committed Black teacher and the central character in one of the most recent films about education, *187* (1997). Garfield ends up dead after deciding that the only way to stop the terrorizing gang members and save the good students in his Los Angeles high school is to take matters into his own hands by murdering the gang leader and attacking one of his disciples. In retaliation, gang members come after him, forcing him to kill himself. In the final scene of the movie, as Garfield's lifeless body lies in the county morgue, a student in whom he saw a lot of promise, Rita, is making a graduation speech. She tells the audience that she would not be graduating from high school had it not been for Mr. Garfield.

Win or lose, our teacher heroes always put up a good (and frequently, bloody) fight, and they usually manage to make the other teachers in their schools look bad—lazy, stupid, burned-out, or uncaring—in the process. There is the scene in *Up the Down Staircase* (1967) when suave English teacher Paul Barringer hears that another teacher, young and idealistic Sylvia Barrett (Sandy Duncan), was threatened by a student she was trying to inspire. He tells her she should take his advice about not caring so much. "You'll live longer," he says. The undaunted Barrett, still looking for a ray of hope, proceeds to tell Barringer about her student, who has requested more creative-writing assignments.

One such scene in *Blackboard Jungle* (1955) occurs after young Richard Dadier (Glenn Ford) is able to reach several students in his class of poor troubled boys through the use of cartoons. This leads to a lively and engaging discussion with students exploring the symbolic meanings behind the animated drawings. After the bell rings, veteran teacher Jim Murdock comes in to Dadier's class, noting that the boys in this dark urban vocational school may go for movies, but that will not teach them to read. Dadier, still excited about his pedagogical breakthrough, explains that he is using the cartoon as tool to get his students to use their imaginations and reach out for something—to get their minds out of comic books. "Minds?" Murdock replies. "A mind would indicate a brain."

The knack that these heroic teachers have for making their teacher colleagues look bad makes for many confrontational scenes in teachers' lounges and faculty meetings, as the idealists refuse to buy into the cynicism and hopelessness that permeates their schools. One of the most memorable of such faculty meeting scenes occurs in *Stand and Deliver* (1987), when Escalante announces he wants to teach calculus. The chair of the math department tries to prevent him, saying that these students cannot handle calculus. He says: "If they fail, it will shatter what little self-esteem they have. They are not the type to bounce back." A determined Escalante proclaims, "I teach calculus, or have a nice day." Often times the heroic teachers are White and most of the students are African American or Latino, which presents an interesting racial image of the "great White hope," arriving to save students who cannot or will not be saved by people of color. This great White hope phenomenon was most obvious in *Up the Down Staircase* (1967), *Conrack* (1974), *Dangerous Minds* (1995), and *The Substitute* (1996).

Despite their strong will, teacher heroes in movieland are prone to periods of self-doubt and proclamations that they are quitting, giving up teaching entirely. Generally, either students or a significant other (or both) convince the teachers to stay by telling them they are making a difference in the lives of young people. This talk-them-back-into-teaching scene occurs in a wide range of films, from the *Blackboard Jungle* (1955) to *Summer School* (1987). But it is particularly dramatic in the movie *Teachers* (1984), when Alex Jurel (played by Nick Nolte) decides to cave in under a political attack from a corrupt superintendent and resign before she tries to fire him. A former student turned lawyer who is suing the school district for educational malpractice steps in for a climactic scene. She takes off her clothes and runs naked through the halls of the school in a symbolic gesture, recalling when Jurel told her she does not know what goes on in Kennedy High School because she hides behind her memories and other shields. He said that until she walks naked through the halls of the school she will not understand the challenges the teachers face there every day. She takes him at his word, accusing him of being the one who is afraid to walk naked. "There's a whole room of kids in there and they need you and you need them," she says, ripping off every article of clothing. She succeeds in shocking Jurel into realizing that he must stay and fight for his job and for the students.

A GOOD PRINCIPAL IS HARD TO FIND

A few movies offer variations on the central theme of teacher as savior. Occasionally, the principal, not a teacher, is the hero. This was the case in two movies from the year 1987—*Lean On Me*, with Morgan Freeman as principal Joe Clark, and *The Principal*, starring James Belushi as principal Rick Latimer. Both of these characters have their share of faults: Clark degrades and bullies his teachers, and Latimer is a failed educator, "demoted" from a teaching job in a wealthy suburban school to be principal of a poor and violent high school on the other side of the tracks. Still, they both end up heroic, saving the good students in their schools from gang members and unmotivated teachers. And in Clark's case, he also succeeds in raising student's scores on the test of basic skills (of course, the fact that he also threw out many of the lowest-achieving students, could have had something to do with that). Still, much like the heroic teachers in other films, these two principals overcome seemingly insurmountable barriers to make their schools better places for the hard-working and dedicated students.

Of course, Clark and Latimer stand out all the more vividly in a sea of celluloid principals from hell. Perhaps the two most extreme such examples are in two recent films aimed at a young female audience. Never in any moviegoer's wildest imagination could more vile characters than Miss Trunchbull in *Matilda* (1996) or Miss Minchin in *A Little Princess* (1995) be found. Both of these headmistresses are angry old spinsters who seemingly have nothing better to do than torture young children. Miss Trunchbull actually hurls children through the air like a shotput and locks them in a creepy closet. Her motto is Use the rod, beat the child, and one of her hobbies is throwing darts at pictures of her students. Miss Minchin, another thoroughly deplorable character, prefers mental torture of the most vulnerable young girls at Miss Minchin's Seminary for Girls. She seemingly does everything in her power to break the spirit of the always hopeful Sara Crew. After the reported death of young Sara's father, Miss Minchin takes all of the child's worldly possessions and banishes her to a cold, bare, leaky attic, forcing her to clean up after and serve the other students for her room and board. When Sara's imagination and dreams prove stronger than Miss Minchin's evil spirit, the headmistress shakes with rage: "It's time you learn, Sara Crew, that real life has nothing to do with your little fantasy games. It's a cruel, nasty world out there, and it's our duty to make the best of it, not to indulge in ridicules dreams, but to be productive and useful."

Still there is something so extreme and so fictional about these two crazed women that they are less daunting than the more realistic and pathetic principals in charge of the film world's large urban high schools. Here, we find a plethora of principals who are corrupt, inept, immoral or spineless, or all of these, and who often serve as metaphors of a failed public education system. In two 1996 movies, *The Substitute* and a spoof called *High School High,* the principals use the schools as fronts for their drug-dealing operations. Although most movie principals are not quite that bad, virtually all of them try to thwart the valiant efforts of their heroic teachers. And although most of these principals demonstrate a lack of commitment toward or belief in the students in their schools, they frequently side with students who are in confrontations with teachers, in part due to their often stated fear of lawsuits.

One of the worst movies for principals of this genre is *187* (1997), in which teacher Garfield faces not one, but two nonsupportive principals who are more worried about getting sued than they are about the safety of teachers. The first principal, a White man in Black and Latino Roosevelt Whitney High School in Brooklyn, jeopardizes Garfield's safety by telling a gangster student that Garfield is failing him. When Garfield comes to the principal distraught over the markings of *187* (the police code for homicide) in a textbook the gangster left for him, the principal is more upset about the cost of the book than the implications of the threat to his teacher. He implies that Garfield is blowing the markings in the book out of proportion. He is at once dismissive and degrading, telling Garfield, "On the one hand you think someone is trying to kill you, and on the other hand, you actually think kids are paying attention in your classes." On the way back to his classroom from the principal's office, Garfield is brutally attacked by the feared gangster in the hallway of the school.

Months later, working as a substitute teacher in a high school in the San Fernando Valley, in Los Angeles, Garfield's watch is stolen by a gangster student in his class. The student complains to the principal that Garfield has accused him of stealing the watch. The principal calls Garfield into his office with the student and his friend present to interrogate the teacher about his reasons for suspecting the student. When Garfield asks the principal to search the lockers of these students to look for the watch, the principal refuses, stating that the school cannot afford another lawsuit and that he "works hard every day to think of the students at John Quincy Adams [High School] as my clients." An outraged Garfield asks the principal, a Mr. Garcia, whether he has ever been a teacher. Garcia explains that he "has never had the privilege" of being a teacher, adding that "being a principal and being a teacher do not necessarily go hand in hand."

Hollywood principals regularly make disparaging remarks about students and their lack of intelligence or promise. For instance, Mrs. Doyle, the principal in the comedy *High School High* (1996), proclaims that the students are "bigger boneheads than I thought, and everyone knows it except this fool," referring to heroic teacher Richard Clark (played by Jon Lovitz). Mrs. Scott, the Black principal of tiny Yamacraw Elementary School in the movie *Conrack* (1974), tells the children, "Most of you are slow. All of us know that. You don't think good." The image of a bankrupt public education system, mired in a set of rules and regulations that tie the hands of educators, make discipline of students impossible, and keep incompetent and uncaring teachers and administrators on the payroll, emerges from lines delivered by these rotten principals. Most are portrayed as control freaks who do not really care about students. There was, for instance, the principal at Parkmont High School in *Dangerous Minds* (1995), Mr. Grandy, who would not meet with a student coming to him for help and protection because the student did not knock before entering his office. The student is killed hours later by the very people from whom he had sought protection.

The bankrupt public education system also includes self-serving school superintendents and school board members who try to get rid of the heroic educators, or, as in the case of *Mr. Holland's Opus* (1995), eliminate entire departments. But, more often than not, it is the principal who plays the heavy, and thus becomes the symbol of what is wrong with public education. Yet, we do not mean to imply that private school principals— generally called headmasters or headmistresses—are portrayed in a more favorable light. As we mentioned, both Miss Minchin and Miss Trunchbull were more reminiscent of terrorists than of educators. Although they may not serve as symbols for a top-heavy and highly bureaucratic government-run system, they are symbols of a cold, calculated, cutthroat world of power and privilege. The headmaster in *The Browning Version* (1994) is just one example of a private school leader who will stop at nothing to please the powerful trustees and wealthy parents who are the schools' benefactors. After forcing teacher Andrew Crocker-Harris (Albert Finney) to resign because of his unpopularity with the students and trustees, the headmaster denies Crocker-Harris a pension and asks him to relinquish his customary right, as a senior teacher, to speak last at the prize-giving ceremony, for fear the less popular teacher will be "anticlimatic."

PUBLIC SCHOOLS AS WAR ZONES

Recent movies in particular leave moviegoers with an image of increasingly violent public schools enrolling dangerous and delinquent students. Although this trend started in 1955 with *Blackboard Jungle* and was prevalent in 1960s films such as *Up the Down Staircase* (1967), a flood of films released since the early 1980s, including *Class of 1984* (1982), *3:15: The Moment of Truth* (1986), *The Principal* (1987), *Class of 1999* (1990), *Dangerous Minds* (1995), *The Substitute* (1996), and, most recently, *187* (1997), have taken this theme to new extremes. Meanwhile, even though suburban schools in films such as *Fast Times at Ridgemont High* (1982) and *Rock 'n' Roll High School* (1979) are portrayed as less threatening and violent, they have their share of problems (after all, *Rock 'n' Roll High School* ends with the students blowing up the school). Still, teen sex and pregnancy are not at all uncommon in suburbia, nor are drugs. Also, the disdain for adults and the utter lack of respect for teachers and what they do is not unusual either.

In this latest era of films, inner-city public schools have become war zones. Metal detectors are de rigueur—no school is without one. School security guards play more prevalent roles. Surveillance cameras are as prevalent as light fixtures, and high fences (sometimes with barbed wire) are as common at city schools as are picket fences in suburbia. Threatening graffiti is smeared on every wall—inside the schools and out. Corridors are dark, dangerous, and depressing. Classrooms are not much better. Theme music has evolved from "Rock Around the Clock" in *Blackboard Jungle* to loud, pulsating gangsta rap with violent lyrics and ominous tones. The students, who are increasingly African American and Latino instead of White, have become more angry and more severe.

A public school teacher wrote about these movie images: Unflattering stereotypes of urban educators and students abound; administrators are either bumbling and inept, or are cold and slightly sadistic bureaucrats; teachers are burned out, incompetent, arrogant, fearful, or all of these; students are tuned out turned off, cunning, and often vicious, belong to street gangs, and carry weapons. (McLean, 1995) In many of these films, teachers and the nonviolent students walk in fear, facing constant verbal and physical threats. A sense of total disregard and disrespect for teachers and for all other adults prevails. Even in the relatively tame *Fame* (1980), a Black dance student named Leroy emerges as a threatening figure who somehow manages to progress from 9th to 12th grade in spite of his inability to read and his tendency to throw temper tantrums and break things. But this is nothing compared to later films.

In the early scenes of *Lean on Me* (1987), before principal Joe Clark shows up with his baseball bat, Eastside High is in a state of anarchy; student attacks on educators include a horrific scene in the cafeteria, where a student pounds a teacher's head into the floor. Clark and his security guards take an aggressive stance to kick out violent students. This turning point is illustrative of a shift taking place in films about urban public schools, as increasingly, our heroic teachers have become warriors, armed and ready to battle gang members who terrorize their schools, classrooms and hard-working students.

In the *Class of 1984* (1982), we see a mild-mannered music teacher turn, before our very eyes, into a Rambo-style vigilante, who, in the last scene, takes on and kills five gang members almost single-handedly. In *The Substitute* (1996), would-be teacher Shale (Tom Berenger), a mercenary, goes undercover as a substitute for his girlfriend who was attacked by a gang-member student at Columbus High in Miami. In the end, he calls on his former army buddies, and fellow mercenaries arrive to help break up a gang-related drug ring operating out of the basement of the school. And, as we mentioned, in *187* (1997), teacher Trevor Garfield, abused and abandoned by his principals and the "system," takes matters into his own hands and murders the most bothersome gang member. In *Class of 1999*'s (1990) Kennedy High School in Seattle, where security guards wear Darth Vader–like gas masks, robots posing as teachers are brought in by the "department of educational defense" to wrestle control of the schools from the gangs. When the robots—recycled from their military service—go haywire, they begin killing students for even minor infractions. The final scenes include a very violent and bloody battle between members of two student gangs and the robots.

What is interesting and perhaps most disheartening about how these films reinvent and reimagine the lives of inner-city students, is that they show (and so often grossly exaggerate) the anger and rage inside these students and how that shapes teens' behavior in schools. But these films rarely deal in any in-depth way with the societal causes of that rage and anger. Furthermore, whereas it appears that the movie industry has turned up the volume on violence in the schools, data from the National School Safety Center shows that the number of deaths that take place in schools has declined since the 1992–93 school year.

PRIVATE SCHOOLS AS OPPRESSIVE PLACES

At the same time that public schools are getting a bad rap in Hollywood, private schools, including the most elite boarding schools, are also fairing poorly on the big screen. While bratty students have been part of the private school film genre since *Good-bye, Mr. Chips* (1939) and *The Belles of St. Trinidad's* (1954), even these upper-class students have become more menacing in recent films. For instance, in *Another Country* (1984) and *School*

Ties (1992), boarding school students in both England and the United States are portrayed as vicious and vindictive Waspy boys who manage to make boarding school life horrible for a homosexual student in the first movie and a Jewish student in the second. Yet although these private school students are threatening in their own powerful way, they are rarely physically violent, as are the public school students in the inner city.

Furthermore, the private schools themselves often come across as stifling places, bounded by traditions that frequently seem so irrelevant to the needs of their wealthy but emotionally starved students. In *Good-bye, Mr. Chips* (1939), the headmaster of Brookfield School, Mr. Whetherby, says to the young Mr. Chipping on his first day of teaching, "Our profession is not an easy one, Mr. Chipping. It calls for something more than a university degree. Our business is to mold men, it demands character and courage and above all it demands ability to exercise authority."

Yet, the movies also show us that much of the authority that shapes elite private schools and their pedagogy appears to come from forces external to the institution, especially demands by powerful parents and college admissions offices. This theme holds at Brookfield, when at least 30 years later, another headmaster instructs an aging "Chips" to quit "clinging to the past" and teach the new pronunciation of Latin to make Brookfield an "up-to-date" school. Chips responds that he has watched all the traditions die one by one—grace, dignity, a feeling for the past. "All that matters here today is a fat bank account."

By the 1980s and 1990s, it appears to be very important to many educators and students in Hollywood's private schools to cling to "traditions" of power and exclusion and to suppress romantic ideals. In *Dead Poets Society* (1989), the four pillars of Welton Preparatory School are "Tradition, Honor, Discipline, and Excellence." Resting on these pillars, Welton is the self-proclaimed "best preparatory school in the country," sending 75% of its senior class to Ivy League universities. This is, after all, why Neil Perry's father has sacrificed to send his son to Welton, and not to go read poetry in a cave or to play the lead role in a Shakespearean play.

In *The Prime of Miss Jean Brodie* (1968), the romanticist teacher (played by Maggie Smith) at the Marcia Blaine School for Girls in Scotland is portrayed as horribly misguided in the end, sending a young girl off to die in a political struggle that neither she nor the student knows very much about. Still, the headmistress at Marcia Blaine, Miss Mackey, comes across as an infinitely less likable character, as she nags Miss Brodie to rein in her "progressive attitude" and to teach in a more conservative manner. She also inquires as to how Miss Brodie spends her weekends. At one point, when Miss Mackey is trying to force Miss Brodie to resign because of her unorthodox teaching and personal life, which has raised some eyebrows among the trustees, Miss Brodie exclaims, "I am a teacher, first, last and always . . . it is true, I am a strong influence on my girls, and I am proud of it. I influence them to be aware of all the possibilities of life—of beauty, honor, courage—and I do not influence them to look for slime where it does not exist." And yet, as in the other movies about private prep schools, the forces of conformity and authority prevail, drawing fairly rigid boundaries around educators and students alike. They cannot and will not question the status quo, namely the existing power relations that shape their futures and their advantage.

CONCLUSION

Sociologist Herbert Gans (1993) reminds us that creation and distribution of motion pictures is not purely an artistic endeavor, but is also a business, relying on the sale of theater tickets and video rental for profits. He notes that "entertainment caters to a set of specific and fickle audiences, and has to be, virtually by definition, deviant, daring, and even oppositional to the values of these audiences." Popular movies and TV programs are not about everyday marriage but about passionate or violent affairs; they do not deal with car theft, they deal with murder; they ignore life in the suburbs for life in the Mafia.

Clearly, Hollywood's portrayal of education reflects a grandiose, mafioso interpretation of life in schools. It may entertain us and occasionally keep us on the edges of our seats, but it will certainly not help foster public support of schools or educators. Nor is it likely to help solve the problems of unequal educational opportunity in this country, although it may give us hope that if we only had a few more heroic teachers to go around . . .

BIBLIOGRAPHY

Cohen, S. (1996). Postmodernism, the New Cultural History, Film: Resisting Images of Education. *Paedagogica Historica, 32* (2), 395–420.

Gans, H. J. (1993). Hollywood Entertainment: Commerce or Ideology? *Social Science Quarterly, 74* (1), 150–153.

hooks, bell. (1996). *Reel to Real: Race, Sex and Class at the Movies.* New York: Routledge.

McLean, M. M. (1995, September). It's a Blackboard Jungle Out There: The Impact of Media and Film on the Public's Perceptions of Violence in Schools.

MOVIE LIST

Another Country (1984)
The Belles of St. Trinidad's (1954)
Blackboard Jungle (1955)
Bright Road (1953)
The Browning Version (1994)
A Child Is Waiting (1963)
Class of 1984 (1982)
Class of 1999 (1990)
Conrack (1974)
Cooley High (1975)
The Corn Is Green (1945)
Dangerous Minds (1995)
Dead Poets Society (1989)
Fame (1980)
Fast Times at Ridgemont High (1982)
Good-bye, Mr. Chips (1939)
High School (1940)
High School High (1996)

Kindergarten Cop (1990)
Lean on Me (1987)
A Little Princess (1995)
Matilda (1996)
Mr. Holland's Opus (1995)
187 (1997)
The Principal (1987)
The Prime of Miss Jean Brodie (1968)
Rock 'n' Roll High School (1979)
School Ties (1992)
Stand and Deliver (1987)
The Substitute (1996)
Summer School (1987)
To Sir with Love (1967)
Teachers (1984)
3:15: The Moment of Truth (1986)
Three O'Clock High (1987)
Up the Down Staircase (1967)

A Gentleman's C
for TV's Education Coverage

GEORGE R. KAPLAN

As IT ENTERS its 6th decade as an encompassing force in American life, television has yet to come to terms with what 9 out of 10 Americans habitually place at or near the top of their worry lists: the condition of public education. The connection should be a natural for a medium that both entertains and informs, often brilliantly. But, to understate the obvious, education's story has enjoyed a less than spectacular run on TV. Although well over half the population depend on television as their primary news source, the medium has only intermittently delivered the goods on this crucially important domain of American life. As a result, the national conversation on our schools that this pervasive medium should be facilitating has yet to take its place as a fixture on national TV.

It is hardly a revelation that school people crave the recognition and legitimacy that television seems to confer on its subjects. And television's insatiable appetite for material to fill its endless program hours should play right into the waiting arms of the schools. But the real drama of the learning experience that touches every student somehow still eludes the incredibly versatile medium that has brought us Don Larsen's no-hitter (in practically prehistoric 1956), front-line coverage of numerous wars (starting with the Vietnam conflict in the mid-1960s), moon walks (a long generation ago, in 1969), and even the infamous O.J. Simpson trial of the 1990s.

The record of the commercial broadcast networks in covering education has been uneven at best and more often than not, plain dismal. Except for relatively brief stretches, the networks have not customarily employed

Imaging Education: The Media and Schools in America. Copyright © 1998 by Teachers College, Columbia University. All rights reserved. ISBN 0-8077-3734-8 (pbk), ISBN 0-8077-3735-6 (cloth). Prior to photocopying items for classroom use, please contact the Copyright Clearance Center, Customer Service, 222 Rosewood Dr., Danvers, MA 01923, USA, tel. (508) 750-8400.

full-time education reporters (nor has the supposedly education-oriented Public Broadcasting Service, since John Merrow's 5-year, 100-appearance stint with the *MacNeil/Lehrer NewsHour* ended in 1989). Yet, the networks do not hesitate to feature and often glamorize specialized correspondents for sports, foreign affairs, business, science, the law, health, politics, and assorted others. The schools have always beckoned, but their familiarity to TV audiences and their shortage of high drama and visual excitement have made them a tough sell. Even as the medium burnished its image as the nation's "Great Educator," much of its coverage of what is or ought to be happening in our schools has struck mass audiences as plodding, colorless, and forgettable. And, as a result, they pay scant attention to the limited amount of education coverage on network television. Ralph Waldo Emerson aptly noted that the very word *education* has a cold and hopeless sound to most Americans. "A treatise on education, a convention on education, a lecture, a system," he wrote, "affects us with a slight paralysis and a certain yawning of the jaws"(Aaron, 1989, p. 34).

Some of the blame belongs to the education establishment, which perceives little need to enliven its basic message: Providing a first-rate (sometimes erroneously called world-class) education for the children of the 1990s and beyond is an overarching national imperative and not a quiet stroll in the park. But most of the blame falls to a cutthroat, profit-driven commercial television enterprise that hungers for the breaking, visually compelling stories that lure audiences to the tube. The best that education ordinarily offers viewers are repetitive scenes from decaying inner-city schools and the banalities of too many White, middle-class, male school leaders in lifeless interviews or discussion panels. Hardly the stuff to stimulate advertisers. Sad to say, the kinds of school-connected stories that grab most viewers have little to do with learning or with issues that bedevil education's decision makers. Time after time, television highlights drug busts, violence, pregnant students, or the fulminations of religious fundamentalists on the allegedly lax moral and curricular standards of our schools. And even these succulent themes score poorly in commercial TV's relentlessly competitive race for ratings.

Although audiences for network coverage diminished precipitately with the growth and maturation of cable TV and the arrival of new electronic media forms, the early evening broadcasts of the major commercial networks were still America's most watched TV news programs in the mid- and late 1990s. Despite their claims of responsible impartiality, however, they have historically shortchanged children and schools. All three—ABC, CBS, and NBC—as well as cable outlets—CNN, Fox News Channel, and MSNBC—still churn out roughly 22 minutes of news per half-hour. In a typical year, though, only a microscopic proportion of the stories in those

22 minutes are on education. Occasionally, as in the case of ABC's long-running "American Agenda" segments on its early evening news program, education has received top billing. Regrettably, these well-meant 5- to 7-minute exposures have comprised only a small fraction of the news and feature-story content of the single commercial network that has consistently—and with some justification when compared to its peers—prided itself on its reporting on education. Ordinarily, though, it takes such an event as a school visit or speech by a president or first lady to rate instant and universal coverage from the networks. President Clinton's 15-minute effusion on education in the 1997 State of the Union address attracted a predictably high volume of reporting and postmortem analysis, but much of the emphasis was on its political and economic implications and not on the implications for schooling.

The ritual flurry of education-focused programs that fill the screens and airwaves when a window of opportunity opens at the start of the school year are usually relevant and sometimes of top-notch quality. Once the school year is properly under way, though, the TV spotlight blurs, and coverage of the schools reverts to its haphazard ways, with education's constituency struggling for every minute of decent airtime it can get on network news or as a documentary subject. Although the urge to scandalize often prevails, television's limited treatment of this huge continuing story can also be sober and well intentioned. Sometimes, as when the National Education Association aired eight weekly half-hour programs called *School Stories*, there is reason to hope that provocative and well-produced shows, whether commissioned by a teachers union or the Christian Coalition, might reach appropriate audiences, especially parents, school people, and political policy makers. The subjects of *School Stories* were eclectic—reaching emotionally disturbed children, sparking students' imagination, connecting with business, and plugging into technology, for example—with an underlying theme of how teachers and students are, in the NEA's words, "overcoming today's education challenges."

The series was solid, on-site television and a worthy companion to the NEA-underwritten *Teacher TV*, a continuing series intended mostly for teachers and other educators that, according to the NEA, drew favorable responses from lay audiences. But two possibly avoidable factors inhibited *School Stories* from garnering wide critical praise and reaching the audiences it deserved. Instead of appearing on a commercial network, CNN, or PBS, all of whom might have rejected the series on grounds that it could be interpreted as an "infomercial" or a long paid advertisement by the NEA, the programs appeared on The Learning Channel at 12:30 P.M. on 8 Sundays from October 13 to December 8, 1996. Unfortunately, The Learning Channel's actual audiences are, at best, in the low six figures, as compared with the millions who watch most network shows. Also, at 12:30 P.M. on autumn Sundays, the hoopla surrounding the National Football League's weekly games has already begun. For better or worse, potential viewers are lunching after church, settling in for a long afternoon of football or light fare on TV, or preparing for family activities. Reruns of *School Stories* continued past the football season, but, in the absence of a commissioned survey, there was no way of determining whether they reached a respectably sized audience.

One of the oft-cited deterrents to estimating the impact of TV programs dealing with education is the chronic uncertainty about the size and nature of the audience. Does it represent the desired mix of concerned parents, educators, policy makers, and the public at large—in essence, the audience that favors such offerings as the Disney Channel's annual teacher awards and the quarterly Merrow Reports on PBS? Is such praiseworthy fare seen mainly by public education's core of true believers, or do its critics also benefit from or even watch it?

Lamentably, there are no hard and fast answers to these questions. The ratings services such as A. C. Nielsen, which track commercial television's programs, also monitor PBS and such cable giants as CNN, ESPN, HBO, Disney, USA Network, and C-SPAN. But there is no reliable way to judge the size or composition of the viewing audience of such less-known education- and public affairs–slanted cable channels as The Learning Channel. The NEA did not commission a ratings service for *School Stories*. And even the virtuous PBS does not always represent itself entirely accurately. PBS, like National Public Radio, at budget-submission time boasts of audiences that mirror the diversity of the nation. But when the same services appeal for corporate support to underwrite more and better programs, they often depict themselves as serving primarily an economically and culturally advanced clientele.

EXPANDING OUTLETS WITHOUT
EXPANDING EDUCATION COVERAGE

In sum, the nation finds itself with choices that could hardly have been imagined a decade ago and that will inevitably have a potent effect on how the electronic media, especially TV, inform people. These options include CD-ROMs, computer conferencing, new-generation satellite arrangements, sophisticated VCRs, compact discs, various TV-telephone-computer combinations, and, of course, the now ubiquitous Internet with its Web sites. The array of possibilities of the emerging interactive digital age is staggering. Some will work out and others will not. But whatever the most workable configuration turns out to be, the lineup of electronic communications vehicles is destined to change.

Paralleling these advances in communications technology has been a series of seismic shifts in the patterns of program delivery. Until the early 1980s, the lineup of TV channels available in most communities was pretty well set: the three national networks, a PBS station, one or two local independents, and, for fewer than 20% of the country's households, some cable channels offering an uninspiring diet of sitcom reruns, vintage films, and some local-access content. Some of us also had soon-to-be-obsolete Betamax videocassette recorders. But on the whole, American families were satisfied with, even grateful for, what was available on the 1.7 TV sets in each household. Today, with a once unimaginable choice of TV fare available across the country, the number of TV offerings on education has also increased. But determining whether more and different people are watching the programs is guesswork at best.

As the century winds down, an overwhelming volume and variety of choices of programming is available, though quantity does not necessarily mean quality, nor does it mean more coverage of education. Americans have become so inured to—or cursed by—the rapid changes in technology that even the widely hailed prospect of having 500 channels at their beck and call, and in high-definition at that, does not bedazzle them. The panoply of choices already available to the nearly 70% of American households that subscribe to a cable service in the late 1990s reaches 50 or more channels, and many cable providers routinely offer such public affairs-oriented channels as Arts and Entertainment; the Discovery, Learning and History Channels, C-SPAN, and CNBC—nearly all of them and diverse others available around the clock and offering some kind of educational content 7 days a week, 52 weeks of the year. Add the Fox News Channel, MSNBC, and as many as a half-dozen local access or institutional channels, many of them originating in schools and colleges, and the potential for a reasonably curious person to stay in touch with nearly any subject appears to be limitless. Educational issues will inevitably get more play than they did in the mid-1990s.

Of the unsung features of this user-friendly electronic bounty, one of the most underrated is the remote-control clicker, which makes surfing across the channels a cinch, while exerting at least indirect pressure on networks, local TV stations, and cable channels to dish up eye-catching program content or risk being zapped. Even the only mildly curious viewer has the capacity to replace sluggish TV offerings with something livelier and possibly more informative. This caution applies in varying degree to all program providers, but, as more noncommercial local access channels become available and, in time, learn how to produce viewer-friendly, socially useful TV, it would seem to be especially relevant to them. For an exercise in unrelieved boredom for most viewers, though, it may be hard to beat a live televised rendition of a discussion panel of parents and local educators or, worse yet, a typical school board meeting. In most American households, both would be prime candidates for elimination by the nearest clicker.

The problem here, as sponsors and station managers attest, is that people simply do not care to watch TV programs on education The subject itself may be to blame. When PBS airs a documentary segment on, for example, air safety or alleged Balkan atrocities, interested and curious audiences are unlikely to tune out; they may not know as much about these subjects as they would like, and, for them, viewing a thoughtfully produced program is mind extending. But try capturing the same audiences for a potentially award-winning network special on, say, an inner-city school's success in shedding a legacy of failure, and, unless controversial local interests are at stake, the channel presenting it might as well be dark. After 12 to 16 years of school—even more in the case of audiences for public television and the "high-brow" cable channels—and additional years as parents of school-age children, TV-viewing Americans may be forgiven if they regard themselves as well-informed, even expert, on public education.

Conceptually and artistically, documentary TV about education tries mightily to compete with the major players. It surely does not warrant the indifference that greets it. Although few productions on any topic approach the standards of *High School,* Frederick Wiseman's 1968 trailblazer, typical in-depth shows on both commercial and public TV usually deliver an adequate, if inoffensive, blend of footage of children in classrooms, conversations between TV celebrity hosts and teachers and specialists, and brief interviews with experts or policy-influencing "deep thinkers." This predictably fail-safe, if unimaginative, format leaves viewers with a nodding acquaintance with the topic but little sense of its larger implications.

Fortuitously, public television, at least, can boast one huge deviation from this standard: the body of work of John Merrow, the Michael Jordan of electronic media coverage of education. His current incarnation as the producer-host of The Merrow Report on PBS furnishes an ongoing lesson in how to communicate what American education is about and how it connects to the larger society. No theme is off-limits, and no ideological mindset prevails in Merrow's uniformly thoughtful and provocative programs. They are always stimulating and often downright entertaining as well. With a Harvard doctorate, teaching experience at several levels, an imposing inventory of well-written publications and scripts, an attractive TV presence, and the instincts of the prize-winning investigative reporter that he would have been on any beat, Merrow is superbly equipped to bring education's story to the nation's TV viewers. Over a 25-year span—he was still in his 20s when his career in nationwide broadcasting on education began at National Public Radio in 1973—he has covered every story of consequence that might tell us something about how children learn, think, and live.

One of the signature features that separate The Merrow Report from the rest—whether on commercial, public, or cable TV—is the program's insistence on tracking and revisiting issues and people. No creditable reporting, says Merrow, should stop with a single exposure to a news-worthy story. He scrupulously chronicles evolving attitudes, successes and failures, and the march of issues and events to give the interested viewer the depth of knowledge and understanding that should undergird respon-sible citizenship. Picking up on this point in the Martin Buskin memorial lecture at the 1996 national seminar of the Education Writers Association, the noted historian of education David Tyack complimented Merrow for his "wonderful television documentaries . . . [which do] not just [present] one-time snapshots, but [go] back time and again to see changes over time."

The return visit, a Merrow trademark, may cover one topic at one school in several visits over a year's time. It may also offer hour-long dissections of such front-page topics as the problems and prospects of charter schools in Arizona, California, and Minnesota over a year or 2 or on the odyssey in Philadelphia of a controversial new superintendent who promised to leave the job if his 10-point plan to reform the city's schools didn't succeed. In sev-eral documentary "magazines" in his "Learning Matters" series for The Learning Channel in the 1992–93 school year, Merrow tracked the profes-sional journeys of three first-year teachers. More recently, The Merrow Re-port has followed groups of first-, second-, and third-grade children as they coped with reading and mathematics, as taught in various ways, during a school year. Some of his findings, especially on the merits of phonics versus whole language-based instruction, have doubtless disturbed progressive school people, but the purveyors of education's more conventional wisdom are equally susceptible to the Merrow treatment. He has been a relentless observer/reporter of the uses and abuses of technology in schools, a con-cern that has brought his viewers into countless classrooms where the won-ders—and problems—of infusing cyberspace into daily classroom instruc-tion are becoming facts of daily life.

Once past John Merrow, the journey is far less rewarding. The occa-sional Bill Moyers education special on PBS—the best of the rest in most respects—is usually well done, especially when it provides insights into the thinking of such people as the writers Jonathan Kozol and Mike Rose. But the inevitable panel discussion with students, parents, educators, and a semi-informed politician or two is customarily labored and unfocused.

Sad to say, the level of discussion in TV documentaries or news specials on education in general is usually pedestrian, and notably so on nationally broadcast shows, where discourse seldom rises to the level of analysis. These programs are devoid of complexity or subtlety as some participants parade their ignorance of anything that happened in America's schools before they got there. They are supposedly balanced by the commentators, who appear unshakeably convinced that nothing that has transpired since they left school 35 or more years ago can match the quality of their schooling in education's no-nonsense good old days—whenever they were.

The high-quality single-subject documentary has been dying a slow death on commercial television, but its nominal successor, the one-hour TV magazine containing several unrelated stories, may be an even less felicitous vehicle for covering education, unless someone as closely attuned to the scene as Merrow creates it. Patterned after CBS's venerable and enormously successful 60 Minutes, such pretenders as 48 Hours, Prime Time Live, 20/20, and Dateline simply do not have education in their line of vision. Nor, unless a principal burns a school down or a teacher murders a student, is an educational topic likely to get there more than a few times in a typical year. For any story to get what passes for decent coverage on these documentary "magazines" it must (1) be shocking or outlandish (scandals in Washington are foreordained winners); (2) feature a free-speaking celebrity of the moment (Howard Stern or Madonna will usually do); (3) receive heavy advance billing as a newsworthy scoop (for instance, H. Ross Perot's various announcements and pronouncements on Larry King Live on CNN); (4) dissect a best-selling book with its author on hand to promote it (Bob Woodward of All the President's Men fame, is a biennial regular); (5) purport to expose the real truth about a current development or personality in sports, politics, or show business; or (6) present a real live hero (General Norman Schwarzkopf of Gulf War renown, for example). Sometimes, as when a magazine is riding high, it may get lucky and nail all six of these in one of its four 12-minute segments.

Along with such back-of-the-book subjects as religion and science, education is not on the regular dockets of these shows. And its customary absence from the daytime shock shows of the likes of Maury Povich, Jenny Jones, and Montel Williams is probably a blessing in disguise. Their political siblings, the mud-wrestling "shout 'n' scream" offerings such as The McLaughlin Group on PBS (and a few non-PBS stations) and The Capital Gang on CNN, occasionally mention education in passing, but often to make the larger point that our civic institutions are headed for the dumpster, and the schools are leading the way. Almost without exception, these commercially successful shows treat education as a throwaway subject, one to be mentioned only in passing. Participants are only too eager to get to the stuff that sells beer and cars: moral decay and political corruption.

Sadly, this bottom-line value system does little to satisfy the curiosity and concern most Americans have about public education. But network and cable executives generally favor contentious panelists of media celebrities and magazine-type offerings because they are cheap, profitable, and easy to produce. Typical of the state of the art of magazine shows is CNN's *Impact*, which made its debut in March 1997 with an offering of drug corruption in Tijuana, Mexico, sexual harassment of women in iron-ore mines in Minnesota, the implications of cloning, and a segment on *Rent* (the rock version of *La Boheme*) and the death of its creator. The second show highlighted ethnic cleansing in Serbia, unsafe sex among homosexual men, the smuggling of rare birds, and a television miracle healer. No room for education to make the cut in a series of this type unless it can provide an elevating segment on date rape by student-athletes or the murderous intentions of a parent of a high school cheerleader in Texas.

Perhaps being left out is preferable to being subjected to this kind of attention. It is punishment enough, even for television addicts, to sit through foolish sitcoms representing school life as peopled by wacky teachers, irrepressible kids, and bonehead administrators vying with each other to do outrageous things such as staging a school fund-raiser at a strip joint. This is a far cry from the earnest, socially responsible *Mr. Peepers, Room 222*, and *Mr. Novak* of an earlier TV generation. One can only imagine the reactions of immigrant parents and children on witnessing the distorted, context-free version that network TV so often presents in its dramatic offerings on life in the nation's high schools. Elementary school children seem to be largely off-limits as sitcom subjects; their antics are evidently not sufficiently outrageous.

Nor, at the other end of the student age spectrum, is higher education a favored subject for sitcoms or, perhaps more significantly, for critical analysis in any TV format. The medium almost never showcases the nation's colleges and universities. Indeed, were it not for the networks' and cable's coverage of college basketball and football, and occasional mention of the universities where faculty members may have carried out noteworthy research, weeks could go by without reference to these institutions. Unlike public school educators, though, postsecondary education's experts in numerous fields are regular participants, sometimes even hosts, in some of television's most worthwhile documentaries and forums. The late Carl Sagan of Cornell, Stephen Jay Gould of Harvard, Robert Dallek of Boston University, and countless law professors, political scientists, and medical school faculty members, in particular, have long been familiar figures on TV, although mainly on PBS and the less-watched education-oriented cable channels.

But these academic stars do not appear on television to talk about the problems of higher education or even to represent the institutions that pay their salaries. They are highly valued knowledge-producers and commentators whose research and opinions can only help fuel the already widespread public impression that our colleges and universities are pretty special places and thus immune to the constant criticism that bedevils K–12 education. To most Americans, the issues that worry the domain of higher education—such dependables as rising costs, faculty tenure, student performance, admission standards, and the rest—do not begin to compare, either in scope or gravity, to the multifront array of concerns that face our schools. Perhaps they should, but TV's decision makers do not see it that way, and higher education gets what amounts to a free ride.

As a general rule, news divisions of local stations, whether independents or network affiliated, have always offered the most consistent and inclusive reporting on education. With local school systems gobbling up as much as half of a community's tax revenues and often dominating its political discourse, viewer interest is more than casual. Local stations have thus become a relatively dependable information source on elementary and secondary education in most areas of the country. Presumably reflecting our national concern, coverage that was once confined to school closings or sports scores now casts a wider net. Even hour-long documentaries or series on local educational issues, produced on the proverbial shoestring, are not uncommon. But stations are more likely than not to schedule such programs in non-prime-time slots or as throwaways in prime time against such competition as *Seinfeld* or the Super Bowl.

It is remarkable, given the often meager news budgets of local TV and radio stations and demands on the time of staffers covering several beats, that so many of these outlets cover their communities' schools so well. And with the growth of regional and local all-news all-day cable outlets, reporting on a locality's educational issues should in time come to display more insight and incisiveness than it has to date. But even now the series and individual programs on local educational topics that surface as candidates for various media awards are setting a refreshingly high standard for the specialty.

The same cannot yet be said about many of the citizen-access channels that cable companies are obligated to provide for use by colleges, school systems, and local government as part of their service contracts with municipalities and counties. Though underfinanced (some simply cannot afford to be on the air for more than a couple of hours a day), unwatched, and often amateurishly managed, a growing number of these channels offer a stimulating variety of homegrown, sometimes delightfully off-beat, programming that is responsive to the needs of local people and organizations.

In some exurban, rural, and otherwise remote communities, they have been almost literally a lifeline to trends, events, and contemporary thinking that might otherwise have passed them by. And education plays a prominent, frequently leading, role in such areas. How much of an effect the Internet will eventually have in supplanting or supplementing these services is still difficult to tell; much will depend on the availability and cost of the equipment.

TALK, TALK, TALK—BUT NOT ABOUT EDUCATION

The advent of all-talk, as distinct from all-news, cable TV and the vast expansion of its radio counterpart in the 1990s has done little to alter the electronic media's coverage of education. All-talk broadcasting has dispensed blizzards of opinion that have surely colored the views of the relatively small numbers of those who watch all-day talk TV and the millions who have become devotees of the radio version. The latter often have a smorgasbord of choices, and education is a favorite subject. No longer straightjacketed by what used to be called the "equal time" or "fairness doctrine" requirement of the federal government that was eliminated in the 1980s, and thus free to offer commentators of any political persuasion that they feel will attract viewers and listeners, networks and stations have usually gone the conservative route. This is the proclivity of most owners, and, equally important, the right-wingers are customarily more lively and therefore more attractive to sponsors. The end of the "equal time" obligation has meant that Rush Limbaugh is free to promote his unfailingly conservative daily take on hundreds of radio and TV stations without sponsors or stations having to worry about giving time to those who would presume to represent the other side. No challenger has come close to matching his ratings.

Watching and listening to Limbaugh, Kate O'Beirne, Robert Novak, Armstrong Williams, and sundry other conservative icons could convince some audiences that public education is a toxic waste dump, that private school choice represents the only real alternative, and that teachers unions should be abolished. And these are the reasonable opinions. In a zone of their own, armed with all kinds of data and opinions of doubtful veracity that they unload as ultimate truth, are the more extreme commentators on the Right, mesmerizing communicators who treat public education as yet another manifestation of godless statism, dangerous socialism, and even diabolical satanism. All government is evil, but public schools—or government schools, as some apostles of the hard Right call them—typify it at its worst.

These hard-core conservative commentators are wondrously articulate and persuasive masters of the memorable TV and radio sound bite. Unlike all but a few of public education's public backers, they are colorful characters, always ready to rail, electronically or in person, at the evils, not just the ills, of public education in general and urban school systems in particular to any audience that will watch, listen, or both. Since the publication of the Reagan administration's reform manifesto, *A Nation at Risk,* in 1983, the national debate on school reform has raged, but the debate lost some of its edge with the death in 1997 of the American Federation of Teachers' Albert Shanker, a towering and profoundly respected force in every serious debate on educational issues for over 20 years. Unfortunately, however sound and principled their case may or may not be, most of public education's defenders and supporters of reform-from-within are professors, bureaucrats, education writers, and functionaries of Washington-based education associations and not professional publicists. They are far removed from education's real battlefields. Most register, even with sympathetic audiences, as well-meaning but humorless functionaries possessing few of the skills demanded by TV and radio.

By a substantial margin, the most telegenic and authoritative presence on national education issues in the 1990s has been President Clinton. Enviably knowledgeable about and dedicated to improving the country's schools, Clinton is a master at packaging public education's messages. He can outtalk most others who wade into the fray without taking a deep breath when the subject is education. But in his second term, the one in which education was to top the national agenda, Clinton's pleas for public support of sensible reform, frequently issued in TV and print photo-op visits to inner-city schools, were often drowned out by the media's—and the nation's—preoccupation with the political scandal *de jour.* Few experiences could be more disillusioning for education's backers than watching a network TV report on a presidential visit to an urban school degenerate into a a testy exchange on campaign finance with persistent reporters. Somehow, some distraction like this always seems to come along to deflate the hopes of education's advocates that, energized by an education president to whom TV has always been kind, the schools will have their day on the ever seductive screen. No time could have been more propitious for TV viewers to get up to speed on education than the moment in history when President Clinton began his second term blessed with a prosperous national economy and no major international problems to worry about. The ever potent bully pulpit of commercial TV stood ready to be used, but the idea of preaching about schools and children when the presidency itself was in trouble over ethical matters was far less attractive than it might once have been.

Perhaps television was never meant to be cast in the role of education's honest broker or publicist-in-chief. With the networks and the most popular cable channels engaged in a permanent competition for viewers to watch their escapist fare, the idea of upgrading, or even perpetuating, the long-running national debate on the schools on TV is not especially appealing to the medium's movers and shakers. There will always be public TV or something like it for viewers desiring less frivolous programming, but much of its generally serious-minded and usually better-educated audience is already on board, reasonably well posted on the school scene and not dependent on TV for very much. Preaching to the converted does little to advance an idea.

The impact of another factor, the concentration of ownership of the networks and stronger cable operations in the hands of a few entertainment superpowers, may prove to be substantial and even positive for education. Although network TV had attained once unthinkable levels of witlessness and editorial blandness long before the arrival of Disney (ABC), General Electric (NBC), Westinghouse (CBS), Time-Warner (CNN), and News Corporation (Fox), the prospect that these media giants would encourage bold stands on most public issues was none too hopeful. But acting responsibly toward public education has long been one way for the profit-obsessed megacorporations to make points with many viewers while not going too deeply out of pocket in the process. Several of the networks' parent companies have traditionally traveled this route.

Such largesse, if that is what it is, may do little for a media corporation's bottom line in the short run. But over time, as thousands of firms have learned, a proschool stance, accompanied by a few relatively low-cost programs such as the venerable, highly respected Westinghouse Science Talent Search, can help build relatively agreeable corporate profiles. This does not mean that most of the TV operations of these media behemoths will not continue to insult the intelligence and offend the sensibilities of thinking viewers of all ages. Nor does it improve the likelihood that the networks will exert themselves to provide any more programming about education than the meager ration they now offer.

The people who run commercial TV are sophisticated marketers of their products. Their constant search for what does or does not constitute decent TV while racking up profits must be feather-tip sensitive to public tastes. And no amount of market research is apt to reveal that the viewing public prefers to learn more about national educational standards, tax credits, or literacy than it does about the merrymaking of that wild and crazy *Friends* gang. When tired footage of classrooms fills the screen as talking heads pontificate on these issues, a high boredom quotient is bound to result. For better or worse, the stock items of The Great Education Debate simply are not attractive TV material. To paraphrase the late Spiro T. Agnew: Once you've seen one inner-city school, you've seen them all.

Like the other media, TV has no obligation to cast public education—or any subject—in a positive light that serious investigation has determined may not be warranted. But worthiness does not necessarily rank among the principal criteria for broadcasting news, documentaries, or even sitcoms. In contrast to public radio—the electronic medium that consistently produces coverage of education—television, by and large, has proved to be inadequate in providing viewers the full, all-sides treatment the subject deserves and the medium should be offering. At best, it earns a gentleman's C. It understands the subject and recognizes its importance. But it is not making much of an effort to master it.

BIBLIOGRAPHY

Aaron, D. (1989, October 9). The worldly puritan. *The New Republic*, p. 34.

Educating Television

JOHN LEONARD

LIKE TELEVISION, I'm going to tell some stories, so that maybe from the mustering of a few intimate details we will arrive at the Bigger Pixel.

There was Jonathan Kozol on public TV on a Thursday night in September in 1996 talking about how little money our nation spends on educating the children of the poor, and how much we seem to resent even these pinched pennies. The splendid rage of this Citizen of Virtue—if Robespierre came to mind, so did Spinoza grinding lenses—reminded me of 30 years ago in Boston, where the very same Kozol had shamed me into teaching reading and composition to an attic full of teenaged girls in an Episcopal church in the Roxbury ghetto. These quick-witted, slow-burning, high-flying Caribbean birds of paradise had been discarded by Boston's School Committee: bagged, tagged, and trashed. Yet they'd show up 2 nights a week in our attic, to read Paule Marshall and Ralph Ellison, to discover metaphor in the lyrics of Bob Dylan, to proceed from diary keeping to short story writing, and to tell me things I had not wanted to know about the streets. Much later, I would receive invitations to several graduations from colleges such as Spelman and Shaw. But this was some years after all we yogurt-faced do-gooders had been told to leave Roxbury in the spring of 1967, pursuant to the secret resolutions of the Newark Black Power Conference. Or else.

As furious as I was to be bagged, tagged, and trashed myself, in obedience to the new line of Fanonized yard goods, I was also relieved. Teaching was harder work than writing novels. I would try it again, for a year in the late 1970s, commuting by Metroliner between New York and Philadelphia for a fiction workshop at Penn, which was harder than writing articles

Imaging Education: The Media and Schools in America. Copyright © 1998 by Teachers College, Columbia University. All rights reserved. ISBN 0-8077-3734-8 (pbk), ISBN 0-8077-3735-6 (cloth). Prior to photocopying items for classroom use, please contact the Copyright Clearance Center, Customer Service, 222 Rosewood Dr., Danvers, MA 01923, USA, tel. (508) 750-8400.

for the *New York Times*. And I would try teaching for a third time for several years in the late 1980s at Columbia, by bus to Morningside Heights for weekly seminars on practical criticism, which was harder than reviewing books for National Public Radio, television for *New York* magazine, and the politics of culture for *New York Newsday*—especially since all the J-school grad students wanted from me were trade secrets on the *trick* of attitudinizing, as if they already knew how to think.

I miss Roxbury, but not teaching. The pay's lousy, and not only do students talk back, but they're also needy. They have alcoholic fathers, passive-aggressive mothers, problems of sexual identity and anxieties about money; and I am not worthy. I know just how unworthy I am by looking around me. I am surrounded by real teachers. My wife teaches history and political science at a private school in Manhattan. My daughter teaches the Middle Ages and the Reformation, and my daughter-in-law teaches comparative literature and postmodern theory, to college freshpersons on the Left Coast. My stepdaughter, when she isn't writing for the slicks, tutors troubled kids in English, French, and math. They are heroic, and there is no good reason why they shouldn't be celebrated on prime-time television, that honor roll and rap sheet of the culture, at least as much as doctors, lawyers, cops, and cowboys. Most of us, after all, will spend more time in school than we will in hospitals, courts, or prisons, not to mention on a horse.

But it hasn't worked out that way. While, if I may be briefly postmodern, the TV schedule is subject to periodic seizures of enthusiasm for the classroom as a contested site for competing narratives—for instance *five* new teacher series in the fall of 1996—the audience resists. The audience has always resisted. *Gunsmoke* moseyed on for 20 years in prime time, and *Perry Mason* kept winning cases for 17, but you won't find a single teacher show in the top 100 TV series since 1948. *Mr. Peepers*, with Wally Cox teaching science and Tony Randall teaching history, lasted 3 years in the 1950s, and got its highest rating when Mr. Robinson married the school nurse. *Our Miss Brooks*, with Eve Arden teaching English and Richard Crenna teaching biology, lasted 4 in the same decade, though Miss Brooks didn't get to marry Mr. Boynton until they made a Hollywood movie. *Mr. Novak*, with James Franciscus teaching English and Dean Jagger and Burgess Meredith as principals, lasted just 2 seasons in the 1960s. *Room 222*, with Lloyd Haynes teaching history and facing up in the inner city to drugs, dropouts, and racial bias, had a comparatively long run of 4½ seasons, through January 1974.

Although *Fame*, set in New York City's High School for the Performing Arts—and introducing us to the talents of Debbie Allen, Lori Singer, Cynthia Gibb, Janet Jackson, Nia Peeples, Carrie Hamilton, and Eric

Pierpoint—also lasted 4 years in independent syndication, it had been can-celed by the NBC network after a single season, in 1982–1983. Likewise, the CBS network had canceled *Paper Chase*, with John Houseman as the imperious professor of contract law, after a single season, in 1978–1979, before it went into another couple of years of cable TV production. *The Bronx Zoo*, with Ed Asner playing a high school principal very much like Lou Grant, also vanished after a single difficult season, 1987–1988, during which Ed himself got shot. *TV 101*, a dramatic series about a high school media workshop, got the ax after one controversial season during which it had the temerity to suggest that a pregnant teenager might actually contem-plate having an abortion. Perhaps it isn't fair to mention *Gideon Oliver*, with Louis Gosset Jr. as a Columbia University anthropology professor, since he was too busy fighting tongs and cults ever to bother with a college class-room, but he was canceled, anyway, after only half a year in 1989. Nor did Montel Williams do much better, despite the help of veteran filmmakers such as Joan Micklin Silver, moonlighting from his talk show for one ab-breviated season in 1995 as an ex–Green Beret teaching high school science.

Slapstick seasoned with stupidity apparently contributes to a longer run. *Welcome Back, Kotter* lasted 4 years on ABC in the late 1970s, with Gabe Kaplan indulging a Brooklyn high school remedial class of "sweathogs" that included John Travolta. *Head of the Class* lasted 5 on the same network, from 1986 through 1991, with Howard Hesseman as the substitute teacher of a class of nerdy geniuses—among them Robin Givens before she mar-ried Mike Tyson—who knew everything about physics, literature, and the density of oxygen on Mars, but nothing about sex or baseball. (From *Head of the Class*, besides jokes about Einstein, Phil Donahue, Marilyn Monroe, William F. Buckley Jr., and "getting it on with Sara Lee," we also learned that all of the poems of Emily Dickinson can be sung to the tune of "The Yellow Rose of Texas.") We seem more comfortable spending classroom time in the company of scholar-athletes, as in *The White Shadow*, with Ken Howard as a White coach of a mostly Black high school basketball team, which lasted 3 years on CBS, and *Coach*, with Craig T. Nelson in charge of a state college football team, which ran for an astonishing 8 years on ABC. Nostalgia for the old *Cosby Show* perhaps accounts for our putting up with *A Different World* for 5-plus seasons on NBC, even after Denise Huxtable (Lisa Bonet) vanished from a Hillman College campus where nobody ever went to class anyway. *The Wonder Years* isn't usually counted as a school show, although, in the 6-season span of this growing-up-in-the-sixties sitcom, Fred Savage spent more time daydreaming at Robert F. Kennedy Junior High School than he did at home with his bewildered parents.

Of those five new teacher series in the fall of 1996, four were canceled in the summer of 1997: *Dangerous Minds*, a movie spin-off with Annie Potts in the Michelle Pfeiffer role of an ex-marine who brought to her class-room the compassion and cunning of a social worker and a nun, plus the survival skills of a navy Seal and a Zapatista; *Pearl,* in which Malcolm McDowell as a god-like college professor met more than his caustic match in Rhea Pearlman as the blue-collar grandmother (with idiosyncratic opinions on Moby Dick as Charlie the Tuna) who had decided that it's never too late to go back to school; *The Steve Harvey Show,* with the comic as a 1960s soul musician reduced to teaching music and drama to an out-of-control hip-hop generation ("I haven't worked this hard since I filled in for one of the Pips"); and *Mr. Rhodes,* with Tom Rhodes as a worst-selling novelist who, between Michelle Pfeiffer jokes, would rather teach *The Electric Kool-Aid Acid Test* than *Silas Marner* at a stuffy prep school. The worst of these five survived for a 2nd season on the fledgling seminetwork WB: *Nick Freno: Licensed Teacher,* in which Mitch Mullany, as an out-of-work actor, "emotionally stunted man-child," and Jim Carrey wannabee, substitute-taught with Forrest Gump shrimp boat jokes while leaving his needy students in the lurch whenever there was a part in a soap opera to audition for.

Never mind that most teachers aren't former musicians, or unemployed actors, or failed novelists, or ex-marines. They're actually in it for the teaching, sort of like Prometheus. And never mind, either, that the five series varied wildly in quality. It was still cause for cheer that Plato, Shakespeare, Keats, Melville, George Eliot, Robert Frost, John Steinbeck, and both Tom and Thomas Wolfe were spoken of in prime time as if they mattered; that, while politicians demagoggled about uniforms and vouchers and curfews and bell curves, television was reminding us that once upon a time public schools embodied the very meaning of this country—before we decided we'd rather not pay property taxes.

Annie Potts was in fact far more persuasive in the TV version of *Dangerous Minds* than Pfeiffer had been as a black-belt biker chick in the movie. Dressed as if in a hurry at night in a burning building, oddly vagrant like a rock-band roadie, fiercely inward, with memories of guns in Texas, Potts had some cool and edgy street in her. From previous duty in sitcoms such as *Designing Women* and *Love and War,* she brought not only her usual smart mouth but also a "been-there" credibility to this inner-city "academy" program for grown-up-too-quickly *problem* children, with their high IQs and low self-esteem and gaudy self-sabotaging behaviors, their gang colors and their babies. She was her own subtext, teaching *Of Mice and Men* as if with a rodent in her pocket, teaching *Look Homeward, Angel* as though she'd run away with a circus. She was lots more hands-on than is strictly permissible in today's supersensitive public school system, where an incautious hug can get you suspended for child molestation, and not above bribing kids to perform, and one began to wonder if all her students would wind up living in her house, like in an R. D. Laing therapeutic commune. But good educators always break the rules to save a child. *Dangerous Minds* was at least nostagic for the bygone era when all of us had cherished teachers—instead of border guards—who sought to engage us in classrooms that weren't impossibly overcrowded, in buildings that weren't falling down, in neighborhoods that didn't resemble Belfast or Beirut; back when public schools were trampolines from which we bounced into our futures, instead of warehouses with metal detectors or detention camps for refugees.

Never mind, because generally speaking the public has been impatient with even the best teacher programs, whether they're set on a college campus, at a high school, or even in a day care center. You may not even remember *Day by Day*, a short-lived half-hour NBC series with Linda Kelsey, formerly a reporter on the *Lou Grant* show, as a lawyer who, on the occasion of the birth of her second child, with her stockbroker husband dropped out of the rat race to run a depot for tiny tots in her own home. The timing, 1988, was unfortunate, in the middle of the crazy witch hunt for satanic ritual abusers in day care centers all over the country. The TV audience found it easier to identify with Linda's money-loving and child-disdaining yupscale chum, Julia Louis-Dreyfus, who would go on to costar in *Seinfeld*, that immensely popular cheese doodle of urban fecklessness, Chinese take-out, and penis jokes, in which everybody wears a prophylactic smirk.

Likewise gone, after a single quality season, in 1993, on Fox, is *Class of '96*, a dramatic series set on a New England college campus. Perhaps because executive producer John Romano had actually professed some English at an Ivy League college before he migrated to Burbank, the goings-on at "Havenhurst" were not only literate but guilty of association, like language itself, with rational comment and abstract ideas. The working-class scholarship hunk (Jason Gedrick) was an upwardly mobile reader of Melville. The suburban princess (Lisa Dean Ryan) was so embarrassed to be rich, she unpacked her luggage into cardboard boxes and dismissed her father's limo before setting dainty foot on campus. Other freshpersons were Black, or blonde, or a computer wonk, or the daughter of a famous actress nobody else had heard of, or a son of whom so much was demanded by his father that he drank himself dumb. Adults included Mason Adams as the college president, Madolyn Smith Osborne as a new dean who had once been a student radical, and various familiar faces as professors of English, history, mathematics, and economics.

Without neglecting hormones or rock music, *Class of '96* was neither porky nor jaded. Everybody at Havenhurst seemed to know that there's something else to do with your mind besides blow it. If the students were fresh, nomads of knowledge, so, too, were shocks of recognition, rushes of friendship, the giddiness and terror of inventing brand new selves, the discovery that life is sometimes true or false and sometimes essay questions. This wasn't at all the sense of college we got from, say, the Bennington novels of Donna Tartt, whose *Secret History* degenerated after 200 pages into an excess of Greek love among vampire support groupies, and Bret Easton Ellis, in whose *Rules of Attraction* the life of the mind was less compelling than the immune systems and urine samples of the characters. Or even from the campus novels of Mary McCarthy, Randall Jarrell, Bernard Malamud, and William Gass in which students, whenever mentioned at all, hung upside down like bats in the belfries of the crazed and horny professors.

I mourn even more the brief passing of *My So-Called Life*, which came and went on ABC in 1994–1995 while persisting a season longer in reruns on MTV. Think of it as *fifteensomething*, a lowering of their sights from boomer weltschmerz to Gen-Y angst by the executive producers of *thirtysomething*. If you thought the folks on *thirtysomething* spent too much time feeling sorry for themselves, they were only lukewarming up to curdle. It's taken most of us most of our lives and several momentous occasions ever to feel as bad for 10 minutes as the suburban high school kids in *My So-Called Life* feel *all* the time, and they have apparently felt that bad since Pampers. What's amazing is that we love them, anyway. We would have to be insensate indeed, comatose in our comfort zones, not to remember what it felt like to open our lockers on a heart of darkness, to discover teen sex and adult hypocrisy, mean streets and betrayed friendships, black holes and vertigo, as well as the subversive texts that break the code and the subversive music that seems to sing it. When 15-year-old Angela (Claire Danes) was 12, "my mother gave me these sex talks and I don't think either of us has ever recovered." Though she used to be close to her father, "my breasts came between us." While she's supposed to be reading Kafka, all she thinks about instead is Jordan Catalno, a hunk so inarticulate he is either an Aztec god, a Nordic rune, or a cementhead: "Why is it *he* gets to be the one with other things on his mind?" From what she has seen at home and school, Angela develops grave doubts: "If we all did what was in our hearts, the world would grind to a halt." These doubts are seconded by her closest friends.

If skeptical, morose, goofy, romantic Danes is an unfinished symphony with more phases than the moon, A. J. Langer as Ray-anne, voted "best potential slut" in the sophomore class by a poll of jocks, is light, heat, energy, and sarcasm. Wilson Cruz as Rickie, their half-African, half-Latino, wholly androgynous Third Musketeer in these high school wars, is a marvel of dignified vulnerability; gay-bashed, he will insist on eyeliner, honoring his own confusions. What's more, mirabile dictu, they are actually learning something in school. They read Anne Frank, and then discuss it with a cop who brings them home to their troubled parents. They connect the dots between a science lab experiment on a pig's heart and what goes on in the parking lot at a school dance. They find in Kafka's "Metamorphosis" a variety of their own irrational self-loathing. As Angela navigates on sympathy and cunning through an opaque world, she has a better built-in moral compass than she seems to think, and a voice as distinctive as J. D. Salinger's Holden Caulfield or Mark Twain's Huck Finn, before Huck lit off for the territory on that famous raft. That the great waste of unwashed Nielsens so resoundingly rejected this series—an honorable alternative to *Heathers* on the one hand and to *Clueless* on the other—leads me to believe that it's time we stopped asking what television has done to the attention span of the American public, and begun instead to wonder what the attention span of the American public has done to television.

Christy, a 1994 CBS series based on Catherine Marshall's lovely (if sentimental) novel, was another mass-market failure in the teaching sweepstakes. It was based on an idea as old as the Republic, and as recently expressed as the Peace Corps and Vista programs in the Great Society '60s: You can't afford to waste a single child, and the privileged young invest themselves, and everybody learns how little we really knew about each other. Kellie Martin, who grew up as Becca in the wonderful series *Life Goes On*, starred as Christy, an idealistic 19-year-old who left genteel Asheville, North Carolina, in 1912 to teach in a missionary school in Appalachia. There, to assist her in her own education, were Stewart Finlay-McLennan, as the widowed doctor who gave her a dress to wear. And Randall Batinkoff, as the handsome young minister who started the school. And Tess Harper, as the mountain woman Fairlight Spencer, who can do everything but read. And Tyne Daly, as a gun-toting Quaker surprise: "Were you meant to come here and serve, or were you only running away from home?" Plus, of course, the children, all 12 grades of them, as young as 5 or older than Christy; sleepy, because they got up before dawn; barefoot, because they couldn't afford shoes; a girl who wouldn't talk; a boy who lied all the time; hogs under the floorboards and a pet raccoon.

In one episode, Christy's failure to understand the local moonshine culture caused her school to burn down. In another, having acquainted her class with where they'd come from—with Bonnie Prince Charlie and the Scottish Highlands—she had to depend on a bagpipe-playing ghost to save a wayward waif. I'd have thought we'd all identify with Christy; ache for the misapprehensions and the condescensions, the quick temper and quicker despair, the huge ambition and modest results, the terrible doubts and romantic entanglements; and then rejoice in her ability to bounce—

because, of course, one of these children was secretly reading *David Copper-field*, and another would grow up to write his own novels, and a third would maybe invest herself in passionate teaching, and, out of moonshine, cabinet making, history lessons, cartwheels, bagpipes, and an ax, the Republic would compose its music. But *Christy*, after such promising ratings for its 2-hour pilot, fell off the charts into an occasional holiday special, like the long-gone John-Boy *Waltons*.

WHY IS EDUCATION A TERMINAL CASE?

Why don't school shows work on television? Maybe most of us hated high school and would rather not be reminded of our psychic pimples and never again want to take another test. Maybe most of us are cowboys, preferring the saloon tart to the civilizing schoolmarm. Maybe the culture itself thinks teachers have it too easy in the Darwinian tooth-and-claw, taking the summer off to read books and plan courses, which is also why we underpay them. And maybe the answer is as simple as our pulp appetite for brutal closure. Like many another noble noodle, including presumably the readers of this book, instead of one more cop show I'd personally prefer a weekly series in which social problems are solved through creative nonviolence after a Quaker meeting by a collective of vegetarian carpenters.

But our abiding narratives are deathward—and have been since at least those first westerns, the Old Testament and the *Iliad*, not to exclude a no less bloody-minded *Mahabhatata*—all about clout, turf, sexual property rights, and how to look good dying. And America—from Wounded Knee to lynching-bees, from the Knights of Labor to the Ku Klux Klan, from Haymarket and Homestead to Harlan County and the Black Hole of Ludlow, from race riots and Ghost Dance Wars to Hell's Angels, Black Panthers, Attica and Altamont—has a history of violence as gaudy as any in the industrialized world. Oddly enough, we now blame TV for promoting this violence among our youth, whereas once upon an earlier time we blamed the public schools for what went wrong with the little people. So a buck-grubbing, status-grabbing, commodity-obsessed tantrum-yoga culture that measures everyone by his or her ability to produce wealth, and morally condemns anyone who fails to prosper, blames its angry incoherence not on itself, but on anything else, from original sin to recessive genes, alien abduction, demonic possession, Arab terrorists, Madonna and the designated hitter. But I digress . . .

How we loved Christa McAuliffe, the schoolteacher who left New Hampshire for the stars in our stead, on board the Challenger. We loved the TV movie about her almost as much. We had perhaps dreamt of our-

selves as lifting off to probe either Mars or the music of the outer spheres
. . . of gravity's slingshot and ghostly white against black nothing, of earth-
rise and earthset, of immensity and silence, free fall, space curve, time warp,
light wave . . . On January 28, 1986, with the children of America watching
on television, for 73 seconds McAuliffe was air-borne. And then the seven
Challenger astronauts were dead. And Peggy Noonan wrote a lovely
eulogy for the president to lip-synch. And everybody talked about O-rings
in the solid booster rocket. And maybe that's what happens to teachers in
the real Darwinian world, when they put on airs.

The 1990 ABC docudrama *Challenger* was a meticulous account of the
6-month NASA training period for those seven astronauts prior to launch.
It hurt to watch. It seems to me unfair of the producers to have cast Karen
Allen as McAuliffe. In the opinion of many of us, Indiana Jones went down-
hill after *Raiders of the Lost Ark* because Allen wasn't in the sequels. Frizzy-
haired and freckled, with a smile like a field of sunflowers, she so much
embodied McAuliffe's eagerness to please, to experience, to share, that we
ached all over again. No wonder everybody was always giving her an
apple. Not that the *Challenger* space shuttle wasn't an equal-opportunity
disaster. The flight deck was also stacked with another woman, a Japanese
American from Hawaii, and only the second African American ever to be
sent into outer space, Dr Ronald McNair, played by that Brother from
Another Planet, Joe Morton—perhaps the most complex of the astronauts,
a sax player, a karate black belt, and a laser physicist.

As the docudrama moved these astronauts around, however, from
Houston to Huntsville, Alabama, to the Kennedy Space Center at Cape
Canaveral (authentic NASA locations, like the sacred sites of departed Dru-
ids, Stonehenge as a launching pad) and introduced both their families and
their contractors (Lockheed, Rockwell, Morton-Thiokol) and advised us of
gale winds that forced recovery vessels back to port, of the lowest tempera-
tures ever for a shuttle liftoff, of so much solid ice at the launching site that
it looked on the TV monitors "like something out of *Dr. Zhivago,*" we were
also moving around some mythic baggage. The rest of them were pros; this
was their career. McAuliffe was an amateur, a stranger in this strange boy's-
book land so full of hardware and mysticism, Sputniks and Star Wars. And
thus, when they slipped the surely bonds of earth to touch the face of God,
she was our innocence. To gravity's rainbow we lost our teacher and were
no longer permitted to be children. That's narrative: no school tomorrow.

This, I admit, is a harsh reading. But education is in increments, not
explosions. It has been better served by television as a 24-hour machine
for grinding out narrative, novelty, and distraction, surprise and empathy
and news and laughs, an electronic classroom of high-culture snippets and
vulgar celebrity, a place to celebrate and a place to mourn, a circus and a

wishing well, than by television as a representation of what teaching really feels like. On television before midnight: anthropology. After midnight: archeology. Via public TV, that remedial seriousness, we commune with the spoon-billed bee-eaters and the midwife toads. From the networks, we ought to have learned to recognize the predators and parasites in Washington and on Wall Street. Commercials themselves are a crash course in advanced capitalism: overproduction and forced consumption. Whereas the humble little red schoolhouse or concrete bunker, well, when it's not about babysitting and vocational guidance and guns and drugs and pregnancy and AIDS, it's about making distinctions and connections; about surprise, wonder, passion, and regret; about citizenship and critical intelligence.

After serving her time in public schools from Oakland, California, to Bedford-Stuyvesant, Brooklyn, my wife ended up in a Manhattan private school for girls, and still feels guilty about it, but is nonetheless determined to teach internal contradictions to the daughters of the ruling class. Which explains her long afternoons of coaching debate or running off to another symposium on multiculturalism, her longer nights of planning and grading, those frantic phone calls from seniors needing college recommendations, the predawn spice smells of Chinese or Mexican food for a classroom banquet after the latest Third World survey, the missing weekends when she's gone to Washington with busloads of the best and brightest for a protest demonstration or to Bard to bring back a whole new way to teach reading, her disappearance for 2 years into meetings of the committee on faculty development and evaluation, as if into the black hole of a dead star, those summers she spends pretending to look at palaces and pyramids while secretly dreaming up entire new curricula, full of feminist jumping beans, on macroeconomics and comparative political systems, brand-new menus of distinctions, connections and mighty scourging doubts. So many children, in the kitchen, in the garden, on the stoop, their eyes the true color of Byzantine icons, of smoke and flame.

Before we were married, I thought history was what White men did in the daytime. Imagine, then, living with a Braudelian, an Annaliste: Weather, she will explain, and infant mortality statistics; the compass and commode; plague and gunpowder, sewage and forks, the Inquisition and the Invisible Hand; the Paris Commune, the Industrial Revolution, gunboat diplomacy, women's suffrage; surplus value, false consciousness, bad faith, brainwashing and foot binding. On the occasion of her birthday several years ago, her eighth graders staged a surprise party in the classroom, and this is what they sang to her, just like Judy Collins:

As we go marching, marching/ in the beauty of the day,
A million darkened kitchens/ a thousand mill lofts gray,

Are touched with all the radiance/ that the sudden sun discloses,
For the people hear us singing:/ "Bread and roses! Bread and roses!"

There is, of course, a second verse:

As we go marching, marching,/ we battle too for men,
For they are women's children,/ and we mother them again.
Our lives shall not be sweated/ from birth until life closes;
Hearts starve as well as bodies;/ give us bread, but give us roses!

This, alas, is the sort of education we seldom hear about on television, where no teacher ever seems to have more than one class, instead of the usual seven, as well as the sort of education we seem to have stopped insisting on in the true colors of the scorching day.

Toward Greater
Responsibility by All

GENE I. MAEROFF

EDUCATION AND the media are locked in a symbiotic relationship that—like a bad marriage—leaves both parties feeling uncomfortable and, often, less than satisfied. What occurs in schools and colleges, like it or not, has news and entertainment significance and the media are not apt to ignore these events. The media need education in the same way that they need government, politics, culture, international affairs, sports, and the other areas of endeavor that provide material to fill the hungry column inches and voracious airtime that must continuously be fed. What emanates from schools and colleges provides a portion of the fodder that is the raison d'être for the media's very existence.

Disgruntled educators might say that the relationship is one-sided and that they could just as readily forgo it. Educators may very well find appeal in the notion that newspapers that ignore schools and colleges would then report no bad news about them. Late-night news reports on television, devoid of any coverage of schools, would cease to show them as places of unremitting violence, sexual misbehavior, and ignorant students. Similarly, the demise of college guidebooks would remove a thorn from the side of administrators. An end to the reporting of test results by the media would mean diminished pressure and less misunderstanding. And if Hollywood omitted from its films any depiction of educators and places of education, it would spell an end to portrayals that seldom are positive except for the role of the lone, heroic teacher who stands up against a corrupt and violent system.

Imaging Education: The Media and Schools in America. Copyright © 1998 by Teachers College, Columbia University. All rights reserved. ISBN 0-8077-3734-8 (pbk), ISBN 0-8077-3735-6 (cloth). Prior to photocopying items for classroom use, please contact the Copyright Clearance Center, Customer Service, 222 Rosewood Dr., Danvers, MA 01923, USA, tel. (508) 750-8400.

But the public would be poorer for the loss. Admittedly, coverage of education is not all that it might be. The public, however, deserves to be well-informed about education. States and localities spend more tax monies on education than on any other single expenditure item. Students in elementary and secondary schools and in colleges and universities are engaged in pursuits that in no way should be hidden from public view. The answer, in light of the standoff between the media and education, is not less coverage but better coverage. In much the same way, if television sitcoms and movies depict education in stereotypical terms, what is needed are stories that more closely track the truth. Education belongs in the media. The media, ideally, belong to the people, and if any aspect of life goes uncovered, then the people will lack the full disclosure that helps democracy flourish. This may sound overly dramatic, but the First Amendment affirms the special status of the media in the United States. A news blackout—whether on behalf of education or any other field of potential coverage—is not in the public interest.

This, of course, does not necessarily mean that one should derive satisfaction from the situation as it exists. Above all, the consensus of the contributors to this book holds that the media perpetuate a negative image of American education—from student achievement to teacher performance to higher education's tuition policies. The negativity probably feeds on itself. Once cast in an adverse light, a person or an institution cannot readily escape the penetrating glow of unfavorable attention. Even positive developments become marginalized by reporters fearful of being duped.

Surely, much that happens in the nation's schools and colleges merits praise. Many youngsters grow into strong and swift readers. Many of them also conquer the arcane aspects of mathematical esoterica that would set their parents' minds spinning. Many, as well, though not enough, gain dominion over problem solving—able to analyze, sythesize, and diagnose in ways that assure their ability to function as rational, incisive beings. And many go on to acquit themselves with distinction in the halls of academe.

On the other hand, a regular visitor to the typical inner-city classroom can hardly find cheer in what he or she encounters. Education in such places struggles to occur. And even in the classrooms of many suburbs, unengaged students may go through the motions, not causing trouble so long as few demands are made of them. This is the "treaty," described in *The Shopping Mall High School* (Powell, Farrar, and Cohen, 1985), that lets everyone—teachers and students—go his or her own way, a sort of Gresham's law that robs the educational transaction of most of its potential substance.

On top of these egregious failures, the curtain rises on the school as the stage on which so many of society's tribulations play themselves out. Is this the fault of the schools? For the most part, no. But those who write about schools can hardly overlook such realities. The battered child, the child who is kept up late at night, the child to whom no adult ever reads, the child who has no quiet place to do homework, the child who is seduced by the ways of the street—all figure, from time to time, in the articles on education that critics denounce for their negativity.

The onus for improving the quality of education coverage usually is placed on the media, but this narrow view overlooks the responsibilities of the education establishment and of the public. If what appears in the media is to improve, then the media cannot act alone to make this happen.

The education establishment must show more respect for the public's right to know and a greater understanding of the media's role as an intermediary between the world of education and the public. Reporters complain endlessly about "access," about educational officials who try to stifle their efforts to obtain information about schools and colleges. Educational institutions should strive to maintain a free flow of information, while, of course, respecting legal rights to privacy. At the same time, education should do all it can to explain complexities to the media and to facilitate articles that show understanding and insightfulness.

The public, for its part, ought to evince more interest in what occurs in the nation's schools and colleges. Some of the most outstanding articles and television programs on education go unread and unseen by the masses. People do not avail themselves of the best that is available when it comes to education coverage. If members of the public were to clamor for more thorough coverage, as they do when it comes to sports, then the media might respond. And if educators knew that the public cared more deeply about reportage on education, they might view the media in less adversarial terms. Reporters, after all, are the emissaries of the public, helping to ensure that the interests of students, taxpayers, and society in general are served by the educational system.

The media must place themselves in a mode in which they constantly reassess their educational coverage. Dozens of daily newspapers—out of some 1,500—around the country put a premium on covering elementary and secondary schools. In many instances, an editor oversees a staff of reporters who carry full-time assignments in education. Such newspapers deserve plaudits for their efforts. Less frequently, daily newspapers assign someone to work full-time on the higher education beat. One of the most important contributions that newspapers could make would be to assign veteran journalists to the education beat and leave them there long enough to know a lesson plan from a curriculum unit. As matters stand at all too many newspapers, education is a beginners' beat, a wading pool from which to acclimate oneself to the temperature before diving into the deeper waters on assignment to cover municipal government or the courts.

More than that, television has to start taking education seriously. Too frequently, broadcast coverage of education epitomizes the worst of sound bite journalism. Complexities are consumed by the quest for brevity. Television executives should give their viewers more credit and provide them with substantial segments devoted to educational issues. A network or local station that is unwilling to establish a full-time education beat should at least let the same person cover the occasional education story to gain some familiarity with the field. But regardless of who gets the assignment, the sad fact is that education news on television must contend with the same tendency to merge news and entertainment that afflicts the coverage of all serious topics in that medium. The obsession with providing viewers with amusement threatens to melt whatever lines remain between real news and entertainment. This trend transcends the problems of education coverage, representing one of the least responsible parts of today's broadcasting.

When it comes to television and movie productions that are purely artifacts of entertainment, the best one can hope for is that producers, directors, and writers will think more deeply about their treatment of educational topics. Entertainment, after all, is entertainment; it is not journalism, and it is unrealistic to expect films and television programs that make no pretense to journalistic aspirations to conform to the standards by which the news is judged. But why not set some of the stories in schools that are not off the edge? Just as not all physicians work in emergency rooms and not all police officers work in gritty urban settings—you would never know otherwise about either group from watching movies and sitcoms—not all teachers are confined to life-threatening assignments in schools where everyone's life is at risk. Sometimes, just sometimes, the educational venue might be changed for one of these stories.

In the end, getting back to the news, the education establishment and the public have the right to expect truth from the media. This should be the goal of all coverage, an aim that any good journalist would endorse. Along with expecting honesty, however, the education establishment and the public should also prepare themselves for a sobering dose of candor from a responsible media. The media cannot, should not, and, one might hope, never will be a public relations vehicle for education. If that were to happen, the media would lose their credibility and the puffery would not be worth the newsprint or videotape on which it appeared.

BIBLIOGRAPHY

Arthur G. Powell, Eleanor Farrar, and David K. Cohen. *The Shopping Mall High School: Winners and Losers in the Educational Marketplace.* Boston: Houghton Mifflin, 1985.

About the Editor and the Contributors

Gene I. Maeroff directs the Hechinger Institute on Education and the Media at Teachers College, Columbia University. His previous book, *Altered Destinies: Making Life Better for Schoolchildren of Need*, was published earlier this year. In 1997, he was one of three coauthors of *Scholarship Assessed: Evaluation of the Professoriate*. Two of his earlier books, *The Empowerment of Teachers* and *Team Building for School Change*, were published by Teachers College Press. Maeroff spent 16 years on the staff of the *New York Times*, where he was national education correspondent.

•

David C. Berliner is a professor in the College of Education at Arizona State University, where he serves as interim dean. He is a past president of the American Educational Research Association.

Bruce J. Biddle is a professor in the psychology department at the University of Missouri-Columbia. He was coauthor, with David Berliner, of *The Manufactured Crisis*.

Larry Cuban has been a professor of education at Stanford University since 1981. Earlier, he was a school superintendent, for 7 years, and a high school social studies teacher, for 14 years. His most recent book (with David Tyack) is *Tinkering Toward Utopia*.

Patricia A. Dabbs works at the National Center for Education Statistics in the U.S. Department of Education. She serves as technical liaison between the National Assessment of Educational Progress and several other organizations. She formerly worked in institutional research and policy analysis in the University of Maryland system.

Denis P. Doyle is an education analyst, consultant, and writer. He wrote *Reinventing Education* with Louis Gerstner and others. He is also the author of *Raising the Standard*, published in 1997.

Don Hossler is a professor of educational leadership and policy studies and acting vice chancellor for enrollment services at Indiana University, Bloomington. His research and teaching interests include student college choice, higher education finance, enrollment management, and higher education reform in the former Soviet Union.

George R. Kaplan, an independent education policy analyst, is the author of *Images of Education.*

John Leonard is literary editor of the *Nation,* television critic for *New York* magazine, and media critic for *CBS Sunday Morning.*

Richard W. Moll, the former director of admissions at Bowdoin College, the University of California at Santa Cruz, and Vassar College, is the author of *Playing the Selective College Admissions Game* and *The Public Ivies.* He lives in Boston.

Laurence T. Ogle is a statistician with the Office of Educational Research and Improvement, U.S. Department of Education. His specialty is large-scale testing, and he is currently working on the Voluntary National Tests Initiative in reading and mathematics.

Todd W. Serman is an attorney and a high school teacher in Los Angeles.

Rochelle L. Stanfield, a staff correspondent for *National Journal,* covers education, housing, urban affairs, federalism, demographics, civil rights, and social policy.

Leonard B. Stevens consults nationally on race-related school issues. He worked for 7 years as a journalist in Rhode Island and New York before deciding to earn a doctorate in education.

Dorothy S. Strickland is a professor at Rutgers University and a co-editor of the Language and Literacy Series of Teachers College Press.

Deborah Wadsworth is the executive director of Public Agenda, a nonpartisan, nonprofit organization that fosters public dialogue so as to improve communication between the country's leaders and the public.

Aleta Watson is assistant city editor responsible for education coverage at the *San Jose Mercury News.* A former president of the Education Writers Association, she has won national awards for education writing.

Amy Stuart Wells is an associate professor of educational policy at the Graduate School of Education and Information Studies of the University of California at Los Angeles. She was the coauthor in 1997 of *Stepping over the Color Line.*

B. Ann Wright has taught English and was director of admissions at the University of Rochester before becoming dean of enrollment management at Smith College. She is now chief public affairs officer at Smith, living in Northampton, Massachusetts.

Index